How to Plant a Billion Trees

How to Plant a Billion Trees

A Memoir of Childhood Trauma and the Healing Power of Nature

Nicole Walker

BLOOMSBURY ACADEMIC
NEW YORK • LONDON • OXFORD • NEW DELHI • SYDNEY

BLOOMSBURY ACADEMIC

Bloomsbury Publishing Inc, 1359 Broadway, New York, NY 10018, USA
Bloomsbury Publishing Plc, 50 Bedford Square, London, WC1B 3DP, UK
Bloomsbury Publishing Ireland, 29 Earlsfort Terrace, Dublin 2, D02 AY28, Ireland

BLOOMSBURY, BLOOMSBURY ACADEMIC and the Diana logo are trademarks of Bloomsbury Publishing Plc

First published in the United States of America 2026

Copyright © Nicole Walker 2026

Cover design: Jen Huppert
Cover painting by Rebecca Campbell

All rights reserved. No part of this publication may be: i) reproduced or transmitted in any form, electronic or mechanical, including photocopying, recording or by means of any information storage or retrieval system without prior permission in writing from the publishers; or ii) used or reproduced in any way for the training, development, or operation of artificial intelligence (AI) technologies, including generative AI technologies. The rights holders expressly reserve this publication from the text and data mining exception as per Article 4(3) of the Digital Single Market Directive (EU) 2019/790.

Bloomsbury Publishing Inc does not have any control over, or responsibility for, any third-party websites referred to or in this book. All internet addresses given in this book were correct at the time of going to press. The author and publisher regret any inconvenience caused if addresses have changed or sites have ceased to exist, but can accept no responsibility for any such changes.

Library of Congress Cataloging-in-Publication Data Available

ISBN: HB: 979-8-216-27887-0
ePDF: 979-8-216-27889-4
eBook: 979-8-216-27888-7

Typeset by Integra Software Services Pvt. Ltd.
Printed and bound in the United States of America

For product safety related questions contact productsafety@bloomsbury.com.

To find out more about our authors and books visit www.bloomsbury.com and sign up for our newsletters.

Contents

Acknowledgments   vi

1. Burn It All Down   1
2. Heartwood   13
3. Just Up and Move   21
4. Dry as Smoke   39
5. Failure and Succession   49
6. A Single Tree Is Not a Forest   67
7. Well-Fertilized Soil   83
8. Reseeding   103
9. Vertical Trees, Horizontal Forests   115
10. Breathing Old Growth   127
11. Bodily Infestations   143
12. Fires That Burn Too Hot   157
13. Trees Are Not the Only Fruit   179
14. On the Trail   193

Glossary   210
Notes   211
About the Author   215

Acknowledgments

I am grateful to so many people for the people who brought this book into being—and that includes the support of so many friends and family who helped me make it to this point. As this book tries to make clear, my mom and my sisters, Valerie and Paige, buoy me and always have. Rebecca Campbell, whose artwork graces the cover, showed me it was possible live as an artist. Beya Thayer, who seems to hold the world together with her bare hands, keeps me together with those same hands. And thank you to David Carlin who collaborates with me on everything from writing to books to presiding over NonfictioNOW to picking the better Airbnbs. I'm grateful to the people who I met in college and still count as dear friends, Misty Cummings, Van Havig, Emily Headen, Kris McNeill, Andy McClain, and Gabe Brandt, and those I met in graduate school, Lynn Kilpatrick, Steve Fellner, Margot Singer, Matthew Batt, David McGlynn, Jeff Chapman, Eric Burger, Kate Rosenberg, Maggie Golston, Steve Tuttle, Peter Covino, Mary Anne Mohanraj, Samantha Ruckman and Heidi Czerwiec and my writer friends Ander Monson, Lawrence Lenhart, Karen Renner, Andie Francis, Ann Cummins, Matt Bell, Katharine Coles, Jackie Osherow, Donald Revell, Karen Brennan, Robin Hemley, and David Shields each made me believe in myself and in the power of storytelling. Jane Armstrong passed away just as I was writing these notes. I hope she knew how much help she had been in the crafting of this memoir. I wish my dear friend, Julie Paegle, had lived to read this. She always believed in me and my writing. I could not have written this book without the support and love of Angie Hansen. Thank you to my dear literary agent, Malaga Baldi, who works tirelessly on my behalf and thanks to Richard Brown and Victoria Shi for believing in *How to Plant a Billion Trees*, for Martin Tribe for copyediting, Peter

Perez for publicity and Maria Rhode for marketing. It takes a billion people to make a book. Thank you to my colleagues, KT Thompson, Shewin Bitsui (and LL again), Geetha Iyer, Oscar Mancinas for the work they do to make our MFA program a great one. I also want to thank all the people who worked so hard in the 2024 election to protect reproductive freedom and abortion rights, Maggie Downing and the folks at Free & Just at the Hub in DC, Dawn Penich, and Jasmine Viehe among so many others. And I want to acknowledge and thank Fannie Lou Hamer, Florynce "Flo" Kennedy, and Toni Cade Bambara who were pivotal figures in the 1960s fight for reproductive freedom, expanding the definition of choice to include the unique struggles of Black and poor women. And I want to thank Andrea Askowitz, Allison Langer, and Jane Marks who invited me into their powerful storytelling lives. I want to thank all of my students and all of my teachers for building this forest. And, truly, thank you to Bruce Hungate for writing with me and for practicing radical optimism! Of course, my people—Erik, Max, and Zoë. Thank you for making my life a home.

I wouldn't be me and this book wouldn't be this book without each of these beautiful humans. These people are my trees, my mushrooms, my forest, my heart. I am lucky to share the world with them.

Some of these chapters have been published in different form in *Ecotone, The New York Times, The Southern Review, The Georgia Review,* and *Longreads.*

1

Burn It All Down

I live inside the largest contiguous ponderosa pine forest in the lower 48 states. The ponderosas bear extreme climates—very cold and very snowy some winters, and pretty hot and pretty dry other winters. Those trees grow so tall, and so slowly you might miss their abundant accumulations in both height and thickness. In this ponderosa pine forest, it may snow a hundred and fifty inches a year. Those winters, snow collects in layers like the Kaibab, Coconino, Supai, and Navajo sandstones that have layered the Colorado Plateau over the last 100 to 300 million years. But unlike that long-lived stone, the snow turns over, year by year. It falls in chunks. It melts before the branches break. Seventy-five-mile-an-hour winds bend the trees over, their branches touching ground, like excellent yogi. A slight shift in wind turns those yogis to catapults—the snow flies. Incoming.

And then it doesn't snow again for eight months. It doesn't rain for five.

But then it does rain, thanks to monsoon storms which arrive, usually, in July, pouring water through the soil and into aquifer as a promise that we'll be able to draw water up through wells during no-rainfall reason to the next snows. In this place where the sun shines 300 days per year, I live for those other sixty-five. A good monsoon reveals an active forest. I go hunting for mushrooms, even in arid Arizona. I mainly find lobster mushrooms, funnel shaped and as brightly orange as a boiled crustacean. These mushrooms are actually a fungus that grows on top of another insipid tasting mushroom, rendering it non-toxic and edible. Even delicious. The lobster fungus renders the russula invisible but that doesn't mean it's not there. In the forest, one organism tops another which tops another. Nothing ever really disappears. In the fall, the ponderosas lose dry, orange needles, sinking nitrogen and carbon back into the ground to feed themselves later. Unlike humans, trees do not mark the moment when everything turns to shit. When things turn to shit, they say, "All the better to soak the ground with bacteria that dissolve dead leaves so the soil can uptake their carbon and push it toward the roots of the ponderosas." They are long-winded, these trees. Perhaps because they live so long. Perhaps because they're full of shit. But in a good way.

What I love about forests is that though they have a system, they don't have what I think of as culture. Systems are made of pressures, signals, adjustments, physical things. Cultures are made of ideas, opinions, feelings, and fears. Trees do not have an opinion about adaptation or vulnerability, what is beauty, truth, garbage, or rot. If a sickly tree sends signals through a forest's networks asking for help, the microorganisms, mycelia, and mycorrhizal fungi (mycelium is the vegetative structure of a fungus, while mycorrhizae are fungi that form a symbiotic relationship with plant roots) form webs of information that send nutrients to a tree. The healthier trees, the better for the whole forest. No one makes fun of the scraggly tree for being needy. No one sends the waste to live in a landfill on the other side of the mountain. No one declares supremacy. There are super tall trees. There are shorter trees. Trees who have both male and female cones. Every organism has a purpose. The trees are looking out for one thing: forest health. In the human cultural ecosystem, stronger beings are apt to take from the smaller ones. The taller trees presume they deserve their height even at the expense of shorter ones. What I love about the forest: all forces are present, available, and eventually knowable even if nearly invisible. This is true for each organism, whether microscopic or one of the largest entities on earth, like redwood trees or the aspen clones. Human culture amounts to an assemblance of opinions and imaginings masquerading as something real. These are invisible forces. Their impact is difficult to measure. For example, I imagine that you're looking at me. Why are you looking at me? Should I feel ashamed? Proud? Desired? Beautiful? Hideous? I cannot get behind those eyes to know what you're thinking. Maybe I don't want to know.

I do hope I can explain my situation—what happened to me as a kid and how it changed my life in ways that I now compare to my understanding of trees. Everybody loves trees. The researchers I work with at the Center for Ecosystem Science and Society study how forests serve as some of the most important carbon sinks. Without them, how can we hope to absorb the tons of carbon dioxide that we pump into the atmosphere, raising global temperatures to 1.5 degrees Celsius? Some researchers and environmentalists want to plant up a trillion trees that can soak up that carbon. If only that single solution was so easy. I spent a lot of my life looking for a single solution to fix what went wrong with my life. I looked to the magnanimity and the supremacy of the singular. As in a poem I wrote for my sister whose boyfriend killed himself when she was fourteen, I held on like a drowning man clutches a burning rope. As we pin our hopes on forests, the number of wildfires increases every year. As I tried to restore the joy of my childhood, I keep desperately planting. Will I ever know a truly healthy forest again?

The fires get worse every year. They rage closer to metropolitan areas. It's impossible to name all the fires in the west I've had to pay attention to since moving to Flagstaff but here are a few that burned in Arizona: Watson. Schultz. Museum. Pipeline. And also California: Eaton. Palisades. CZU Complex. Camp. Recently, I've had to pay attention to fires in the Midwest and Eastern United States. The Black Swamp in North Carolina. The Buffalo in South Dakota. The Big Ridge in Georgia. Square miles of forest twisted by flames into self-annihilating tornadoes—as if the tree wants to eat itself. All that carbon, once stored, now free.

Fire permeates everything. Stand on the edge of the burn. Watch as the globe warms before your eyes. The heat pinks your cheeks. It's not the heat of your own body—your hands in your pocket, letting your soft body warm them. This isn't the heat of a campfire—hands warming gently over flame. The smell isn't just of burned wood—the squirrels and owls and bear cubs and salamanders flake their hot death into your hair. Mosses and mushrooms, so cool and wet, turn into infertile ash. In the past, Indigenous people set controlled burns to keep the fires low and slow. Hundreds of years of forest management where managing meant quashing all flames. Now the forests are set to go up! It's almost as if the forest managers, led by white men for the last couple of centuries, didn't know what was best for forests or bears or squirrels or salamanders or really anyone at all.

In 1982, when I was ten years old, a fifteen-year-old boy molested me. He was supposed to be babysitting me and my younger, twin sisters, Paige and Valerie. After the twins went to sleep, the babysitter and I sat on the couch, watching "MASH," which aired after the news. The babysitter started caressing my arm. Then my neck. Then he took off my shirt and my pants. Then his clothes. He laid me down. He lay on top of me and had sex with me. I had a vague idea of what was happening. My parents had been forthcoming about how babies were made, and during long and lazy summers in the suburbs of Salt Lake City, I had watched plenty of instructive soap operas.

I remember his naked body on top of me, the woven wool couch scratchy on my back. He was heavy for a fifteen-year-old. I could see the tiny blackheads all over his nose. I wished he would get off me. He was crushing me and his face so close to my face felt claustrophobic. Are you looking at me, I wanted to ask. Why are you still looking at me? I wanted to rewrite the situation. If I didn't have to look at him, I could imagine a different story. I wish he'd asked me if I was OK. I wish he'd said thanks. I wish he'd put his clothes back on and my clothes back on and talked to me. Instead, after he whispered, "no one can ever know about this," he sat by me continuing to watch B. J. Hunnicutt and Hawkeye Pierce swirl their glasses full of gin they'd tapped from their homemade distillery. The five minutes of flapping flesh was not the stuff of soap operas that I had watched. Had I watched the episode where Luke rapes Laura in the disco on *General Hospital*, perhaps I would have understood the filth of what had happened. But *General Hospital* had moved on from that unseemly scene. I let my imagination do the same. Now Luke and Laura were in love and living inside a mall, unseen during the day, dancing through the mattress section of a department store in the night. Perhaps by next season, the babysitter would put his arm around me, or hold my hand, and declare in front of his friends and family his love for me. Although soap operas don't have seasons. They run endlessly, year after year. The characters don't grow or age. Stuff just happens to them over and over again.

I didn't really know how wrong the babysitter situation was. I was flattered by the attention, but also confused. Why me? What does this mean? Was he my boyfriend? Why did we have to keep it a secret? I haven't always used the word "molest"—I felt too guilty and complicit. Sometimes, I used the words "sexual interference," although the noun version sounds permanent and unmoving. Assault sounds violent, which the situation may have been emotionally, although there was no blood. I am still prone to feeling conflicted. Is being forever unsure a product of the molestation? Or do I feel inherently responsible for everything that happens to me? Can the two be disentangled?

Although I grew up between the mouths of Little and Big Cottonwood Canyons where Douglas fir and cedars decorate the granite canyons, I didn't know the *system forces behind* real forests until I visited the uncut expanses of the old growth forests of the Pacific Northwest, or, later, moved to Flagstaff which is located within the largest ponderosa forest in the lower 48. But as a kid, even without knowing all the chemistry that happened between sky and earth, I loved trees. I climbed them. Sat under them. Helped my mom put up their fruit in late summer. Swung from them. Ran around them. Stood behind them while playing hide and seek. My cousin Trev and I climbed the cherry tree at his house, although he went higher than I. He also fell and broke open the skin on his head. We climbed the plum tree in my grandma's backyard, although he was the only one who went high enough to climb onto the roof of their carport. At the MacDonald's, their cherry tree performed its acrobatics high into the sky. Annie and I ate cherry after cherry until we looked inside and saw white strings squiggle about that we tried to believe were not worms. Does swinging on a tire swing from a wide on my grandparent's giant willow tree count as being part of a tree? That willow tree shed so many branches every year. The babysitter's sister and I scooped them into black garbage bags as part of our volunteer service for the one year we joined the Girl Scouts, back when I was a good kid. My mom, no matter what else had changed in our family still calls me a Druid. I think my mom understood I had an affinity for trees, but I don't think, like a Druid, that I worshipped trees. I think I wanted to be one. The associations we make with trees: tall, strong, beautiful. Everything I felt after what happened with the babysitter I wasn't.

When I tell people I felt complicit for engaging with the babysitter, for going over to my best friend's house for a sleepover where he happened to live, they argue: "You couldn't consent. You were ten years old," they say. And, I see that, now that I've met other ten-year-olds. It does seem gross and rotten and it's hard to remember exactly how I felt. I think of my mom reading this and feel not only a burning shame but also her pain. Maybe the work of writing about this is like restoring a forest, but I think every time she remembers, her forest burns all over again.

I try to draw the shape of the story. I try to understand why someone would think a ten-year-old kid would want to have sex with a fifteen-year-old. Perhaps I thought he was my connection to a world where I never felt a part. I wonder what my life would have been like if it didn't happen. I adapted. But one thing about adaptation is you don't know you've adapted. You grow around the dead parts making burls in the softwood. You grow thicker bark. You cinch up your roots. You fake it 'til you make it, try to keep up with your fellow trees, try hard to bury the detritus into which your roots sink.

Although I'd kept what the babysitter had done and continued to do from my parents and sisters and from his parents, I needed to tell someone. If I explained my version, perhaps I could explain how it was OK, that I was in love. I would adapt the story to make it palatable. To make it seem less like the sordid story it was.

I sat on the floor by my friend Kelly's bed and told her about my boyfriend.

"He really likes me," I told her.

"How do you know?" she asked.

I know the babysitter had said not to say anything, but since he had continued to babysit, to ask me to sit beside him on the couch, to pull off my shirt, did that meant we were progressing relationship-wise? Eventually, Luke and Laura move out of the mall and get married. Love grows, right? When he came and got me from his sister's room when I slept over at her house, he left the music on. Foreigner's *Waiting for a Girl Like You*. You would only play that song if you really liked the person whose nightshirt you lifted off her head, right? I knew all the words to John Cougar Mellancamp's *Jack and Diane*. The babysitter and I were just two American kids. The babysitter was just asking me to run off with him behind a shady tree. My Bobby Brooks slacks dribble off as easily as any pleasing American girl's.

I told Kelly about the music. I also told her that he kissed me, although he hadn't. I told her we had been naked. I cannot remember what else I told her, but I must have said something like the word *sex* because Kelly's mom called my mom the next day and told what I had said.

My mom, picking me up from dance class, asked, "Nikki, Kelly told me about you and the babysitter. That he was touching you."

My stomach turned. If she focused her senses, she would see the way my flesh had festered. She would smell the fallen, decaying tree I had become. I was quick with a cover story. "Oh no, Mom," I said. "That was just a story. I was just saying I had a crush on him. And then telling her about Luke and Laura on *General Hospital*."

My mom stared hard at me, like if she could hold me in the tractor beam of her eyes, I couldn't weave and dodge my way out of this. But I had told Kelly about *General Hospital*. And, even though he was already man-sized and had blackheads on his nose, I suppose I did have a crush on him. My mom picked the babysitter up from school the next day and asked him what was going on between us. He told her that he knew I told a lot of stories. That I had an active imagination. And that wasn't even really a lie.

This storytelling, a.k.a., lying, scenario convinced my mom to find me a therapist. Here, she planted the first tree in my forest-turned ash. Dr. Tony LePray, a psychologist with a PhD in Children's Psychology, asked me why I'd lied to my friend about this babysitter.

"I guess I just wanted attention?"

It was important to maintain the "I had a very active imagination" storyline for everyone—for my parents' friends, my parents, my sisters. We were a regular family. We swam at the pool in the summer, skied at Brighton or Alta in the winter. My sisters and I went to school and, even when I didn't make it into Gifted and Talented, our teachers loved us. The twins, on April Fools, switched classes for the day. Could an abnormal family can get away with that? We were a family of gentle, protective lies.

Not all stories are good ones. If you have to lie over and over again, it's probably not so much a story as a den of iniquity. Sure, you can take shelter there but if you don't come into the light, the waste matter builds up. There's nothing to eat inside that stench-filled place. The story begins and ends in darkness. Perhaps the lying was part of the process. A healthy forest needs waste matter for its webs. The body will out, though. At least my body did. Did my body want my mom to know? Doubtful! The body just does what it does. I shouldn't be so ashamed to type it, but I do not want to tell this story. I think I may well wish I were still in Dr. LePray's office, lying away.

Personal trauma may have misshapen my memory and my mind so profoundly that straightforward storytelling cannot fully or correctly express it. Stay with me. My jagged lines will converge. These braided parts will feed each other, I believe.

It is beguiling to invoke that adage of the road not taken—as if there were ever only two roads diverging in a wood. But narratives are big on turning points and turning points suggest a particular path leads directly to the inevitable now, without remarking that the now keeps moving, as does the story, as does the path itself. At what point do we determine where the "now" came from? Isn't it always moving forward? Doesn't determining cause and effect require a definitive "now" moment? Here's the effect. Where? The effect. Where? Now, it's right here. As I remake my story, I indubitably plant more trees to make it look like I have grown a very solid forest. But you've seen the trees alongside Highway 26 on your way to Mt. Hood, yes? They are only a thin façade of trees. Behind them, clearcuts. A forest of stumps. It will take me this whole book, and most of my life, to figure out what a forest really is.

Western classical literature defines narrative as a story that moves directionally forward, each turning point a development that leaves the traveler responsible for her choices. Is the pre- and post-lapsarian conditioning the only lens through which we can view the past? There was a tree. There was an apple. And there was a bite. A before and an after. Was the eating of the apple the moment when we stopped seeing a forest full of possible steps and instead saw only one of two ways we had to go?

In non-Western cultures, the path that moves forward like a road, pushing toward some destination, isn't the only narrative model. Instead of a train track or a freeway or even a path in the woods, some cultures hang their narrative structures on non-linear images. Navajo storytellers consider rain, spider webs, and spirals as possible models instead of the usual track or arc. Donna Haraway's *Staying with the Trouble: Making Kin in the Chthulucene* spells out an argument that to stave off the worst effects of climate change, we'll have to change the way we think. Changing the way we think will require us to change the way we narrate our lives. Early in the book, she considers the string game Cat's Cradle and what it means for Navajo story-making.

> In the Navajo language, string games are called na'atl'o ... these string figures are thinking as well as making practices, pedagogical practices and cosmological performances. Some Navajo thinkers describe string games as one kind of patterning for hózhó, a term imperfectly translated in English as "harmony," "beauty," "order," and "right relations with the world," including right relations of humans and nonhumans.

Haraway considers what might be possible if we think using different frameworks, languages, and contexts from our conventional ones. Perhaps then we could see different ways of restoring balance to the world. The difference, to my mind, between paths or roads and rain or nests or spiderwebs is that the way may not be made only by racing from point a to point b on a singular narrative trail. As Haraway says, "Not *in* the world but *of* the world, that crucial difference in English prepositions is what leads me to weave Navajo string figures."[1]

These prepositions matter. Staying *with* the trouble is not the same as staying *in* trouble. One of the worst responses I developed from the sexual interference was trying to move past it, pretend it wasn't that big of a deal, trying whatever I could to make everything all right. I do that now—gloss over the hard things. If I really did go wrong somewhere, it is there. I'll do anything to "make things fine." Donna Haraway's advice to stay with the trouble is good for not only climate change, but for other kinds of trauma. It's the root of therapy—don't just glide on by. Stay and let it sink in. We don't want to sit with climate change any more than we want to sit with childhood sex trouble. But maybe if we stay and look at how messed up it really is, we'd realize we have a lot of work to do.

I rely on innate optimism. I don't know where it comes from. It's different from hope. Hope requires evidence. Optimism is foolish. It leads to disappointment. But, when I crawl on the forest floor, looking under a fallen log for mushrooms, certain that I will find a chanterelle there, I can't help but feel like even I do not find an orange, crenellated cap rising in the moss, a sun lifting its sky, there will be another one under the next tree.

I believe there will always be one more tree to look under.

I believe that if I root around in the dirt of my own story, I'll find the parts of me that had been discombobulated by the babysitter and rearrange them in a manner that makes me an organized human.

Researchers at the university where I work have visited the CZU Lightning Complex fire scar in Big Basin State Park in California that burned from August 19, 2020 to January 5, 2021. Thousands of acres of thousand-year-old trees that once stretched their green cathedrals far into the atmosphere became ghost woods—ships transporting the dead from this green earth across the River Styx, which is also charred and full of ash. But their research shows even dead-looking redwoods can sprout baby redwoods from the resources of their deep, cellulose carbon stores. Up the ladder of these now limb-less posts a fuzzy carpet of green sprouts climbs two hundred feet up those poles. These sprouts, looking as ambitious as asparagus in spring, grew using carbon the trees had absorbed and stored over a hundred years ago. The researchers covered the buds with black plastic so the sun couldn't reach them, preventing any present-day photosynthesis. The research showed that the trees hadn't resprouted from present-day carbon dioxide in the atmosphere. Instead, the sprouts dug into sapwood to convert old-timey carbon the coastal redwoods had eaten years ago into new growth.

The German botanist Stephen Endlicher named these redwoods *Sequoia sempervirens* in honor of Chief Sequoya or Sikwayi who invented a phonetic alphabet of eighty-six symbols for the Cherokee language. The Semper Virens part means ever-flourishing, the sprouts rising from the dead tree giving new meaning to ever-green. This immortality is not a consequence not of pull-your-bootstraps up individual determination but of shared resources and common interest. As my friend, George Koch, Professor of Ecosystem Science, said in an interview that my husband Erik filmed about the research results, "the study is about understanding better the details really at the chemical level almost of how these trees are able to come back to rebuild a crown of vigorous green foliage after losing everything." If only I had George Koch's research study, or even his words, as I looked into the wilderness or into the wasteland of a future that seemed like it would ever be twisted by the babysitter. What if he had been there to explain that maybe what appears to be an entire devastation isn't necessarily so. Inside the tree, substances act. Seemingly invisible chemicals can spawn new growth.

I wish we could rely on the forests to save us. What a beautiful, green, green world. A trillion trees could soak up carbon output and clean up this planet we've made dirty. But trees can't restore what is lost already. Eight trillion tonnes of ice from the Arctic Ice Shelf lost in the past twenty-five years. Animal populations have plunged 69 percent since I was born. The southwest has been in a mega-drought for twenty-four years. I look out at the ponderosa pines from my porch and see nothing but green at all, but these trees can't be the ones to save us. With drought, they are dying themselves.

I'm trying to learn to stay with the trouble. There are two hard stories I plan to tell. One is about being molested. The other is about trees and climate change. But what I want to find are the other stories. The ones I didn't know, because these stories have narrowed my focus for so long. It's dishonest to look away from the mess. The hard facts shape the story. If I didn't want to face the facts, I wouldn't have embraced the braided essay as a form where one combines research and personal story to press hard upon each other like two fingers against a blackhead until the pus erupts. That is a gross image but I'm trying to embrace the gross. Still, let me try a more beautiful metaphor: Writing all this is like mycorrhizal fungi pressing against the forest floor until, from the strain of both, the fruiting body pops up in the form of a chanterelle mushroom.

Here's another gross thing: When I was eleven, the babysitter impregnated me. I use the active verb, with *me* as direct object, intentionally. To "get pregnant" suggests he threw the baseball and I, knowing it was coming, caught it. I did not mean to catch anything, nor did I know how to avoid doing so.

I was sitting cross-legged on my bed when my mom opened the door, and asked point blank, "Are you pregnant?"

2

Heartwood

How do mothers know things they couldn't possibly know? When she asked me that question, my body, inside and outside, seemed on full display: my genitals, my uterus, my breasts, my face, my eyes. I wanted to disappear, to fly from my bedroom window into the field and even beyond the field, up Little Cottonwood Canyon, over Park City, to Evanston, Wyoming where my mother had been raised, and where my great-grandmother lived, and I could hide out there until the rest of the story resolved itself without me, but imaginations do not have the substantial wingspan to lift our human bodies.

At the Woman's Clinic, the only place in Utah to get an abortion at the time, the staff wouldn't let my mom come into the procedure room with me. She had to stay in the waiting room. As I lay upon the table, looking at the faces of two nurses, one doctor, and a bright fluorescent light, the doctor said, in front of the nurses, "You should not be having sex this young."

The nurses didn't ask if I had been molested. They assumed that I was as complicit as I felt. I remember nodding at the doctor, absorbing the idea that I must have wanted to have sex at ten years old. It was so much easier to believe it was my fault. Like being the author of a novel, I was the agent of my own sentences, the author of my own story. Victims are always direct objects. The phrase, "he molested me" I can do nothing about. "I fell for my fifteen-year-old babysitter," is stupid and gross, but it's a sentence and an image of my own devising where I try to make something small and vulnerable from something toxic and seemingly irreparable.

After *Roe vs. Wade* was overturned the summer of 2022, I wrote an Op-Ed for *The New York Times* called *At Age 11 My Abortion Wasn't a Choice. It Was My Life*. The essay received 1,046 comments before the *Times* editors closed them. Most of them were supportive. The main complaint was that my parents hadn't had the babysitter arrested. I don't know if this is me being complicit or another example of where I went wrong, but I couldn't imagine in the 1980s that prosecuting the babysitter was even a consideration. I couldn't imagine testifying. And, the babysitter was only five years older than me. Did he even know what he was doing? How much responsibility does a fifteen-year-old have? Whatever made him do what he did was as much a product of how our culture provides cover for males, their wants and needs. Privilege is a wide carpet of mycelia—it builds a forest of advantage that many? most? boys will take.

In the metaphor of forest burning down, the Sexual Interference was the fire. The extreme event that destroyed so much of the terrain came from how old I was, from people knowing what happened, from shame and complicity. In some version of the story, the abortion might have raised the temperature—caused the fire to burn more acreage, destroy even the canopy of trees and the mycelia underground—more shame, more loss, more ravaged sense of self. But, in fact, it was the next batch of trees sprouting. If my mom hadn't called the Clinic, if the babysitter's parents hadn't contributed $300 to the $600 cost, if abortion had been illegal not only in Utah but the United States, what would have happened to me? Now that I'm 1,000 years old, I can imagine that life, almost. If I had survived giving birth at age eleven, I would have lived with my parents. I wouldn't have gone to Reed College. Maybe I wouldn't have gone to college at all. I probably wouldn't be a professor. I wouldn't live in the middle of the largest contiguous ponderosa pine forest in the lower 48. I wouldn't have my kids, Max and Zoë, nor would I have met the people who would form the incredible support systems like my friends and sisters' friends and mom's friends and in-laws and colleagues and teachers and writing groups and students who undergird this revamped forest.

When I first suspected I was pregnant, I remember sitting on the toilet, looking at the white white white toilet paper. My copy of *Our Bodies Ourselves* opened automatically to the signs you are pregnant pages. I knew what white toilet paper meant. I pinched the skin where underneath my ovaries were supposed to be. "No, no, no," I told them. But it was too late. They weren't listening. I looked at my belly button. If I could tunnel in through there, maybe I could untie whatever knot had been tied. I could fly Superman around my uterus and undo.

At some point, I got off the toilet and pulled my pants up. I punched my eleven-year-old thigh. I thought shit, shit, shit since I hadn't learned how to say fuck yet. I thought of the numbers in pi and the way cells divide. The numbers would just keep multiplying. This was out of my control. *This* being my body. *This* being. Body. It wasn't mine to do with anymore. I didn't tell my mom. I told the babysitter, as he sat at the piano in his parents' living room. I thought we were in this together, like Luke and Laura, through the good and the bad, the fantasy and the real.

"I think I'm pregnant," I said. In front of him, I didn't feel ashamed. Just perplexed and ready for a good plan. I don't think I thought he would ask to marry me, but maybe I did. My imagination whirled like the VHS tapes where Superman kisses Lois Lane, or Luke Skywalker kisses Leia, or on my soap opera, Luke kisses Laura on *General Hospital* although in retrospect all of those kisses were awkward and inappropriate. Luke had raped Laura and *then* they started dating. No wonder I had a skewed sense of what love was supposed to look like. I lived in a story of my own making—a parallel universe where I was older and we were properly dating and all of this was as normal as six-legged frogs, in this particular incarnation of our world. My imagination, if not my body, embraced its full autonomy. I was allowed to think anything I wanted.

I wanted the babysitter to walk up to me and tell me everything would be all right. I wanted different dialogue, different place, different time, different bodies. I had written this scene in my head. I'd tell him I was pregnant. He'd say, "Let's tell our parents together. We can get married. I know you have a favorite doll named Amber. Perhaps we can name the baby Amber."

Instead, he yelled, "fuck" so loud I thought my mom across the street might hear him. But I didn't shush him. He went over to the stereo to put on ABBA's "Super Trouper" and stared out the window, saying "fuck" a million times to himself under his breath. I wanted to sing along to the music. Maybe I did.

Can a forest recover from devastating fire? Big Basin won't look like it did before the fire for hundreds, maybe even thousands of years. That is another thing forests have on their side: time. The oldest tree in the world: Methuselah tree. Methuselah is a Great Basin bristlecone pine (*Pinus longaeva*) that is currently, as of this writing, a mind-bending 4,854 years old. Trees in old growth forests are 250 to 1,000 years old. Old growth forests themselves are millions of years old. According to current scientific understanding, the first forests on earth appeared during the Devonian period, roughly 385 million years ago; with the oldest known forest discovered in Cairo, New York, preserving fossilized root systems of ancient trees like *Archaeopteris*. Is there enough time in a human life to get this old growth forest back? Perhaps if you stick a ten-year-old girl in the middle of a therapist's office, you might begin to amend the burned soil. The therapist tells her that even with her predilection for storytelling, even though she spat out a bunch of bullshit, she, herself, is not shit. He tells her she is a good storyteller. That the truth comes in many forms. You told the mom that no, the babysitter did not molest me. You lied to your mother when all she wanted to do was save you. I told my friend Kelly that story because I'd been reading *The World According to Garp*. But the story covered the story that eventually revealed the material truth. The mom hugs you even if she's not sure whether to believe you. Then, the dad, even though he fills what we thought was a water glass full of vodka, still asks you to input data into Excel spreadsheets for him because he trusts your accuracy and your eyes. Your grandmas, who know or don't know the lies or the truth, still take you for ice cream and fried chicken at the Red Barn. Your sisters know or don't know but they still let you carry them around the house, one in your arms, one hanging on your back. You run up and down the stairs with them. You get out your stuffed animals and play "how to live in a forest." Your imagination will cover for you, which can be a gift. But imagination can also hide from material truth. Some stories *are* garbage. But detritus is as much a part of the forest as anything else. In a balanced ecosystem, waste is cycled into some other use. You will grow that ancient forest again.

"The act of telling itself changes the tale," Dr. Van der Kolk writes in *The Body Keeps the Score*. To me, the fact that telling stories that are bent, crooked, sideways isn't a flaw our culture but a corrective. Sometimes the dreck must be told even if it feels shitty to do it. Sometimes, the culture has to listen to the dreck if it's going to become self-sustaining. Van der Kolk concurs, "The mind cannot help but make meaning out of what it knows, and the meaning we make of our lives changes how and what we remember." Each story forms its own potential meaning. It is its own bit of mycelia that, unfurled, reaches out toward something hungry—meaning, a reader, understanding, a little tree-root, looking for something only the fungi can give it—selenium, perhaps.

At the end of the *NYT* piece, I wrote that without my mom getting me away from the babysitter or getting me an abortion,

> I wouldn't be texting my mom from my home in a beautiful mountain town. I wouldn't teach at the nearby university. I wouldn't be working on a book about climate change and how to shatter predetermined destinies. I wouldn't be married to my husband or have my two children. My life would not have been my own. I would be a prisoner subject to a body's whims—and not *my* body's whims, but the whims of a teenage boy who, as best I can tell, experienced no consequences for inflicting what his body wanted upon my own.

I do not argue that I came through this scot-free any more than I argue that planting a billion, or even a trillion trees, will stop climate change. But I did come through it without some of the worst effects. Et tu, climate, with the help of trees?

I attribute any of my success, if that's what being a writer and a mom of not-screwed-up (yet) kids and a professor is, to rebuilding that burned forest, the reforesting my mother began when she found me a therapist, the planting of friends in that ashen scrub, to a fairly healthy early childhood that formed the mycorrhizal fungi and that I tried very hard, for my writing and for my curiosity, to pay attention to the microorganisms and hyphae, to the tiny details.

As carbon cycle expert Dr. Richard Houghton, at Woodwell Climate Research Center and advocate of the "Trillion Trees Project" project notes, climate and forests are connected ecosystems. Whether researchers study how tiny things within ecosystems work in situ or if they take them into the lab and encourage them to absorb carbon or clean up rocket fuel, scientists see how these tiny things work. As climate change threatens forests with drought, infestations, and subsequent wildfires, scientists are discovering how the smallest changes, from enzyme changes to new growth spouting from the sapwood of trees, make an impact on the whole system.

In the metaphor of human culture as forest, there are forces that remain invisible. This big ecosystem of human culture has many moving parts—some that made the babysitter do what he did, some that made it easy for me to convince myself it wasn't that bad, some that forced my sisters to watch the forest burn even as they didn't know forests were that flammable. Therapy probably saved me from the most deleterious effects of the molestation, but as psychotherapy is practiced today, it promotes anti-ecosystem understandings of human culture—that it is individuals, not whole groups of people, who are overgrown, under-managed, and rife for a catastrophic blaze. The babysitter's family, my family, and even Dr. Tony LePray is tied into the same climate—one microorganism twitches and the whole system shudders. Yet communities do not go to therapy together. Perhaps they should. Maybe instead of outcasting the uncooperative, the weird, the bent, the gross, they could dig deep into the content and find some beneficial micronutrients in the dirty, pervasive ground.

In Ovid's *Metamorphoses*, Arachne, a mortal renowned for her tapestries, challenges the goddess, Athena, also renowned for her weaving skills, as well as her wisdom and warring prowess, and that she'd popped herself from Zeus' head fully formed, to a weaving contest. Athena could find no flaws in Arachne's work. Not renowned for her ability to measure her emotions, Athena beats her with her shuttle—the wooden tool that pushes threads back and forth upon the loom. Arachne, embarrassed and bruised, hangs herself. Athena, out of admiration or honor, transforms Arachne into a spider so Arachne can weave her story again.

According to Navajo culture, the holy deity Spider Man, brought the people the loom of sunshine, lightning, and rain, and the holy deity Spider Woman, taught the People how to weave. Blanket weaving comprises layers of Navajo existence: in ceremony, as clothing, as commerce, and as story. Each blanket woven tells a story. Sierra Teller Ornelas, writes about her mother, a weaver and contributing author to *Spider Woman's Children: Navajo Weavers Today*, in "Every Rug Tells a Story," seeing her own rugs on display in Santa Fe.

> She'll spot her piece and walk over to it. Compelled by the memory it evokes, she'll tell me everything about the rug and what we were going through at the time. ("I had just started dating your dad when I wove that ... I got most of the wool from your Grandma Margaret ... We used some of the money to go to San Francisco for the first time ... ") She'll tell me who bought it and if they were fair in the negotiation. She'll point to areas of pattern and explain their significance. ("That dot is you. That one is your brother.")[1]

Perhaps taking the cautionary tale of Arachne to heart, Navajo weavers leave a loose string as an imperfection, acknowledging there is no perfect weaver but the goddess Athena.

Perhaps trauma survivors are evidence of the imperfections in our human communities, but these imperfections shouldn't be submerged or hidden or cast out. A forest moves, unlike a finished rug. The forest envelops whatever comes, perfect or imperfect. In fact, the forest doesn't judge perfect vs. imperfect. It just makes more forest out of whatever detritus it is given.

What does the intricacies of forest systems have to do with repairing peoples' lives? Perhaps human culture is the problem itself. It's that our culture doesn't account for all the tiny details—which, of course, it can't, because as Hamlet says to Horatio, "There are more things in heaven and earth, Horatio,/ Than are dreamt of in your philosophy." But would that imaginations, opinions, politics, media, ideas—the abstractions of culture—attend to the microscopic, the things you can measure, even if they're difficult to see. Would that the ways humans move and judge and support one another include seeing the elite and majestic peaks of trees as well as the moldering, nutrient-transferring debris that decays along the forest floor, feeding the mycorrhizal fungus which in turn, feed the trees. Trees are big but the underground systems that sustain them are bigger than we could imagine.

If all the fungi within a half gram of forest soil were lined up, they would form a line that's half a mile long. That same half gram of soil includes bacteria that number in the hundreds of thousands. These fungi and bacteria, through their nutrient cycling and other valuable ecosystem services, sustain the forests that dominate the Pacific Northwest. It's why mycologists joke that trees are the photosynthetic appendages of fungi.

(https://www.fs.usda.gov/pnw/sciencef/scifi207.pdf)

Ecosystem research lets me imagine how much gross and rotting stuff contributes to the forest's health. That's the stuff upon which healthful microorganisms grow. Like stories, all that fallen detritus is where mushrooms get their zhuzh. Underneath the piles of rotting needles and leaves, slug trails, fallen trees, and soil are thin threads of mycelia chat make up the carpet of mycorrhizal fungi which undergirds so much of the living forest. This rangy, webby underlayment pushes up mushrooms to reproduce, but its most magnificent job is pushing nutrients into the hyphae—tiny hairs that reach out from the mycelia into the roots of trees. These fungal threads can be very fine, branching between soil particles, and even exploring the shells of dead insects. The mycelia send nutrients up to the leaves of the tree. The trees, doing their own photosynthetic magic, send different nutrients back down to the mycelia. This microscopic push and pull is the kind of synergy I wish I had, that we all had, among our families and communities. When one nutrient is lacking, the entire forest works together to provide, through the interconnected webbing of the forest. The stuff of sky-light and energy, these ethereal things, are converted into bodily substance, with the help of that decaying rubbish on the ground, and, together, they push substance through the trees leaves and needles, back into air. The babysitter story was nothing but an ethereal myth until I hooked the muck-ridden and dirty truth into the telling. And then it became something that I could shape like clay.

3

Just Up and Move

The trees are moving west. Unlike the pioneering white settlers, the trees are not moving very fast—about ten miles a decade. It will take a long time for the trees to decimate buffalo populations, turn prairie grass to wheat, decimate Indigenous populations, and establish Walmart as the largest employer. Still. They're coming. Thirsty trees of the east move westward, as, due to climate change, rain in the east, especially the southeast, is drying up. Fortunately, in the Midwest, rain grows heavier. The trees, tempted by this moisture, send their seeds a little further to the left. It's mainly deciduous plants like scarlet oak that want to move. Beware Gambel oaks, you scrubbier version. The big trees are coming for your water.

Freedom to move is seen as a fundamental right to American culture. Manifest Destiny and apple trees, Mormon pioneers, and Dunkin Donuts—the right to replant yourself in other territory is embedded in our sense of self. The United States is so large! Why not try all fifty flavors? Bring your tulips of Michigan to Arizona, your chestnuts of Massachusetts to Oregon, your cotton to New Mexico. If you think of an ecosystem as big as the planet, all the new species will sort themselves out, right? They'll be checks and balances on the invasions—except for a few overly aggressive ones, like the tamarisk trees that slurp water from the Colorado River through their non-native straws or the Emerald Ash Borer that drills into ash trees, leaving a wound as big as a quarter, we'll find a way to manage these new visitors.

Utah loves its trees. Who would imagine the state whose terrain that is often compared to Mars would be so verbose with the number of named trees: white Fir, Rocky Mountain Maple, Bigtooth Maple Boxelder, Serviceberry,

Netleaf Hackberry, Mountain Mahogany, Desert Willow, Douglas Hawthorn, Utah Juniper, Rocky Mountain Juniper, Engelmann Spruce, Blue Spruce, Bristlecone Pine, Lodgepole Pine, Pinyon Pine, Ponderosa Pine, Narrowleaf Cottonwood, Fremont Cottonwood, Aspen, Chokecherry, Douglas Fir, Gambel Oak, Peachleaf Willow.

    Drive along South Temple, huge maples, elms, and lindens canopy like flying buttresses over the street, shading your car from the very-hot, high desert sun. From South Temple and State Street, you can see all the way out to South Jordan, Draper, Sandy which used to be populated by orchards of apple, peach, cherry, and apricot trees and now it is populated with popular landscaping trees like Japanese maples and honey locusts. Northern Utah, unlike southern Utah, is no Mars. The biggest populations centers boast the most trees. The settlers re-routed the mountain streams, attached garden hoses, and colonized the hell out of the dirt, the rocks, the scrappier pinyon pines and junipers.

After the abortion, after the babysitter drove his Jeep up Stonehill Lane without even slowing to see if I was OK. After winter break, when I went back to school, something had changed. No one said anything directly to my face, but my teachers didn't look me in the eyes. Some of my friends, Jodie, Jennifer, Jessica, and Sarah, who already mostly couldn't hang out with me because I wasn't Mormon and because my parents drank wine, played four square without me. I stood on the edge of the square, waiting to be let in, but the girls with the red ball managed something never-before-accomplished: they did not let that red ball out of bounds even one time, creating a forcefield of them, inside the big square that held the smaller squares. That forcefield didn't budge for the rest of the year, no matter if we were outside on the playground or inside the classroom.

    I came home once to see my sister crying, my mom holding her with one arm, the other gesticulating. When they saw me, she stopped crying, my mom stopped explaining. They looked down at the floor. It wasn't until later that I learned that when Valerie was in the lunch line, the lunch lady shook her head and said, "I hope you don't end up a slut like your sister."

Forest fires in the west burn hotter than they did pre-colonization. Fire suppression meant that any lightning strike or campfire run amok was extinguished as quickly as possible. Trees were money and you wouldn't burn good money would you? But now, our forests are kind of messy. When Trump said before the raging fires of 2020, when Californians wore masks for COVID-19 inside and masks for smoke outside, that we should rake the forest, he wasn't exactly wrong. There is a lot of detritus on the forest floor. Pre-settler people let small fires burn, which cleaned up fallen branches, dead leaves, hopeless grasses, sappy, inflammatory pine needles. Now, when a fire gets going, it has all that material built up over centuries of forest management policies, the heat reaches temperatures that the fire-resistant bark cannot resist.

Under these policies, when wildfires destroyed acres of forest, or when forest products corporations clear-cutting swaths of forest, forest managers replanted trees. Hundreds of trees. Sometimes the kind that had been there. Sometimes a kind that grew faster so you could harvest it quickly to cut it down again to make more money. Forests became a kind of crop, like corn, grown for the greatest return. These trees, grown so close together, aren't spaced as they would be in an old growth or native forest. And hot forest fires kill the bacteria and fungi in the soil. These tree farms may look like green forests but the webs of connections between the microbial soil ecosystems, the mycorrhizal networks, and the communication between trees isn't happening. Tree sluts, forest managers and paper companies were. As many as you can plant. The more the merrier.

When school let out for the summer, I didn't have to see Jodie, Jennifer, Jessica, and Sarah anymore. And the babysitter and his sister were obviously off limits. And my sisters had each other. Plus, I probably smelled a lot like fire. Who would want to play with me?

But on the street behind Stonehill, high schoolers lived. I would be starting middle school soon. Maybe that was close enough. So, I rode my bike up and down Tree Farm Lane until one of the boys invited me inside his house.

At first, my job was to watch the teenager boys play Ultima. They were very good at this early role-playing game. I was very bored. Still, it was better than sitting in my bedroom, playing with my doll, Amber, who had begun to age.

She now looked more like a wrinkling old woman than a baby. And I probably looked of age. Of a kind of age. An age older than teenagers, because I had been on *General Hospital* before, at least in my mind.

On the soaps, people change lovers like modern day folks change the channel. What difference did it make, if, once Sean, wanted to see me in the backseat of his Camaro or Tony wanted to meet me outback on the trampoline?

My friend Larissa, my age, but less in need of redemption, and I met two guys at the mall who were old enough to drive us home. We snuck into my basement. Larissa and the boy made out on the couch. The other boy took my arm and pulled me into my old playroom. I don't remember his name. Shane? Steve? I do better these days with the names of trees. I don't remember when he and his friend left or what Larissa and I talked about after. She must have told me what happened on the couch. I told her what happened in the playroom.

I would have liked a little more story to go with my story, like they have in the soap operas. Perhaps, Tony needed comforting because his sister had amnesia. Perhaps Sean had just returned from his own bout of amnesia and thought I was his wife, although she'd been dead for many years. But my story was my story. The girl who had sex with the babysitter and had the abortion. It was a shitty story, but it was mine. The irony that the street was called Tree Farm Lane didn't come until I started writing this book, but the trees, they lined up. They seemed mostly the same as all the other trees to me.

If these men were some kind of substitute for the forest, they were weedy replacements. But I too felt as thin as dried weeds. When you're 13, you're just fine with burning it all down. You get used to the smoke. In fact, you might find it addictive. I don't remember my exact first cigarette. In the story I tell myself, I think it was at Noah's house on Chadbourne Street, part of the sixth concentric outcropping of Salt Lake suburbs. Noah was the same age as the babysitter but things had changed. I didn't watch *General Hospital* anymore. I had moved on from copying the babysitter's music taste like Rush and Loverboy, to listening to The Clash and The Doors. I met Noah through Tony. They knew each other from high school, which Noah did attend on occasion. Tony, who lived on Tree Farm Lane, only wanted to experiment with fire. His parents expected him to date girls his age, get good grades, and go to college. They even bought him a moped. Noah, born to need-to-get-married parents who parents were on-again, off-again, whose mom worked housekeeping at Shilo Inn and whose dad worked sometimes or not at all, and, when he didn't, growled at his kids and punched holes in the drywall above his wife's head, already knew what a burning forest smelled like.

Noah's dad, Randy, smoked Marlboro Reds. Thus, Noah must have smoked Marlboro's. Thus, that must have been my first cigarette. Chadbourne Street was dotted with matching duplexes that alternated yellow, blue, yellow, blue in a neighborhood otherwise populated by detached, five-bedroom family homes. My Aunt Brooke had lived in a blue one after her divorce, before she went back to school to get her graduate degree. It was transitional housing for those who could get out of there. It was where Noah and his family lived—a yellow one—for most of Noah's childhood.

I sat cross-legged on the driveway, scratching the dirt line between concrete sidewalk squares with a stick. If I dug out all the dirt, would the concrete shift? Was the dirt keeping the driveway in place or was it gravity? Instead of joining me in my seventh-grade science experiment, Noah dug his hands into the engine of his VW Fastback, which he'd purchased for $500—money he made working at a body shop. He asked for a wrench. I stood up, unwinding my crisscrossed legs, to bring him the tool.

"Not this kind. Adjustable."

I sorted through the toolbox again, found an adjustable.

"Need me to hold anything?" I asked.

It's not so weird to go from helping your dad nail siding in the hot tub room you built with him at your house to helping your boyfriend fix his VW. My dad had a Karmann Ghia when he first drove. My dad should have, ostensibly, approved. I was working with tools even if my main work was stick-scratching driveway dirt. But my dad neither approved nor disapproved. Unlike my mom, he didn't try to keep track of me. I imagine he was just grateful I wasn't stealing his Benson & Hedges.

A brief interlude about my dad. If I had to choose a tree to represent my dad, I would say bonsai—maybe a topiary, maybe a dwarf apple. He was heavily manicured and a bit stunted. My mom, having read several books about what happens to young people who are molested, said, "I wonder if your dad was molested. It would explain his drinking. His lack of emotional growth." I think the drinking explained the drinking and lack of growth, but it's possible he suffered some trauma in his youth. He didn't talk much about his childhood. My grandma, who I was close to, didn't talk too much about my dad, although she adored him. Maybe my grandpa, who died when I was one, resented her adoration? Maybe punished my dad for it?

He had the confidence of a fifteen-year-old boy who has to talk himself up because he wasn't sure anyone else appreciated his mad financial management skills. He impressed upon me and my sisters the importance of dressing well, working hard, and making money. My sisters and I work when we're on vacation—even in our sweatpants, even on teachers' salaries.

He spoiled us a little—bought us cars when we turned sixteen. My sisters, three years younger than I, didn't get the years of building hot tub rooms, staining desks, crafting ships from popsicle sticks. They tended to him when drinking got really bad and his liver started to go. He shrank. He seemed to get younger, needing people to nearly carry him from couch to bed. He became so young that he finally disappeared entirely, like a bonsai tree cut too sharp.

Watching Noah work on the car was a little better than watching the boys of Tree Farm Lane play Ultima—I occasionally had a job, like wrench delivery. Did I smoke as he worked on the car? I don't think so. If I had been smoking, I would have been sitting cross-legged on the sidewalk, grinding cigarettes rather than sticks into the ground. But maybe we had just finished smoking. Noah's mom, April, didn't mind if we smoked at her house. She didn't like it if we drank her beer but, if we were quiet about it, we could have sex upstairs. The only rule? If we heard Noah's dad come home, we'd hightail it out of there. Noah's dad was a different kind of drinker than my dad. He was the kind that would say to his son, in front of me, as he held onto the wall for support, "Isn't she a little young? Does she even have hair down there?" April chastised Noah's dad with a long, drawn out, "Randy," while she shook her head. But she was careful not to say much more. There were holes in the drywall from Randy being aggravated by April or by one of their three sons. April rushed us out of the house when she got wind that Randy was on his way home. Sometimes, he didn't announce his arrival. Sometimes, he came home in the middle of the day, as if he wanted to catch us doing something indiscreet. As distant as my dad sometimes was, I couldn't imagine not wanting him to come home. My dad came home at 6:30 every evening. Randy's unpredictable hours scared me. Whenever he caught us, I hid behind Noah who was as big as his dad—maybe even bigger.

As Noah grew more and more frustrated, trying to free the intractable metal from the engine block, he hit the carburetor with the screwdriver. Then, he got a hammer. Between the wrench, the hammer, and the screwdriver, he tore the carburetor from the engine. Noah, who took after his father in temperament, threw the carburetor across the driveway, into the street. The metal crashed into the bitumen where it came apart completely in front of the townhouse where my aunt, just a few years earlier, used to live.

My parents' house was only three streets south. Oak Ridge, then Creek Road, then Stone Hill, but across all those bulldozed flattened ridges and hills, their creeks diverted, that house was part of a different ecosystem. Five bathrooms, five bedrooms, for five people! My dad had his own office. On our TV, we were among the first cable-initiates, MTV and HBO curled into our living room and wrapped us up like an invasive snake. In the basement, if we could free ourselves from the encircling cords, Paige and Val and I practiced the piano and choreographed dances to the soundtrack of *Grease* in the same basement where that boy took me by the arm to the playroom.

Behind our house, the construction for the Mormon church hadn't begun yet. My sisters and I dragged a mattress through the field. We slid down to the little bit of Deer Creek left to flow, undammed and unpiped. We threw twigs into the water and ran along the bank to try to reach them before they disappeared underground, when the dirt turned into road. I didn't even remember the creek until recently when I was wondering why trees seemed so important to the story of my childhood. I really didn't spend that much time with trees—at least not wild ones. But there were some wild trees that lined Deer Creek. I don't know whether that stream has been diverted to irrigate fields, or is pumped into the water treatment plant, or retrained to flow behind property fancier than our five-bedroom home. Or, perhaps it is global-warmingly dried up. Or, maybe it's still there, hidden behind fences marked "do not trespass." Or, in the best version of the story, it's still twisting behind the bottom of the hill—free because no one can build on such an incline. No one can find the stream or its trees so it's safe from whatever the current settlers want to do to it.

At the top of the hill, on that well-bulldozed plain, in our backyard, my dad planted fruit trees. He planted roses. My mom, in charge of annuals, tucked marigolds and petunias into the soft beds of amended soil. It's hard to talk about how lucky we were, especially when I consider the fucked-upedness of my childhood. But bad falls are cushioned by landings made soft with extra money and decorative plants.

But money didn't keep me home. After school, I went to Noah's three-bedroom, two-bath duplex, or Noah and I would drive into the next arrondissement of suburb—the one that hadn't been built yet. We called it the four-lane because that's what it was—a four-lane highway cut into the landscape—but where no homes had been built yet. The trees remained, for a while, the only witnesses to Noah and my explorations.

Noah was four years older than me. Almost the same number of years old as the babysitter. But this was different, I protested then and I protest now. My parents knew about it. Dr. Tony LePray knew about it. In fact, Dr. LePray had negotiated an agreement with my parents where, as long as I committed to school and to one guy, I could date. Unlike the babysitter, we dated out in the open. Noah came over to my house for tacos every Friday night. It was different and sanctioned. And yet.

We drove out on the four-lane. Noah asked me what we should pretend.

"Church."

"Church this time. Good." He pulled over. "Sorry the car broke down. I'm sure someone from the Wardhouse will come by and help us soon. Why don't we sit in the shade for a bit. Have some lemonade." We didn't actually have any lemonade, but he did have a blanket which he got out of the back of the car.

"Sit here," he patted the spot next to him. I sat down, pretending innocence although I already knew how this story went.

"You know, you're pretty. I know you're almost ready to start thinking of marriage." This church we pretended to be driving home from was Mormon. The girls he knew from high school got married early. Like right after high school or as soon as their boyfriends returned from their missions. In this story, I was older than I was in reality—but less experienced.

"You know, as your bishop, I'm allowed to give you some advice on marriage and the like. How to practice for it."

"Practice for marriage? Like making dinner?" I asked, with pretend innocence.

"Well, practicing the part that makes babies. Do you know how that works?"

I shook my head.

"Let me help you figure it out. Put your hands in the air."

I lifted my hands, and he removed my shirt.

"When you're married, you'll have garments that you keep on while you lay together. But for now, just keep this bra on."

He took off my pants but left my underwear on.

"The garments will have holes in them for this. But for our purposes today, we'll leave these on too."

He put his warm hand against me until I became warm too. Then, he pulled the leg of my underwear to the side. The elastic must have bitten into him. I wonder, do garments help or hinder? There's something about fabric that makes you feel like you're in the wrong place at the right time, or vice-versa—which my body had learned was the definition of sexy. You're not supposed to be doing this—but here you are, on a blanket, off the four-way, under a cluster of trees that have been here longer than any of your ancestors who claim they were destined to be here a long time ago. Is Mormon sex sexier because of what it tries to hide behind that fabric?

Noah wasn't a selfish lover. He wasn't a molester. He kissed me. Sometimes, I was the experienced one in our four-lane stories. We pretended he was my young student. Sometimes, I was the Sunday School teacher. Who is out of place in this story? Me, at thirteen? Me, who was already heading down that wrong path? Noah and me—our parents had all left the Mormon church in which they'd been raised. If the four-lane was the road to hell, who put us on it? Should I have known to get off this go-nowhere highway?

I tell this story for prurient reasons as well as artistic ones. What happens to a reader's mind when they are confronted with this story? I'm sure shock and maybe disgust. And maybe a little titillation. It is difficult to talk about bodies, especially bodies in sex, especially bodies in sex that should probably not have been having sex, and not have a complicated response. This is not the kind of trouble Donna Haraway asked her readers to stay with, but I wonder if stopping here for a moment and feeling this discomfort—sitting with an array of emotions and concerns shooting out in all directions, might be one way to practice a cat's cradle. What if this troubling narrative spins new narratives, ones previously inconceivable? If a story is a half-gram of mycelia, how many half-miles out do stories stretch and unfold?

It's as difficult to trace all the effects of childhood sexual abuse as it is to imagine how much forest there once was and now how little. Imagination, like imagining these young people having sex under Gambel oak trees off a future road, is like trying to imagine how much forest has been lost and what the accumulation of that loss means. The internet attempts to contextualize the numbers: Over 200,000 acres of rainforest are burned every day. That is over 150 acres lost every minute of every day, and 78 million acres are lost every year. During the 2024 Canadian wildfires, over 5.3 million hectares by total area burned. In the last decade, 7.08 million acres burned in California. When Resource Market Watch calculates how much wood is harvested each year from public and private forests, they don't measure in terms of trees or acres but in terms of cubic meters. "Wood" differs from "tree" in the same way "pork" differs from "pig." Still, 439 million cubic meters is another number we can try, and probably fail, to imagine. It's easier to fantasize about bishops taking advantage of young, church-going women than it is to imagine these numbers of trees.

The planting of trees carries its own number's game. The organization *8 Billion Trees,* presents that 1.9 billion trees are planted yearly, estimating that 158 million trees around the planet are replanted every month. And out of the 158 million trees, 5 million are replanted each day, and approximately 7,000 are planted every minute. The Nature Conservancy offers a program to Plant a Billion Trees. By donating x number of dollars, you can be part of their forest restoration program. They claim that "trees help make peoples' lives better—they filter clean air, provide fresh drinking water, help curb climate change, and create homes for thousands of plant and animal species." But around the world, forests are being cut down at alarming rates for all types of reasons. From harvesting timber to cutting down trees to make room for development, some of these places are now degraded and have lost the ability to provide the benefits we rely on.

"But forest restoration can help bring balance back to these ecosystems while increasing the capacity to store harmful emissions that cause climate change. By supporting Plant a Billion Trees, you can help TNC restore forests that will survive the long term to benefit people, nature and the climate." (https://www.nature.org). Some say this denuding of the forests also "helps make peoples lives better." If we're planting 8 billion trees, that's one tree per person, and yet, I don't think that's quite the balance we're going for. Perhaps a billion trees per person? Or, even better, a billion trees per bear cub, owl, squirrel, salamander.

It's easier to imagine sending twenty-five dollars than it is to imagine planting twenty-five trees. Planting trees is a pain—especially here in Arizona where I have planted several apple trees. I took my shovel into the back yard, picked a spot, pointed the spade part toward the ground and jumped hard on flat end of the shovel. The dirt did not move. Flagstaff's soil contains mainly clay content, which is good for making pots, not so good for growing apple trees. However, the largest contiguous ponderosa pine forest in the lower 48 manages to do just fine. Soil is context and context is everything, making the difference between fertility and infertility, knowing consent and complete fantasy.

Still, I fantasize forests—ones where the trees are spaced well apart, branches too high to reach, but as they reach and cross, become the alphabet that writes the manual for how to enter heaven. Evergreen feels like a kind of immortality. Trees, who outnumber humans and outlive them. No wonder we fall prey to a little hero worship. And, then, we set the axe and match upon our heroes. Perhaps we like nothing to be taller or older or more plentiful than us or that questions how the definition of the word "useful" deviates depending on whether it's humans or trees talking.

I did not want to admit to my deviancy. How different was the context between Noah and the babysitter? I snuck out my house in the night, creeping down the stairs, sliding open the dining room window, slipping out onto the roof of the hot tub room my dad and I had built together, shimming down the gutter pipe onto the AC unit, and out into the fields. Before Smiths Grocery was built on the corner of 7800 South and 3400 East, before the church was built behind my backyard, before the four-lane had houses lined along it, I could stay up all night in the summer where it never seemed to get cold and the haze didn't interfere with the light from the stars, and Noah, and I, and even Linda, who was Noah's age but friend to us both, sat on the landscaping walls that pushed the dirt from neighbor's yards into tidy squares. We weren't always derelict. We weren't always debauched. Sometimes, we swung our feet in unison, imagining how we got here, how wild this sky seemed, how bent into ordinary and domestic our parents wanted us to be. How we wanted to resist becoming them. "Deviant" didn't seem like a bad thing when compared to conforming to the square rules of adulthood like these overwatered green lawns conformed to the rigid landscaping walls.

Escape wasn't necessarily necessary. It wasn't that anything was *that* wrong at my house. My dad left for work at 6:45 a.m. so he could swim at Steiner, the university pool, for an hour before he drove to his job at TerraTek on Wakara Way. His office was located in Research Park, the lucrative offshoot of the University of Utah. Pressed against the foothills, the Park is squared in glass and steel now but when my dad worked there, the brick buildings were more understated, blending in with the rust-colored rocks and cracked straw of the mountain's feet. He worked 11-hour days, coming home at 6:30, sometimes drunk but not too often, not back then.

My mom ironed, put up peaches, pickles, pears, and cherries, like her mom did before her and her mom did before that. But my mom also reconciled budgets for my dad's start-up financial advising company. She took accounting classes so my dad didn't have to hire a CPA. Perhaps, too, she was preparing to leave my dad and wanted to have some skills to get a job and some kind of sense of how much money it took to go it alone. She didn't confide in me too much then, but in retrospect, I can see she was living many narrative threads at once: good Mormon-like wife; distraught, worried mother; woman planning a new life, escaping up into the mountains where, in the future, after she divorced my dad, would work at the pharmacy at Snowbird. In his many-layered selves, dad fixed the sprinklers; he planted carrots; he sprayed the deck. Sometimes, he slurred his words. Twice, he crashed his car. Sometimes, he went down to the bar at the mouth of the canyon and bought a round of drinks so he could pretend he had friends. I, even then, had my own multiple lives. I was a kid with dolls; a reader; a dancer; a singer; a smoker of cigarettes who sat under the growing apple tree, believing neither parent had any idea of what I was up to even though of course they could smell the smoke.

Words have many lives too. I discovered that the street my dad worked on was named after a Shoshone chief. Chief Wakara led the Timpanogos and Sanpete bands of what were thought to be Ute tribes but may well be Shoshone. Chief Wakara had been revered as a trusted trader by Ute and Shoshone, as well as by white settlers. But the easy trading relationship didn't last long once Brigham Young and his followers arrived in Salt Lake Valley in 1847. Gradually, the Mormon settlers began to push the Indigenous people out. When the Ute and Shoshone resisted, the Mormons used more aggressive means to force them onto land less arable, with water far from the crops they would try to raise.

Hunger and frustration drove Chief Wakara to lead his fellow Utes and Shoshones to raid Mormon settlements. Brigham Young retaliated—instigating what would later be called The Walker War (1853-4) after which began the erasure of the Ute and Shoshone culture from the Salt Lake Valley. The fudging of the name here, from Wakara to Walker, I would like to serve as a sign that my dad, Bruce H. Walker and myself, my sisters, and my mom, who still keeps his last name, were on the side of good. But, of course, we weren't there, timewise and if we had been, it would have been on the side of wrong. There are many things you can do with a name—trace your history, begin a story, make an anagram out of it until you can't recognize yourself—but you can't lie about where your name came from.

Before the Mormons arrived, the tree species that grew in the Salt Lake Valley are ones I'm familiar with here in Flagstaff: Quaking aspen, Pinyon Pine, Gambel oak, Douglas Fir. There are more ponderosa here than Utah juniper or cottonwood but as Northern Arizona spans 7,000 feet elevation and nine different life zones, northern Utah expresses similar terrain. But Salt Lake Valley is lower, elevation wise, than Flagstaff, and, thus, a little more temperate. There, the Mormon settlers brought trees and plants from their Midwest environs—greenery that made them feel more at home. The Manifest Destiny here wasn't just to claim territory for white people, although that was indeed part of the plot. Their religious command was to turn this desert land into its own kind of Eden. They named it Zion for the Promised Land—a name and idea borrowed from Jewish people. Salt Lake Valley is nothing if not a hodgepodge of substitutions. white settlers for Indigenous people. Blessings for Jewish people that didn't ask for them. Apple trees for Chokecherry. The Western Goshute, a band of Shoshone, called The Great Salt Lake, Pi'a-pa, meaning "big water," or Ti'tsa-pa, meaning "bad water." Big bad water kind of works, although the millions of birds that migrate to eat the brine shrimp that live there wouldn't call it bad at all.

The problem with my story is that I was named the bad guy. When my mom told the babysitter's parents that the babysitter had impregnated me, they accused me of spreading *Playboy* magazines across their backyard—a form of toilet papering? I don't know. I didn't do it, although I could imagine a version of the story that was me saying to them, "Look at this. This is what your son does. This is what your son likes." But I didn't do it. Nor did I say it. I still wonder who did it. Maybe his sister. Maybe the babysitter did it himself and then blamed me—a kind of "see, she tried to seduce me and rile me up," kind of defense. I understand his mother's willingness to believe. Just as my mother believed that I'd made up the story I'd told Kelly. What mother, who, in the driving winds of a hurricane, wouldn't want to wrap her brain in a sail of "that girl must be fucked-up." And I'm sure I was, in my way. And still am, in my way. But invading the neighbors' backyards with sheets of *Playboys* I didn't do.

The facts I remember seem clear: He was babysitting. I was wearing a tube top. My sister, goofing around, pulled it down in front of him. I screamed and pulled up the shirt, so embarrassed. I ran upstairs to my bedroom.

The babysitter followed. "It's OK," he said. "It's just your goofy little sister. Don't even worry about it." He reached over to the flimsy string that held my tube top up and readjusted it. I felt better. He had a little sister. He knew what little sisters were like. I let my sister off the hook. I truly didn't worry about it. I didn't wonder, like I do now, if my nipples were the same purple as that tank top. I didn't wonder if my sisters maybe thought this was something he would like. Or I would like. I didn't wonder too much about his relationship with his sister. I didn't worry, until now, that maybe he wasn't just flirting with me. Maybe he was flirting with my sisters too. I mean, the whole thing was in good fun, right? He laughed when they laughed even as he followed me to my bedroom. Facts are easy to see. How one fact presses down the lever on one's future are less clear.

Later, the babysitter led me back downstairs. He fed us chicken fingers. I helped him put Paige and Valerie to bed. I was allowed to stay up late enough to watch MASH. My parents wouldn't be home until after midnight. We sat on the couch. He reached for the same string he had readjusted. He worked the string down over my shoulder, pulling until the same purple nipple was revealed. I didn't say anything. He'd touched the string earlier. My brain operated on a strict logic: You break it; you buy it. You touch it; it's yours. A kind of materialism? Or perhaps that possession is 9/10ths of the law cliché that isn't actually true, but you still tell your sisters that when you have taken the Oreos from the kitchen cupboard and hidden them in your room, that they are all yours now. No point in arguing.

I don't think that it was my idea that he take my shirt off. But I don't know. It was the 1980s. I didn't understand what rules there were for how to be ten. Or maybe I didn't think of myself as eleven at all. Maybe I'd read that children of alcoholics grow up fast. Maybe I thought since I was the oldest sister, I was more mature than my age. What would I get out of following him to his room again after that first time at my house on the couch? Attention? Did I feel the need to please people that much? How can you make a narrative out of nothing but questions? I am trying to let all the possibilities extend themselves. I'm trying to stay with the trouble and let all the paths unfurl in front of me, let all the narratives *be* for a minute. I thought I was in a movie version of my life. I wanted to please the babysitter. I might have even thought the sex felt good, although I don't remember feeling that. I might have thought I was capable of consent, that I knew what I was doing. I might have just wanted to be different. Perhaps, I thought this was love and who turns down love?

Three years later, I'm thirteen. I didn't wear tube tops anymore, but I did wear shirts that are removable for the purposes of sex. With Noah, I usually took them off myself. Am I just substituting one rationalization for another or is there the difference between a wildfire/molestation and a prescribed burn/an older boyfriend with weird fantasies? Here's perhaps the difference between the babysitter and Noah: With the babysitter, it was a one-way fantasy, me believing I was someone else and something else. An entirely made-up story so I could bear what was happening to me. With Noah, however strange our fantasies, at least we shared them out loud. An untold story, made to be kept quiet, one which you can't share even with the person with whom you are physically enacting the fantastical, becomes perverse. It creates all the detritus left on the forest floor. Fuel, when you're a forest of one, piles higher—some of its tinders touch the tips of the canopy. The bark of a redwood can withstand some flame, but once the dry bones of "don't tell" reach the sharp green, there's a threat that the fire destroys everything.

Noah seemed like forest enough. I exchanged my Amber doll for trips with him to Deseret Industries, Utah's Mormon form of Goodwill. There, we shopped for baby clothes and used car seats for a future we thought we might have. He wouldn't have minded to exchange drywall full of dad-punched holes for a new forest. And I was like, hello pinecone. My body had been changed by being pregnant. Even though I didn't end up with a fistula in my bladder from giving birth when I was 11, my breasts dripped milk for a month after the abortion with the babysitter. With Noah, two years after the abortion, as I fingered the crocheted hoops of a baby blanket, my uterus felt empty—as desolate as a clear cut. If Noah had said, let's buy this crib, I would have started digging into still hot ashes.

But we were not dendrologists. We didn't know that it took more than sticking a seedling into the ground and praying for rain to build a forest. We didn't know about the underground mycorrhizal systems that supported the trees. We didn't how necessary healthy soil, fallen trees, mosses, and mushrooms were to make a forest. Two trees, one thirteen, the other seventeen, do not a forest make. Our soils, depleted, made good ground for invasive species like Russian olive, not so good for majestic trees like Semper Severis, or for babies.

4

Dry as Smoke

Salt Lake painted itself in God's or, at least the Midwest's, image. They planted any kind of tree—Tamarisk that outcompeted native cottonwoods, Russian olive that thirsted for ground water, box elders that drew box elder bugs. Once the settlers cleared the land of native plants and forcibly moved the humans that had been living there for centuries into the saltier, drier parts of the state, they turned the color of the valley from scrappy sage to vivid green. The valley blossomed with weeds—non-native maples and lindens, apple, and peach trees. Kentucky bluegrass grew thick for the lawn mowers and cheat grass grew tall for the cattle. Weeds of tulips and roses, dahlias and peonies reflected the Midwest and upstate New York and even the England we wanted to remember. It looked very nice and organized.

But then things started to glitch. In the lowest part of winter, in the lowest part of the valley, even when the Utes and Shoshone burned smaller, personal fires, an inversion settled over the basin. High-pressure forced cold air down and then, without wind or storm, the valley-sky accumulated dust and smoke. In the mountains, the air remained clear. Pre-settler, this inversion lasted only for a week or two. As I was growing up, I was told that the Indigenous people called Salt Lake "Smoky Valley." When the Mormons settled, they brought more wood and coal smoke. Then, they brought industries that spun clouds of heavy particles into the sky which fell into the Great Salt Lake. The railroads and trolleys were soon replaced by cars. Bands of freeways wrapped the city in ribbons. What had been a two-week smoke-filled valley became a smog-filled one for a month, then two, now sometimes an entire winter is spent under an oppressive layer of gray. What falls from the sky is frozen ash, not snow. Even the orchards that had been planted in the wake of the forced removal of the Shoshone and Utes were now being removed for bands of housing.

Suburban houses cannot convert the particles in the air into breathable gas like the native trees, or even the apple trees could. Grasses, mown, then stuffed into Hefty bags, can't recycle gray smog into blue sky. Unlike forests, invasive plants don't connect in an underground system of call and response. Every mullein, Dalmatian Toadflax, cheese weed, bind weed, thistle is on its own.

Currently, the west is in its twenty-sixth year of a mega-drought, but the year of the babysitter was the year of the Great Flood. I remember the flood and I remember the babysitter, but it was only when my mom was asked by the fact checker about the article in the *Times* that I knew both happened the same year.

"That's how I remember the year," she said to the fact checker. "They had lined State Street with sandbags, dividing the west side of the city from the east, making it hard to get from the freeway to the woman's clinic."

I think of my mom putting me in the car like the kid she still thought I was. I imagine she told me to put my seat belt on. If it had been our current times, I may not have been allowed to sit in the front seat. Kids under twelve are supposed to sit in the back. Although I, probably recklessly, let each of my kids sit in the front seat when they turned ten.

I didn't know that 1983 was the year. I was eleven when she took me to the clinic. I'd always thought I was twelve when the babysitter impregnated me, but she remembered because it was the year of record snowfall and a hot, quick spring melt that brought the floods. I also thought I had helped shovel sand into some of the bags that lined State Street, but that hero-story couldn't have happened. For the months surrounding the abortion, I went nowhere except to school and therapy. I must have experienced most of the flooding through the TV.

In response to rising waters, the governor responded to the rising levels of the lake by purchasing pumps to drain the excess water further into the desert. The pumps worked for about six months, then, the lake reduced itself to normal size. Then, two years after the flood, the mega-drought began, and the lake reduced itself further. Now, thirty-two years later, the pumps sit silent, many, many miles from the water they once chugged.

By the time the drought had begun, I had started smoking regularly. Noah and I, when his Fastback was running, drove along Wasatch, down 4th South, to Raunch Records where I bought *CRASS* LPs and he found 45s of local bands like The Massacre Guys and The Bad Yodelers. We smoked in front of Cosmic Aeroplane and in front of the Speedway. We smoked inside at the Indian Center where we moshed to music. My claim to fame, Sean Fightmaster, featured in the film *SLC Punk*, kissed me by the water fountain. Did Noah know? Did he care? He probably would have taken it as the hallmark of true punk-dom that his girlfriend was kissed by the guy with the tallest mohawk in town. That's how I took it even though I was just standing there. Boys kissed who they wanted to kiss. I had lips. Deal sealed.

I kept smoking even when Noah disappeared with another girl into the woods one night, not coming home. I know because I called his house every hour all night long. April kept answering, saying, "No, he's not here yet" until even she of the most-patience-with-me took the phone off the hook. I smoked while he said he might come back and I smoked when he didn't. I smoked when Noah didn't call me for a month. I smoked while he suggested that I date Derek, his slightly younger best friend. "You two have a lot in common." Derek didn't listen to Crass's "So What" from *The Feeding of the 5000* which ends its anti-capitalist, anti-institutionalist screed "Jesus Christ can always save my life but I can always use my knife. So what? So what?" ad nauseum or the post-structuralist Subhumans who sang "You'd like to write a book but you're not sure where to begin. It's the story of your life and the end of its your death and every word that's in between is just a waste of breath" and wondered if the freedom we're looking for is just another hand from which we feed. Derek liked Tears for Fears and U2. I tried to go see shows on my own, but I didn't have a car, so I was trapped at home unless I wanted to go somewhere with someone else. I had become used to going. My own family felt foreign to me—or they made me feel foreign, like my terroir had changed. I think I smelled different. When they looked at me, all they could see was she who had been penetrated. Their eyes bore new holes into me. "Slut," the lunch lady had called me to my sister. But as when I was a kid and I stood behind a tree to play hide and seek, Derek was at least wider and taller than I. No one could see me behind him. And, I gave up listening to Crass even though their music drummed hard in my heart singing their anthem, "Fight War, Not Wars," But it was, eventually, easy enough to learn to like U2.

If Noah was a Fremont cottonwood, a riparian native to Utah, that usually grows on its own but sends big wafts of cotton-like seeds across the state, Derek was more of a poplar. Poplars are members of the same species but were often planted by farmers as windbreaks because they grow quickly and can tolerate a variety of conditions. However, poplars can grow into large trees with invasive roots that compete with nearby crops for water and nutrients. Derek didn't have the deep, complicated roots Noah had, but he did stop new trouble coming my way. Even though I'd been transferred, replanted in a new, unfamiliar forest, attached to a tree named Derek, I still sat at Noah's mom's house, listening to The Doors and smoking cigarettes.

Using Camel Bucks that Derek, Noah, and I collected, we bought a windsurfer. We drove out past the now-receding Great Salt Lake to Stansbury Park—a big-pond/tiny lake in a golf community near Tooele (pronounced Tah-Willa). We'd switched from Marlboros to Camels just for the Bucks and for the windsurfer. I couldn't drive yet so if I wanted to go anywhere, I had to go where Noah and/or Derek wanted to go. Noah and Derek sat in the front seat while I sat in the back on the floor of the bus because we'd taken the seats out to make room for the board. I ate sunflower seeds in between the cigarettes I smoked.

Something had made me sad, so I wasn't talking to either of them.

"Don't be such a drag, Nikki."

Who said it? Noah or Derek?

"Just stop pouting."

I don't know if I was pouting or just feeling left out or not sure what exactly my job as a thirteen-year-old girl hanging out with sixteen- and eighteen-year-old boys was. I thought I'd bought my ride by having given them a pack of cigarettes I'd purloined from Smiths Grocery that now stood in the field where Noah and I had first had sex. Maybe I was irritating them by singing Tears for

Fears' "Mad World" too loudly. That song, a handful of sunflower seeds, trying to light a cigarette on the floor of a microbus when the wind blew in from the front seat would have made anyone look pathetic.

I thought it was cool—to smoke, have a boyfriend, hang out with high school kids. Part of me, even though I had first slept with Noah and then Derek, made me think I was just a doll to be passed back and forth between them. But another part of me felt something else—not love or admiration, but that I was just one of the guys. I could keep up with them—tell jokes, talk about how Ronald Reagan's trickle-down economic policies would upend the last forty years of progressive reform, smoke and smoke and smoke some more.

The windsurfing sail was big and heavy for me to lift but the board, wide and solid, could absorb my attempts to balance. If I could get the sail up, I could make it across the lake. To turn around, I had to lower the point of the sail toward the back of the board, dip its tip into the water, and let it skim and then step-turned around the mast. Sometimes, I fell in at this point. Noah and Derek laughed—it was easier for them. They were taller and had more upper body strength. Noah swam out to help me. After we both climbed up on the board, he stood behind me, pulling the boom up toward us. His arms held me and we leaned back together. I fell into him like he was still my boyfriend.

What story did Derek tell himself as he sat on the beach, watching Noah help me? Maybe he just flashed back to when Noah and I were together and he was just our friend. Maybe he thought, better Noah swimming out there than "me"? I'm not sure! Maybe he thought, Noah is my friend, what is mine is his. Maybe he didn't need to tell a story at all. Unlike the babysitter's parents who needed someone to blame for the porn magazines in their backyard, Derek didn't need anything at all—he had access to a windsurfer, a car, a pack of cigarettes, and a girl. Maybe you only need stories when you don't have a purchase on what is real. Who needs to turn the real happenings into an episode of *General Hospital* when you can turn Camel Bucks into a watercraft, a friend into a girlfriend, a cigarette into smoke?

When Derek and Noah went places without me, I hung out with Noah's mom, who made popcorn for us in an aluminum pot, shaking it hard to pop every kernel. That's all she ate. She liked being thin. She was tall, dyed her hair blonde, and drank Black Label beer warm, all day long.

We sat out back, eating popcorn, smoking, listening to The Doors or Donovan. She loved sad music. She loved the 1970s. We laughed at the words "women are wicked."

"Randy says I'm wicked," she said more to the window than to me.

"Why do you stay married to him?" I didn't know then about inertia or shared property or better the devil you know. I didn't understand how difficult it is for a single woman to support three kids on her own, even though Randy only sporadically provided help. Women in Utah didn't have a lot of agency—jobs were hard to come by, community property may not have gone to her, the state wasn't good at requiring child support be supplied.

April had grown up just north of Salt Lake, in Bountiful, in a straight-laced, Mormon house. She told me about the petunias her mother grew in the backyard, the way her dad mowed the lawn every Saturday. It was a proper, suburban childhood. April's conflagration? Getting pregnant with Noah at sixteen. You get married at sixteen in 1967, the year Noah was born. Abortion wasn't legal, especially in Utah. Mormons had been getting married and pregnant at sixteen forever. Why did it hit her so hard? She wanted a different life—one where she could go to Woodstock or march for civil rights. She didn't know how she ended up with three kids on Chadbourne Street. Her favorite book was *Dandelion Wine*. We read passages aloud to each other about the smell of cut grass and the importance of porches, some kind of nostalgia for a time when each mowed lawn smell, each birdsong, each sip of wine was noted and appreciated. That book was about nothing but beauty's short breath—perhaps the kind of staying with the trouble that Haraway wants us to practice.

April pointed to the yard. "We probably have enough dandelions to make our own wine. They're not weeds if you do something useful with them."

My dad was a big fan of herbicides. ChemLawn came every other week to make sure our Kentucky bluegrass was the monoculture he and every other Utahn except April expected it to be. I think my mom thought April was a bit wild and dangerous. She seemed, to my mother, to have no boundaries at all.

I'm struck again by the *NYT* comments about how my parents should have called the police—that the babysitter should have been put in jail. I do hear that. I think of my sisters. What if the babysitter had been grooming them? What if some other neighborhood girl had been the one who left the *Playboy*s in his backyard, calling attention to the nakedness that occurred in the basement of his house, trying to call her attention to him? But also, he was fifteen. Only four years older than I. Noah had been four years older. Derek two and a half. They should have known better. Clearly, they were taking advantage, but it wasn't rape. Clearly, I could not conceivably have consented to the babysitter's advances with full comprehension of what it meant. But once I did know the ramifications of sex, I could consent, right? Or should we arrest them all—this whole American culture, a weedy wasteland? Boys wouldn't take advantage if they didn't think they could or should. It's not just that they get away with it—it's that it's part of the story, the narrative of boys. I would like to have a little agency to my story now, but some of the *NYT* comments make me believe that no, your story is this: you were molested, then you were complicit, then you were corrupted. Then you were gullible and needy. Then you started smoking. You were easy. You were definitely heading down the wrong path. You might end up like April, never sure if your paycheck would cover the bills. Or if your husband would come home with his. Or if the drywall was the only facia in danger.

Here's a little more of the metaphor. My parents planted another tree in the forest of my rehabilitation by trying to sell our house. They wanted to get me away from the babysitter, his parents, stigma perceived or real. They wanted to uproot, if indeed we could still call the family a tree instead of a burn scar, the whole family from this toxic landscape and move downtown, closer to my dad's work on Wakara Way.

But it was a down market. My parents were willing to sell our house for less than they bought it. If you knew my dad, you would have known this was the greatest sacrifice he could make. He liked to accumulate assets, not lose them. My parents lowered the price again. Still no sale. For two years they tried to sell the house. Although in some ways, the sign on the front yard sometimes seemed to read, "Shame Lives Here," most of the time the sign said, "Your parents will do what they can to get you the hell out of this hell of a place."

I will never know if I'm short from smoking cigarettes or having sex too young or if my DNA was written that way. If there's one fact I carry with me from the 1980s that I can't escape it's that I turned out to be only five-foot three. And, although I would like to be tall so I could distribute more weight over height, it's not *my* height I worry about. My son, Max, complains to me that he is short. He pulls me toward him in the kitchen, taking me by the shoulders to turn me around so we can match up back-to-back. He's twelve and the top of his head reaches the top of my ears. He wants to be a basketball player.

"Stop measuring yourself against me," I tell him.

Again, he's twelve so he gets mad fast. "I am the shortest kid in my class!" He runs over to the door jamb where Erik and I have etched each kid's height since we moved into this house fourteen years ago.

"See. Here is Zoë when she is twelve." He points to a high line.

"And this is me," pointing to a lower line.

"Girls sometimes grow more quickly than boys. And anyway, she's a giant. That's why we call her Susan Monster. Don't compare anyway. Comparison is the thief of joy. You are you." My children love it when I quote Winston Churchill.

"I wish I had more of dad's genes."

"There are good things about being short," I said.

"Like what?"

It took me a minute. "I don't hit my head on tree branches like dad does when we're hiking off trail in the forest."

But maybe my height *can* be attributed to smoking. "The study, published online March 17 in the journal *Annals of Epidemiology*, found that teenage boys who smoke are on average 2.54 centimeters (an inch in the US!) shorter than non-smokers." It looks like most of the data I'm looking for applies to boys, but isn't that always how it is? I had a hernia operation at age eight from carrying Paige and Valerie around, one on my back, one on my front. Girls rarely have hernias. Also, this study suggests that girls don't start smoking until they have passed puberty. The sex was pre-puberty—the smoking not very long after. Passive smoke contributes to stunted growth as well. My dad smoked. Maybe I can blame him both genetically and smokily.

I think of the apple tree, so pruned, cultivated. You can buy dwarf apple trees so you don't have to use such tall ladders for picking, so more of the energy goes into the fruit rather than the branches and leaves. I don't usually feel like I lost my innocence. Mainly, I feel like my habits of mind were shaped by things that happened to my body: the babysitter and Noah, my sitting in the passenger seat as my mom drove me to therapy, my hernia operation, my sisters and I dancing in the basement to *Grease*, delicious, toxic cigarette smoke.

Cultivating apple trees is a paradoxical business—force-stunting them is advantageous. Dwarf apple tree branches grow low, making picking fruit from them easier. Style guides are rife with instructions about how to prune to create smaller trees. You can buy scions that grow small even when grafted to regular-size trees. Bred, hybridized, shaped, pampered, tucked, groomed. Sometimes being smaller has its advantages. Oh, what we'll do to grow, and pick, the easiest fruit.

5

Failure and Succession

What I wanted from telling my story is what I want from a painting. I want to move into the paint itself and become part of the image. This is a kind of hiding but it's also a kind of presence. In this painting of my dreams, I want to part the brushstrokes, open them wide, and step between their oily certainty. I want to be part but not the whole of the story. I want to be on even ground with the other figures in the painting—tree, human, stone. I want to be *configured*. Smoothed and readied and wet but unlike as with sex, my becoming only means what it means in light of the color and shapes and chiaroscuro around me. The tree in the painting—it shades me from too harsh light, but it also promises that there is another way to be part of the story—some way that is broad and rich and wide enough that others can come into the story too. We could be sheltered by the story of the tree. Color me understory. One strip of color next to another, next to another. You and me, in this story, a river of cellulose and pigment, lines of electrons and protons as real as energy from the sun. We are photosynthesizing all right in here.

Rebecca Campbell's mom, Betsy, mother of seven, wife of a Mormon bishop, grandma-haired at fifty, was a rebel. She drove Rebecca to art classes. Took art classes herself. And, when asked by the teachers at Mutual—the afterschool program Mormon girls attended—to write about a flower that reminded her of her daughter, she chose not a flower. She chose to compare her daughter to a tree—strong, sturdy, ever-rising. And Rebecca has been that to me for thirty-five years.

    I met Rebecca the year she'd shaved the hair on the sides of her head. She didn't have quite the mohawk that Sean Fightmaster wore and was more New

Wave than punk rock but she snuck out of her house at night to dance at The Bay with her equally New Wave friend, Abby. I had made it through seventh grade but by the middle of eighth grade, my parents were worried that I was not fulfilling my schooling potential. We'd struck a deal, thanks to my therapist, Dr. LePray, that if I promised not to sneak out anymore and got only A-grades, I could go out with Noah, my boyfriend, until 10 o'clock on weeknights, 11 o'clock on weekends. Dr. LePray said trust had to be rekindled in my family. We shook on it which meant, if the dancing didn't start until 10, I was out of luck. I never missed my curfew. I came home in time to watch the news then MASH with my dad.

Although we both grew up between the mouths of Little and Big Cottonwood, Rebecca's story is not like mine. Her house sat next to a stream, under a canopy of Gambel oaks. She lived *in* the mountains—not in a square of organized houses and foreign grasses. Rebecca's parents were Mormon. Her dad had been a bishop. Her mother, though, was starting to question the patriarchy that undergirded the church. Rebecca was a painter. Her mother started painting watercolors to see what it might be like to be an artist as well as a wife. Rebecca's sister Allison knew my boyfriend Noah because they both attended Brighton High. Now that I'd been installed in the ninth grade for my last middle school year, Rebecca and I were classmates in Mrs. Peterson's English. Rebecca found out a little about me through Allison. She decided to befriend me anyway.

I had never been befriended before. All my friends in school were just my friends. We'd been together since kindergarten. As elementary school kids, we sat on the steps of the Kiva, a word I didn't know until I'd moved to Northern Arizona that Canyon View elementary had adopted from the Hopi. Mrs. Gardner rolled the cart with the SRA Reading Labs. We each chose a folded card with a reading passage on the top with a quiz below the fold, depending on the color-coded path we were on—aqua for Matt and me, green for Jeff, Jill achieved the highest status—blue cards—teacher's pet level. We became a friend group probably because of our color caste system. We ocean-colored readers sat on the highest steps of the Kiva, tearing through the cards, trying to catch up to Jill. Jill, who was in Gifted and Talented that year and the years I wasn't and still is, in her art world, to this day.

But between the I-was-mostly-like-the-other-third-grade-kids and the fourth grade, I'd slipped through the waxy cards of the SRA Reading Labs somewhere my pre-babysitter friends couldn't touch. By the time I got to middle school, I'd lost more friends than gained because of rumors about what happened to me and the babysitter. Either way, now I was on my own in a whole new grade and one person with an awesome haircut who snuck out at night said something like, "Do you like The Clash?"

And I said "Yes," because I always say yes.
And she said, "I have a bootleg tape of the Eurythmics. Do you want to hear it after school?"
And I said, "Thank you for being a tree."

No. Rebecca is not a tree. She's a forest unto herself. In high school, she ran the debate club, took her Model UN team to Washington DC to compete at American University, took art classes in school and after school at Realms of Inquiry as well as private lessons. She was going to be a famous artist from Salt Lake City if it was the last thing she did.

She took me into the woods behind her house. Putting a pinecone from one of her mountain home trees in my hand, she taught me how to peel the levers of the cone until I freed the seed. She pointed to an open space and said, "Dig with your hands. You don't need a shovel." We stood around the ground we'd sown and spit onto it. We knew water was scarce in the desert, but she assured me we had plenty of liquid in us to get this fallow land up and starting to produce again.

We both edited our high school literary magazine, *Runes*, where Scott Oates, the creative writing teacher, joined forces with Rebecca in leading me to think making art might be one way to make a life. Mr. Oates didn't teach high school for long—he went on to teach college English. What if we had missed his tutelage? All these years later, he just today sent me a letter about the *New York Times* piece. I wrote back to him that, yes, without the abortion, I wouldn't be here. But the truth is, in many ways I wouldn't be here without him. He let me hunker in his office as his teacher's aide. I took as many *Runes* classes and other creative writing classes as I could. He brought me art as a kind of sustainability—when in doubt, write. He made a space for me and Rebecca in that class, even if he did try to convince us to read Atwood's rather than Plath's poetry.

Although Rebecca wrote poetry and stories too, she focused on making a self-portrait woodcut for the magazine, so we weren't in direct competition, art wise. She took me to galleries. I brought her back copies of Van Goghs from the Musee d' Orsay when my parents took my sisters and me to France. She loaned me her copy of *Gödel, Escher, and Bach*. I read to her aloud from Shakti Gawain's *Power of Visualization*. I told her, "You can't wish you were dead or, according to Shakti, you will get cancer later in life. You shouldn't make wishes with negative words in them. You can't want things not to happen, you can only positively want. Like, I wish for world peace, not, I wish for no more war." We were very into world peace and in wishes and in the idea that we could organize our futures.

My boyfriend, Derek, benefactor of Noah's girlfriend donation, and I had been already dating a year when Rebecca and I became close. Derek drove us to Jack and Karl's apartment to drink beer and listen to Madonna and Prince. Madonna and Prince posters decorated their walls entire. We drank shitty beer we bought from the gas station on the corner of 9th and 2nd even though none of us was twenty-one. The curtains, pulled, let everyone smoke pot in smelly peace. Their apartment was so dirty that they didn't bother to clean the cat shit off the floor. They should not have had a cat. We took the bus from the suburbs downtown to Bandeloops where we drank mint iced tea. At Derek's house, we took mushrooms and ate a pound of Grapenuts drenched in sugar, trying to swallow even when we couldn't stop laughing.

Derek drove us and Trevin, "Rebecca's then - boyfriend," the twenty miles downtown to Memory Grove—a park dedicated to veterans but also served as the entrance to City Creek Canyon. It had wildness spilling down and death underneath and monuments that seemed archaic. But it also had a million trees but it wasn't quite a forest. Maybe some of the trees were native. I didn't know then how to check.

Rebecca broke up with Trevin when she found out he was sleeping with her friend. For a minute she thought it was me but I confessed I didn't sleep with him until *after* they broke up. Trevin, were he a tree, would have been an aspen—he was young and adopted and had scars on his face like the inky dashes against white bark—and didn't know that climate change would eventually extinguish his species. Still, he blocked a little of the weather Derek couldn't. Derek had become himself somewhat cruel. When I wouldn't sleep with him, he wouldn't force me, but he would scream at me until my curfew that I was an insecure, overprivileged, manipulative bitch. I took illegal shelter in Trevin after he and Rebecca broke up. The sex was bad. We lost the condom. Looking for a condom deep inside someone's vagina takes the sexy right out of sex. Comic sex is forgivable so Rebecca, eventually, forgave me.

She moved to Portland for college the year after I did. We lived together with her new boyfriend, Todd. It was a very orange-carpeted house and although I wanted the upstairs room, she argued that she could really use that space as both a bedroom and a studio and so I gave in. I'd slept with her ex-boyfriend all those years ago. Tit for tat.

Years later, after we'd moved back to Salt Lake, while Erik's cousin Emily, Rebecca and I were camping, we fought about who should break up with whose boyfriends. We probably all should have broken up with our boyfriends but instead broke up with each other and didn't talk for almost two years.

When I got pregnant, I didn't want Zoë to grow up not knowing Rebecca. I reached out to her. We met at the Oyster Bar—mirrored walls, black-and-white tile mosaic, black leather seats. Over 59 cent Kumamotos, I told her about the babysitter how young I had been, or thought I was … by this time, I'd aged myself a year to make it a little less sordid, to make it seem like the humus of my forest wasn't as ashen and barren as it sounded.

She'd known something, I'm sure. Noah had told Allison something and Allison must have told Rebecca. Perhaps she had just told Rebecca that I was "fast."

But "fast" must not have meant the same to both of us. As she sat across from me, she looked both shocked and sad.

"I'm so sorry, Nik. Why didn't you tell me?"

You can't be "fast" if you're to succeed in a succession forest.

All kinds of forests—redwood, Douglas fir, maple, oak—are the end-result of succession forests. Succession explains how lichens and mosses replace rocks, then annual weeds replace lichen, then perennial weeds, then shrubs and deciduous trees like aspen and poplar, and then, in the West at least, coniferous species that are finally considered "Old Growth." It can take several centuries for a forest to make it this far and stochastic events like floods and fires can set the cycle back a few decades or a few centuries, depending on how destructive they are. Native Americans managed the forests by setting prescribed burns to keep the detritus from piling up but when white settlers stopped clearcutting most of the United States and set some forests aside for forest management, fire suppression was the primary policy. A century of built-up forest garbage, as I mentioned before, helps make the fires burn so hot and so destructively.

But underneath that forest, burned or no, still lies that network of connections, that web of forest life that, even in some of the hotter fires, still pulses with the lines the redwoods and Doug-firs will need to succeed. Is it overly sentimental to call these life-giving strands art?

My friend in Flagstaff, Shonto Begay, is also an artist. He uses a kind of Pointillism to create his work, dotting the wooden end of his paintbrush against the canvas. I visited him in his studio which sits above Flagstaff's downtown, across from Heritage Square and the Hopi Building, to interview him about his practice. He's painting a boy sitting below a tree, the roots clutching the ground, the branches cradling the sky. Although the scene tilts at a 45-degree angle, neither the tree nor the boy look vulnerable. No one is sliding off this rock. Shonto has his own style—small, devoted dots make up a large, realistic image.

I am not a professional interviewer and Shonto is my friend so I'm happy to just listen to him talk. I set Voice Memo to record on my phone and asked him how he liked to travel to promote his work.

"I don't mind traveling," I prompted. "It's like having a port key to go places. But I don't like it when no one shows up. I just gave a Keynote for the Moab Festival of Science. Only fifteen people came. Don't you need more people to key-in if you're giving the 'keynote?' Or maybe more people in the audience to notice your note?"

He shared, "Once, I was giving a Keynote in Georgia. Afterward, someone came up with a book for me to sign called *Shonto*. It was a book about my life! I'd forgotten that I'd given someone permission to write my story. Now there I was, famous not for my paintings but for my story."

"Let's talk about your paintings," I suggested. Shonto has galleries all over the West, *Modern West Fine Art* in Salt Lake, *Medicine Man Gallery* in Jackson, two here in Flagstaff.

"Of the fifteen boys that I knew in the boarding school, only five of them are still alive. My art saved me," he repeats. "It was a sacred place I could go to. I pretended to do their bidding but inside, I kept myself tucked away."

Shonto changed colors and brushes. He flipped his brush over to work on the roots of the tree—the roots, carved into the side of a mountain, revealed by ages of slipping rock. Each of Shonto Begay's 36-37 styles of brush-butt dots isn't on its own a work of art. The dots must accumulate and then move in response to the other dots surrounding. Shonto lets us see the pixels which remind us of all the small touches that conspire to keep us in the picture. Staying with the trouble means staying with the moment which means digging into the pixels that make up the art, digging into the ground to see how the tiny dots interrelate.

"Have you always painted like that?"

"I have 36-37 shapes I use like an alphabet. I know what shape each layer requires."

He's done talking. I can tell by the way he turns the music up. He's listening to traditional Navajo music, and I hear a version of "In Beauty I Walk" coming through the tiny speaker. Rebecca and I each bought a poster from the Cosmic Aeroplane with the whole "In Beauty I Walk" song typed below a photograph of Delicate Arch outside of Moab. The song wasn't meant for us. It had been co-opted for an incense-filled, new age, mysticism, but we didn't understand at the time. We were young and we thought we were original—shaved heads, safety pins in our ears, Sean Fightmaster not even a character in *SLC Punk* yet.

Rape culture, which means to me that I expect men to be rapists and thus, live and work and teach my daughter accordingly, hiding behind boyfriend and inside paintings to keep safe, is woven throughout. As I write this, another member of the Fundamentalist Latter-Day-Saints has been arrested for child sex abuse. The *Arizona Daily Sun*, our local paper, reported, "Bateman was first arrested in August when someone spotted small fingers in the gap of a trailer he was hauling through Flagstaff. Police found three girls, between 11 and 14, in a makeshift room in the unventilated trailer." It's common in polygamist culture for young girls to watch the older girls have sex to learn the ropes—a kind of reverse *Handmaid's Tale* where the dress is pushed up against the hips, obscuring the face of the girl lying on her back so the younger girl can see how the man pushes himself passed her garments, into her. Perhaps these offshoots of the Mormon church are anomalous. The official stance of the church is against polygamy yet in 2020, Utah legislature overwhelmingly reduced the charge of polygamy from felony to misdemeanor.

You get by on what makes you. In a healthy forest, nurse logs are fallen trees that give life as they decompose. The whole forest starts over on their bodies. Conch mushrooms come to split the outer bark apart. Banana slugs ooze their silky mucus, adding new microbes that chew up the cambium and spit out dust. Into the dust, spores from honey mushrooms find purchase. In the shade of the fallen fir, chanterelle mushrooms bloom from mycelia that have lived underground, sending up crenellated caps above and forwarding nutritional messages from the trees below. A nurse log is similar to a whale fall—when a whale dies, its body floats to the ocean floor providing enriched ecosystems for feed deep sea microbes, arthropods, mollusks, nematodes, and larger scavengers like crabs, octopus, eels, and more.

Where a forest has been severely burned or clear cut, nurse logs don't abound. The soil, depending on how depleted it is, might lay fallow for a long time. With some help, it may support pollinator meadows. One of my students, Megan Quinn, who received her MA in Biology and her environmental narrative certificate with me, presented her thesis about how mosaic meadows grow between patches of trees.

She wrote,

> Within both the older and more recent burn scars, low fire severity increased floral richness, but did not have an effect on any of the other floral resource metrics. Other studies have demonstrated multiple differences between

high- and low-severity fires. For example, some studies have shown a decline in native plant species due to loss of the seedbank in high-severity fire. In contrast, low-severity burn patches in ponderosa pine forests can increase floral richness, with subsequent increases in pollinator biodiversity.

With low intensity fires, this opening creates space for native species like lupine, globe mallow, Indian paintbrush, and pentstemon. But high-intensity fires change the soil and the hydrology, inviting non-native species to take hold.

Rape culture proceeds like high-intensity fires. Bad things happen, thus, one expects more bad things to happen. Then, bad things happen to reinforce that belief. Rape culture simultaneously makes every person think about rape—perpetrators believe that rape allows them to dominate like dandelion toadflax—a weed so toxic and pervasive that no matter how many hikers pull them out by the roots, they dominate our forests. And victims of rape spend their lives wishing they didn't have to tell their story over and over again about how they don't need a whole forest. They'll take any tree.

Art pushes against the idea that rape culture is the only culture. Sure, there is rape culture but also music culture, paint culture, writing culture. Layer and layers of culture—as many layers of culture as Rebecca's thick brushstrokes, as many rotating dots connecting and conspiring to make another picture, to tell another story.

I visited Rebecca's art gallery as soon as COVID-19 numbers fell enough to make it semi-safe to travel. It was her first show at LA Louver in a few years. I tried to make all of her opening receptions. Her work occupied the entire first floor of one of the best galleries in the country. I'm only slightly jealous that she has made so much success with her art. Mostly, I'm just proud of her and lucky to know her. But I'm also jealous enough to insinuate myself into curation.

Inside Louver, on the back wall, hangs a canvas with thick paint outlining a mostly naked woman. The painting is called *Jack and Diane* after John

Cougar Mellancamp's song from the 1980s. The babysitter used to play it in the basement sometimes.

"That's me," I told two women visiting the gallery, examining the twelve foot by ten foot painting. I pointed to the woman, model-me, lying with her back to the audience, wearing nothing but her underwear. Rebecca was talking to Elizabeth, who manages the gallery, so it was my job to explain the painting in which I lay on my side on a blanket of plaid colors that matched the bright red and orange canopy of leaves. The shock of the sky matches the reach of the ground—they marry each other in both shade and energy. My husband, then, when Rebecca took the photo, my boyfriend Erik, stood, hands on the buttons of his Levi's, mostly camouflaged in the background. This painting is huge: 96 inches by 108. It's life-sized. It's bigger than me.

"That's my husband," I announced. "He's peeing in the bushes."

I didn't say the idea here is that we supposedly just had sex because even if it is the idea, it's not the truth. We hadn't just had sex on that autumn-colored blanket because Rebecca had been there, posing us.

"Unlike many figurative paintings in this mode, the woman, me," I repeated, "isn't entirely nude. The man is more exposed. Rebecca likes to subvert expectations."

Rebecca, overhearing me, came over to better explain. "That's a reverse odalisque," she described the way my body is stretched out on the blanket. "The painting is actually about me and Trevin. My boyfriend wasn't very nice to me. He really only hung out with me because I'd have sex with him."

She didn't say it aloud, but the words hung between us. "And you, he slept with because you would sleep with anyone," I imagined her saying. I wanted to interject, "It didn't count as real sex! We lost the condom!" But you can only telepathically communicate in broad strokes. Nuance is better left to the page or the canvas. Still, Rebecca is not wrong about Trevin or my boyfriend, Derek. They dated us because we would have sex with them. They were similar in other ways too. They each carried a suitcase of beer wherever they went. They scouted out places to lay, in Trevin's case, the plaid blanket, and in Derek's case, in his apartment, where we could do our stuff, Bobby Brooks bedamned.

In the painting, I'm lying on my elbow facing away from the audience, looking at Erik. But back when Rebecca took the photos of me in Neff's Canyon, lying on the blanket, I felt more exposed than I ever did with Erik or had with Derek or Noah. The wind running over me gave me goosebumps. I wasn't doing anything. I was just lying there. In my underwear. I was used to doing stuff when I was naked. But now, in her gallery, years later, I don't feel exposed anymore. I feel like I could lie under that canopy of trees forever. If I lay down on that blanket now, my back to the viewer, could you tell how I have changed? The autumn leaves fall upon me, yellow, then orange, then red. Between multicolored blanket and multicolored sky, I am a white patch in the middle of the forest, innocent as a button mushroom. After all this time, thirty years of friendship later, Rebecca's forest helped me grow my mycelia back.

What would she have painted in a normal odalisque? Would she have focused on my breasts that had not yet, maybe would never, suckle a baby? My stomach, rounded forward, never flat again after the abortion, as if it were an empty bowl, waiting for its fruit. She could have turned me into a still life—pears, grapes, peaches, lemons, squash, and apples upon apples. Still lifes celebrate food and wine. They also warn about ephemerality of these pleasures and of the brevity of life. Would she, had she placed me facing the viewer, have painted autumn's harvest, spilling from me? Or would the emptiness of the bowl caught her eye, given her a hint of what she didn't know about me, but would have known, if I'd let her in?

Like Shonto, Rebecca has developed her own style. Thick, painterly strokes form most of the setting—trees are ropey bands of energy, their xylem on fire. The faces, for she mostly paints the human form, she portrays with precision. The scenery invites the audience in. There's room for you, viewer, in this creek, at this beach, among these trees the background seems to say. But the human faces are so accurate, so literal, you know you can't *be* the person in the painting—unless, of course, it is actually you, which it has been me, a couple of times. The faces are completely perfect, and, in their perfection, they don't permit access or entry. They clench against your desire to crawl into the painting. You cannot, even if you can afford it, own the humans in this painting.

One of her most complicated paintings is called *Radiant white*. Twenty young, white undergrads at BYU lean against each other. One of Rebecca's six sisters is one of the sorority girls depicted in the photograph Rebecca used as a model. Her sister told Rebecca that the photographer told them to pretend to be sleeping, hence the heads on each other's bony shoulders. So submissive. So safe in the enclave of the church. Some of the girls closed their eyes. Some looked at each other. Some looked right into the camera. The girls all wore black and white. Their faces were painted white except for one Navajo young woman in the corner.

In an early version of the painting, Rebecca had detailed the Navajo young woman dressed in traditional Diné skirts. Rebecca painted the ceiling a bright yellow and red Shoshone pattern, almost the same colors as the plain blanket from *Jack and Diane*. She reached out to a Native American scholar to see if she'd gotten the color right. The scholar asked if she knew the origins of the plaids, the significance of the cultures. She admitted to him she really didn't. Without knowing more about her, he couldn't advise her to paint Shoshone, Paiute, or Navajo plaids. Not wanting to take meaning away from a culture's symbolism and cultural history, Rebecca painted over both the ceiling and the girl's dress in a fully saturated black paint. The girl disappears into the background. Her story, Rebecca realized, she cannot know. The painting changes meaning and form then. Instead of saying, these girls are so canonical, so dull in their pretend sleep and mono-colored dress compared to this woman in the corner who, colorful, is so much more interesting, now the painting says, no one knows much about this girl in the corner. Where is her family? Why was she in college at BYU in 1978? If her story is about the dress she wore, Rebecca decided it was up to the girl to tell it. She took a brush for house paint, dipped it in a bucket of Sherwin Williams' "Radiant white," and painted huge swaths over all the other girls' clothes. And only I, and now you, know that under the gray black dress in the corner of the painting is a layer of so much color hidden behind that bright white.

I love those paintings, and the people in them, have stories of their own, not all of them traumatic. I wonder what it would be like to be in a body that never knew trauma just like I wonder what it would be like to be tall. Or are there no bodies or selves that haven't suffered some kind of traumatic injury? Trauma is a gradient. Perhaps it's how you tell your story that determines how deeply it's buried or how shallowly it slips around on the surface. What is defined as trauma sets the narrator down a particular path. It's like height—once you reach a certain point, you don't get any taller. You become the story that you tell yourself. But perhaps if you share the story, you the teller, become part of the art as much as part of the trouble.

After the Louver show, Rebecca and I talked about Trevin and Derek and the places we found to have sex outdoors—Memory Grove, the Rock part way up Little Cottonwood, the Four Lane, Neff's Canyon, where Rebecca had painted me in my underwear but where she had *been* in her underwear.

"Remember how my parents told me not to hang out with you? Because Allison told them you were heading down the wrong path?"

I did not remember. She hadn't told me that. At least, I didn't remember her saying so. As Rebecca's older sister, Allison felt it was her job to prevent Rebecca from going down that same path. It was clear that path meant slutty sex.

If she had told me, would it have been impossible for me to get past that humiliation? That Rebecca knew some part of what I had already told her? She and her sister, in their fully-forested perch, looking down at my house below, treed with just a couple of saplings my parents had planted.

But it's probably more complicated than that. Rebecca hasn't led a trauma-free life. When Rebecca gave birth to her twins, one of them, Andi had to be rushed to LA's Children's hospital because she was suffering from hypoxemia. She was on a vent for four months. Josie, who stayed with Rebecca at Santa Monica hospital, was given fluids because the hospital staff thought that might prevent in Josie what happened to Andie. Instead, baby Josie died. If that doesn't count as forest eradication, nothing does. Our lives have run parallel to, crossed over, obliterated, and erased each other. And our narratives, counter, crisscrossing, messy, have spread some of their life-affirming plant and mushroom matter in each other's territories. We make art separately and together. We share our devastations. We replant when we can.

Even if I could cobble together a single narrative arc, I don't think I would. A single story means that I must carry the story and all its attendant meanings alone. I'd rather share it, even if your version doesn't entirely comport with mine. When the NYT fact checkers called my mom, she offered additional details, like the one where the babysitter's parents paid $300 for half the abortion. My story is still mine, but it's also my mom's, and, ever since that night at the Oyster Bar, Rebecca's.

I want to retain authority over my story which means I want to tell it in as many ways as I can. I want you to tell me your version of my story. I want to hear your story. I want to tell you my version of your story. Perhaps that's one of the effects of sexual interference: You become practiced in telling your story in different ways. Telling the story seems enticing but impossible. There are so many threads to follow. So many ways I ended up here but then other ways that I ended up over there.

Other effects include:

1 Wondering where you went wrong.
2 An inability to tell the straight truth.
3 Attention-seeking.
4 Promiscuity.
5 A relativistic sense of morals.
6 Avoidance of sex.
7 Avoidance of intimacy.
8 An uneasiness around people who are certain about how things are.
9 A need for praise.
10 An inability to tell a story without metaphor.
11 A corrosive thinking about the end of the world.
12 Morning beer.

But if I can perform a single narrative, I will. Follow the metaphor—you can't make a forest out of a single tree. The meaning will be different for everyone, depending on how willing you are to step into this painting with me.

The babysitter's house had an atrium filled with plants—orchids and bromeliads, ferns, spider plants, dragon tongues. His family kept a living room as many suburban homes did, that was only used when company came over but, like the rest of the suburban families in Utah, the babysitter's family hung out in the TV room, not the living room. In the living room, the babysitter sat on the edge of the piano bench. The girl told him that she'd gotten her period.

He said, "We'll have to be more careful."

The girl, me, in this painting, said, "We'll have to cut this out of the story. It's too upsetting."

"No, no, keep it in. It shows the dimensions of the whole situation. A knowledge of human reproductive systems. A conversation in the light, not the darkness of a basement or behind closed doors. It shows how there were no parents around. Everyone wants to play house. Let's play house."

The piano. The girl played modern songs on the piano although the 1980s made the music bad. "I've Been Waiting for a Girl Like You," you've heard before. "Jack and Diane" played on the radio nonstop. "Remember how you played the theme song to MASH on your piano?" the babysitter asked.

"I know the lyrics. 'Suicide is painless. It brings on many changes. But I can take or leave it if I please,'" the girl sang.

"It's astonishing how few people know that the theme song to MASH has words."

"The truth is," said the girl, "I don't really know what it means that I've gotten my period. I don't know what it means that I'm standing here, in your parent's living room, wondering why you are speaking in the future tense that we will have to be careful. I cannot feel anything but the shame of the moment. The foolishness that brought me there. And back. Horrible, horrible fool am I."

"Shame. It's the biggest emotion—next to anger. You think you can handle it?" the babysitter asks.

"It obscures everything else. I carry shame like a giant tire around my middle. It keeps everything apart from me, just a little. I can be blasé for the rest of my days, just like Hawkeye, just like the MASH theme song. I can take or leave it if I please."

"What will it take to get through this thick rubber of tire?"

"I don't know. I've tried books and drugs and love and wine."

"Perhaps you need something stronger. I've heard drastic sex acts can help. A tongue muscle that won't quit. A ribbon around your neck. The rough tread of a zipper against your cheek."

"Or I could learn to take the tire off."

"You cannot take the tire off."

"Where is *your* tire?"

"I am the tire," he said.

The tire is the worst. It's a reflex. One tiny nudge of shame and the whole tire springs into action, squeezing *the girl* open. Everyone can see her insides now, which is even more humiliating.

The babysitter looks at the piano. She looks at the rubber plant almost as tall as a tree, seeking light through the top of the atrium. A succession forest's logic might apply inside an atrium as well as out. The atrium pushes air into her lungs like a ventilator. One gets dependent on a ventilator. What would it be to suck directly from the green horns of trees?

Although the trees in neither Shonto nor Rebecca's paintings are anything alike, they invite you in. The faces of the figures they paint are singular. They are portraits of certainty and singularity. Unique to themselves. But the trees are multiplex. I can slip between Shonto's dots or between the lines of Rebecca's thick paint. The trees, like you, can be the subject of the painting without being the *only* subject of the painting. The figures do not have to be of me for me to be part of the story.

Perhaps the roughest part of being a storyteller of an unlovely story is that you feel disconnected from the long, shared, human story. But maybe that human story isn't the only one to be told. Perhaps the trees will be so kind as to let you sit next to the kid in Shonto's painting or with the guy peeing in the back of the painting, behind some trees. Maybe you can sit next to the girl pulsing with light behind Radiant white paint. Maybe she'll whisper her story to you. And you can whisper yours back. Some dots will start to connect. Some plaid will begin to emerge. Some of that hyphae and mycelia beneath the forest floor will feed you. The sense of who you were and who you are making yourself into will converge. And the brushstrokes will lengthen, and you will be painted as tall as a tree.

6

A Single Tree Is Not a Forest

Although I grew up between the mouths of Little and Big Cottonwood Canyons where Douglas fir and cedars decorate the granite canyons, I didn't know the *inside* real forests until I visited the rare, uncut expanses of the old growth forests of the Pacific Northwest, or, later, moved to the Ponderosa Forest. My mom, no matter what else had changed in our family since my cousin Trev and I climbed the plum and cherry trees when we were seven years old, still calls me a Druid.

Maybe it's just easier to love trees than people. In Bessel van der Kolk's book, *The Body Keeps the Score*, he reminds the traumatized person, "Traumatized people are often afraid of feeling. It is not so much the perpetrators (who hopefully are no longer around to hurt them) but their own physical sensations are the enemy. Apprehension about being hijacked by uncomfortable sensations keeps the body frozen and the mind shut." Perhaps the idea of forest seemed safe from sensation. Free from thought. Was there some atavistic part of my mind, that thought, "Things were easier when we were forest people, or, better yet, as Haraway would call us, forest critters?"

In her chapter on *Sympoiesis*, which Haraway defines as "making with," she clarifies her understanding of what "critters" means, "Critters interpenetrate one another, loop around and through one another, eat each other, get indigestion, and partially digest and partially assimilate one another and thereby establish sympoietic arrangements that are otherwise known as cells, organisms, and ecological assemblages." Perhaps a good story is a critter just like a scurry is the collective term for squirrels and cast is the collective term for hawks, cornucopia is for slugs and snails, sleuth is for bears, murder of crows, unkindness is for ravens, bevy is for rabbits, parliament is for owls, a menorah of northern flickers, and a group of cougars is called a range. What's the collective term for stories?

Since I'd skipped a grade, I left for college when I was seventeen. Derek and I drove from Salt Lake, with his cats, through Idaho, landing in Portland at 1:00 a.m. at a Motel 6 in Tigard, Oregon—far, I soon learned, from the campus.

Derek, who didn't have the kind of dad who managed money so Derek could go to college, spent some of his $80 on dinner the next night and some on cat food the next day. We drove out to look at one apartment—a shared room in deep Southeast, practically Gresham. The complex was a lime green, setting itself off from Portland's deeper greens. To make the contrast starker, Douglas fir trees grew right against the neon siding.

"Go ahead," Derek said, gesturing for me to go first up the stairs, whether from chivalry or fear, I didn't know. I was the one going to college. If I was going to a fancy college, I must be able to deal with this not-fancy situation. I knocked on the door. A man with long black hair and a black mustache answered.

"Hello. You're renting a room?"

The man looked up and down at me. Seventeen. Five three. Blonde woman. I saw him register all these body-facts.

"Yeah. I am!" I said.

Derek moved closer to me, into view. "For him." I tilted my thumb in Derek's direction, taking refuge behind the not-quite-yet-togetherness of a boy who I believed, or wanted to believe, had it all together. He's the one who would have to live far from downtown Portland with a stranger with dirty carpet. He was my beard for my girl-self. I took him everywhere to believe I wasn't a short, seventeen-year-old with no defenses.

"Oh. You are the would-be renter," the mustachioed man looked at Derek. Disappointed. Emphasis on the you. "Come in." The carpet, maybe once beige, was mottled with stains. Cans of beer seemed to grow from the ground like mushrooms after a good rain—randomly and abundantly. It reminded me of Eric and Karl's apartment sans the Madonna and Prince posters. The room smelled of smoke and the long history of cats. At least Ziggy and Bud would fit in.

But Derek didn't have anywhere near the full rent he needed. Not by half. Derek beat me down the stairs, back to the car, giving time for the mustache man to say to me, "If you ever need a room, look me up." I didn't look back. Instead, I looked at Derek, who seemed lost.

"Are you OK?" I asked him.

"I just don't think I can do this."

I didn't know what *this* meant exactly. We'd been together for over three years. We shared cats!

But you can't keep cats in your dorm room. My mom put the cats, Ziggy and Bud, and Derek in her minivan to return to Salt Lake with her. Paige and Val would drive back with Dad. Derek left his TV with me. He planned to save up and return in a few months or maybe I'd give up on this silly far-away-from-Utah plan and return to the brown and blue mountains where I once believed I could one day belong.

The next day, I met my across-the-hall dorm-mates. Hans and Christian carried a copy of the Freshman Funnies over to my room. My high school senior picture was included in the incoming freshman photo array. I forgot to call Derek that night on the house phone in the hallway.

"We knew we had to meet this one," Hans and Christian said, and, for a moment, I felt like a normal girl. I was attractive to them apart from my willingness to have sex with them. For all they knew, at that moment, I remained virginal and unmolested. Perhaps these guys, maybe even all Reed College guys, would think I possessed qualities worthy of attention. Maybe, they'd even think I was smart.

I broke up with Derek from the dorm house phone. He sent me letters asking me to please take him back. I read them and wondered, why didn't you send me letters before? Poplars, unlike native cottonwoods, ponderosas, or Douglas firs, don't last very long. I was grateful for the bad things that didn't happen to me because he had been my boyfriend in dangerous, windy places—at concerts, in parking lots, at parties, walking in the parks. I think of all the places I know women have been endangered. Although I had to contribute my part of the deal by having sex with him, Derek blocked a lot of unwanted cocks for me.

I thought I could go it alone as long as alone meant with the attention and support of my dorm-mates, Reed College guys in general, and my new best friend, Renee, who lived a floor above but hung out in my room, sharing the Reese's Peanut Butter Cups my mom sent, drinking straight from the Pepto Bismol bottles that came in packages of two from Costco when we ate too many hallucinogenic mushrooms and our stomachs protested. Hans gave me a nickname, Killer, because I said "Killer" so often in reference to all things good, and, this first semester, all things were indeed Killer. Christian called me Killer too. Hans shortened his version to "Ler," which he still calls me to this day even though I say "killer" only rarely now—mainly to embarrass my kids.

In November, Hans and Christian hosted a "Ler is Legal" party for my eighteenth birthday. It took me a while to understand what they meant. I hadn't thought of myself as illegal before. But then, I took their meaning. If either of them, or indeed any man at Reed College, thought to perhaps have sex with me, it would not have been statutory rape. Coming from Utah, "Statutory Rape" was an unfamiliar crime. Making it clear I was legal for sex did feel a bit like putting me up on an auction block, but I liked the idea that they had been restrained in some way. That someone wasn't in such a hurry. That they were biding their time.

He didn't only throw a party. Hans made me a cake for my birthday. A camas cake. Actually, it was a tulip bulb instead of camas, since camas cakes are tricky, occasionally poisonous if the camas bulb is picked at the wrong time, smashed into pulp and then baked in the dorm kitchen's microwave. The kitchen consisted of that microwave and a refrigerator upon which Renee, and I had drawn a ghostly figure whose most vigorous complaint was, "Oh dismay, I have no butt."

The camas-cake-cum-tulip-bulb had no cakiness to it, no sweetness, and also definitely, no butt. I kept it on the sill of the dorm room until I had to move it to make room for Renee and me to stand in the five-foot-four-inch windows that framed our short selves pounding twin bottles of Pepto perfectly. When I had taken a bit of camas cake, I slugged a shot of Pepto then too. You're not supposed to eat tulip bulbs. You're not supposed to stand in open windows. You're not supposed to advertise at a party that you are now "legal," but Oregon was new, and college was new, and maybe those lines I'd crossed that had set me on my wrong path had been erased. Maybe there were no rules now. No certain destiny. No necessarily correlated cause and effect. Although I had gone down the wrong path, new paths could present themselves, right?

Hans was into cars. Alfa Romeos, in particular. On rainless nights, Hans drove me in his Alfa, cream-colored, low to the floor, fast out Powell Boulevard toward Mt. Hood. He taught me how to drive like a racer—slow down before the turn then punch it at the apex. Hans was the one who explained the sign in his dorm room that read, "These are the tenements of my existence." He explained So Cal punk versus British punk. He pegged me as a lover of the Brits but promised I would learn to love So Cal bands. We listened to Billy Bragg, because truly, he loved the British as I did and Liverpool and blue-collar causes and the difference between proletarians and plebeians. He told me about Jürgen Habermas and the difference between micro and macroeconomics. I retained the distinction between The Descendants and the Dead Kennedys and how to drive fast through curves. About Habermas, I didn't retain as much.

In the cloudy dark, we drove through Gresham, passing the apartment building Derek didn't move into, windows down, singing, "The Stars at Night are Shining Bright, deep in the Heart of Gresham." As we sang, Hans lifted his English cap he wore over his short-on-the-sides, super long on the top that matched Rebecca's ninth-grade hair. He shook his head.

"My hair hurts." He always said this about his asymmetrical hairstyle. He flopped his hair over his part to redistribute the weight.

I pulled my hair up and over my head. It didn't hurt but I liked this idea of balance. It was something I did when I stretched one leg after a dance class. I made sure to stretch the other. Stopping at the first falls, we read the history of the camas bulbs and suspected the green shoots were pressing their way through the black soil. In Oregon, most of the colors are deeply saturated because the substances themselves are deeply saturated with so much water. The saturation helped the succession forests turn to climax forests. So much water causes camas bulbs grow green stubble shoots even in winter.

The Kalapuyans and the Chinook of Western Oregon, the Columbia River Sahaptins, and the Northern Paiute cultivated camas to make delicious non-tulip cakes in the late spring and early summer. Digging large pits, cooks layered camas, then moss, then camas, then moss, then covered with ferns and then fire. The smoke and heat pressed down, the moisture from the moss stemmed up until the camas bulbs turned soft and sweet.

Hans didn't know these details about how to cook camas, but he had read about deadly camas—a variety nearly indistinguishable from the life-sustaining camas that bloomed like blue irises and fed people for centuries. The path to the falls in October is lined with green stalks that could have been either kind of camas. Or tulips. We walked carefully alongside them, pretending to be afraid if the camas touched us, we would die on the spot.

We climbed to the falls by scurrying up the side of hills, racing to stand on boulders where we would be safe from the encroaching dinosaurs from the *Land of the Lost* TV show we both watched when we were kids. We hid from the Sleestacks who slithered their tongues but whose lizardy shape we couldn't see in the dark. This *was* the land of the lost—ferns taller than Hans, who was six feet tall. I lit a cigarette for a little bit of fog-effect. And because Hans wouldn't let me smoke in his car.

We drove onto the next falls—a strobe light effect because even in the darkness, the forest opened square by square. Here's a clearcut. Here's one not.

"I bet it looks like a checkerboard from above." I had moved here for the forest. I didn't want to see the chunks that had been removed for timber and paper as if by a square cookie cutter.

But Hans, lover of the worker and Billy Bragg, who sang, "There's power in the unions," said, "People need these jobs. The loggers have been working here way before we got here."

I'd only been in Oregon for two months. I didn't know about succession forests quite yet, but I did know logging trucks had mud flaps with images of the spotted owl hanged with a noose. Forest managers had halted some cutting events to protect what the EPA had listed as a new endangered species. How could one tiny owl force Weyerhaeuser and Georgia-Pacific and other lumber and paper mill companies to reduce their impact? Hundreds if not thousands of jobs will be lost.

Neither Hans nor I knew the deep history of Oregon. We didn't know that in June 18, 1844, the Provisional Government passes Oregon's first Black exclusion law. It states that Blacks who tried to settle in Oregon would be publicly whipped—thirty-nine lashes, repeated every six months—until they left Oregon. We knew bands of tribes had made camas cakes and we knew the chinook salmon or the chinook winds were named for the Chinook people, but we didn't know that in 1950, 62 of the 109 tribes and bands that were denied federal recognition came from Oregon. When your tribe is "terminated," as, for example, the Klamath tribe was, the government can sell your land and further disperse your people. Now, there are nine federally recognized tribes in Oregon. There once were seventy-one. Native Americans set annual forest fires not only to prevent catastrophic fires but in order to encourage the growth of certain food crops. For instance, the Salish who inhabited Whidbey and Camano Islands burned the forest underbrush to increase the supply of berries and camas. Setting fires also improved hunting opportunities by maintaining and augmenting the amount of open land used by game animals. Cultural burns were practiced for generations by Indigenous peoples living in the Klamath Basin. These burns not only effectively prevented massive forest fires, they also had many other ecological benefits from new seed growth to salmon migration. While the US government stopped this practice for the past one hundred years or so, forest manager now realize that cultural and prescribed burns are necessary to keep forest fires from burning so hot they kill all the life inside them, including the mycelia in the ground.

Hans and I were good at visiting our Land of the Lost, Sleestack, Jurassic past, but not quite as educated about the recent, racist, colonialist past. In Utah, I knew Indigenous people, mainly because I hung out at the Indian Center for punk rock shows. And in Arizona I would soon make many Navajo friends. But in Oregon, when all you see is green and white, unless you go out of your way to look for other colors, green and white is all you get.

The environmental movement is not known for its diversity, unless it's the diversity of animal species. The spotted owl is an indicator species. It lives in old growth forests where 200-year-old cedar, fir, hemlock, and spruce create an ecosystem where each part functions for the whole. Only 10 percent of old growth forests remain and this is from where most logging companies produced their virgin timber, usually shipped whole overseas to be processed in China and Japan.

It is hard to argue for a bird. Even if you love owls, what do you say to a family that has been living in the Pacific Northwest for decades, who know the forest in ways you never will, and who are committed to this particular way of life?

You say, "Well, the owl is committed to his way of life."

And Hans says, "Owls aren't people."

Maybe you counter with, "I don't even like people," but you know this isn't, or shouldn't be, a matter of what you like. You need to dig deeper to explain. You cite, in your now-brain, the fact that hundreds of thousands of forest jobs are lost every day to industrialization and logging companies moving to the tropics, Asia and Africa, and if the lumber industry cared about its people, it would process the virgin timber here instead of sending it to China to be processed. You read Ken Kesey's *Sometimes a Great Notion*. Nothing stays in balance when humans start to mess with ecosystems.

In my now-brain, I could have slipped in nuance and facts. I could have explained the fact that as an indicator species, the health of the owl predicts the health not only of this forest but the forests that stretch all the way to the ocean and then up and through Portland down the other side to the Cascade Range. They have found salmon cells inside trees carried from miles away through mycorrhizal fungi networks. The mycelia absorb post-spawn-now rotting salmon from the banks of the rivers into the deep forest, providing nutrients for the trees.

I didn't want to argue with Hans, but I had a hard time seeing his point of view. Now, I see how interconnected his view was with his sense of fairness, his study of labor movements, and the recognition that money is the main story people live by. I'm sure Hans thought that I was naïve. Soft. Like a girl. To privilege animals above humans is something a girl from Utah would probably do. I may as well have been holding a stuffed animal when I protested that spotted owls can't survive in checkerboard lots of forest. They need connection squares—miles of uninterrupted, old growth forest. The spotted owl is an indicator species. As the forest goes, so goes this owl. The cool thing about old growth forests is how the different kinds of trees, hemlock, cedar, Douglas fir, compete with each other for light, so the understory is dark. It's clean too, in its own way—moss rolls between fern and fallen log, everybody's reaching a bit—there's ambition there, but they take their time turning sun into cellulose. The spotted owl loves this place—he flits between snag and live branch, seeking out voles that eat grasses and tubers like camas. He sneaks and hides as cleverly as Hans and I sneak and hide from Sleestacks along the waterfall road. The difference is, that road, Hans and I know about. As the roads multiply and the loggers' saws bite into bark as hungrily as a dog bites the postman's leg and the fires burn hotter, the spotted owl tries to flee to older forests but when he gets there, the roads and logging and fires have already been there. Once there is a road, humans drive it.

But I let myself believe there would be forest enough for the owl. I had my own denuded landscape into which I had to plant something stable, like a tree. I gave up my singular focus on the spotted owl and turned my eyes to the guy who argued with me about where to cast your lot. I wanted to cast my lot with him. I had one vision: Tree = Hans Tree = Hans Tree = Hans. Hans had many visions. He knew early on that I needed a whole forest and that was a tall order for one person to try to fulfill, even though Hans was at least 6'1." But I went all in anyway. I stopped listening to Jethro Tull and U2. I embraced Billy Bragg, workers' production, London, his bands: The Descendents, Fine Young Cannibals, Fugazi, NoMeansNo, the forest and the forest workers. But, if I had said what I wanted aloud: Be my forest. Be my forest. Be my forest. He would have said, Killer, or, probably Ler, "You have to grow your own."

If you think of interconnection and land, take a bird's eye view of the Pacific Northwest. You can see the web of connections from the Pacific to the ridge of volcanoes that reminds you, the dinosaurs were here among a similar greenery. All you people are new to the town. Maybe the loggers should get out while they can. At this rate, the last 10 percent of old growth forest will be cut and sold in thirty years.

It has been thirty years since Hans and I had this conversation. We didn't talk about climate change then because we quite have an angle on it yet, but the question of the spotted owl is the same. What economies will willingly take a hit to prevent global temperatures from rising beyond the this-far-no-farther point? None of them, is the answer. No company quit doing a single thing to stop the carbon they spewed or, in the logging company's case, eliminating the carbon eaters. But we don't have to wait for companies to make decisions. We can deliver information and new ways of thinking through our tiny mycelia—our internet postings, our emails, our short stories, and essays. It's not over. Unless we shut up.

2.0 degrees Celsius is the point of no return—where everything from the permafrost to the forests kicks positive feedback loops into cycle. The loggers still log, although with far more regulation than they did in the late 1980s and early 1990s. We've learned something about prescribed burns but a little too late because the lightning and human-caused fires burn hotter in this dryer, warmer climate. We're beginning to figure out that in the United States, forests absorb about a third of our carbon output, but we need somebody or something to inhale this other two-thirds. What if they'd stopped logging old growth way back in 1990? 1970? 1945, 1800, or when Europeans first set foot on American soil? What if the white settlers hadn't cut and burned the forest? What if they lived like the people they met here—in the forest. With the forest. What if they'd reconsidered the subject and object of their sentences? What if they'd rethought their prepositions. But the European colonists had one thought—the Native people and the forests are our enemies. We must take them down. And, mostly, they did. Now, we have to back track. Take back our tracks. Unpave our roads. Plant the trees and wait a thousand years for them to become the forests they were. The single solution isn't going to be *the* solution but there are over a billion trees waiting to do the work—not just one.

A single tree can't do much. Can a single bird? This spotted owl? How much did the controversy save it? Not at all, really. Numbers have declined 65 percent from 1995 to 2017. Habitat fragmentation, in part thanks to private land clear cutting, has contributed to the decrease but barred owls have moved in from the East. Barred owls are generalists, which means they'll eat about anything that moves. Spotted owls, singular in their appetites, find narrower and narrower places to nest and hunt. There's a controversial idea to kill all the barred owls. At some point, I imagine the eco-salvagers will give in and say, barred owls are better than no owls.

But while habitat loss to both other owl species and logging affects the spotted owls, spotted owls have learned, over millennia, to appreciate fire. Penn State Biologist, Derek Lee writes,

> Regardless of the amount of high-severity burned forest in core nesting and roosting areas, spotted owls are usually not negatively impacted by fire. In fact, burned areas are beneficial habitat for this species, and thinning and logging intended to reduce fire severity in spotted owl habitat would actually harm the owls.[1]

After a fire, a snag forest can provide even more places to nest, a vista from which to see prey. They don't mind a mess. A fire is the kind of disaster they can work with. A clearcut forest doesn't leave dead trees standing, fallen trees as nurse logs. There's nowhere for mice or voles to hide. The plants that come back are invasive. If you're going to burn a forest down, the spotted owls seemed to say, do it messily.

Do we need to care so much about the spotted owl? Barred owls are cool in their own way. I met a couple in Michigan. Nice babies, no trouble. Is something unique worth saving just because it is? The artist-managers of the Forest Service think so. Barred owl removal has been successful in re-establishing some of the nesting areas for the spotted owls. If art exists to highlight the grand uniqueness that is life on this planet, then the rangers who urge the spotted owls back to their homelands, might be those great kinds of artists that from destruction, create a wild show. As the number of spotted owls continues to dwindle, despite artistic arrangement, perhaps *unique* is just becoming another word for lonely.

What was Hans's art? Driving, of course. His deep knowledge of music history. His flexing on micro- and macroeconomics. His laugh. His jutting bones. At the center of his clavicle, a hollow ran deep. If I wiggled my finger at him, he'd yell, "Don't hook me," and run away down the hall of the dorm or hide under his pillow in his bed to protect me swinging him around by his clavicle. Hans kept his bed high up on Cinder blocks. I had to run and jump to get on top of it. Or clamber up on a chair. I preferred the gymnast's move. His other artistic gifts included carrying me. Because the Commons at Reed served casseroles, which I couldn't eat because they were soggy and too many ingredients melded into each other, I ate only cereal for all three meals my freshman year. Because I ate so little, I was easy to carry. My green satin dress was slippery, but I held on tight around his neck as he carried me all the way from the Student Union to our dorm.

Hans's other art was cleanliness. It made sense, when later he became a brewer, that his fastidiousness contributed to his ability to brew a non-funky, perfectly balanced beer. His dorm room he kept so tidy—no clothes on the floor, no pizza boxes on his nightstand. His records organized alphabetically. The beer our RA bought him organized by height in his mini-fridge. I didn't smoke in his dorm room or his car, but I filled ashtrays in my own room which had no clothes on the floor, but books splayed facedown, spines cracked, empty bottles of Pepto lining the windowsills. Although I might have become legal in November, by December, Hans could tell that the ashes and the smoke swirled around me in such an array that the clean lines of his ex-girlfriend called him back to his So Cal home for winter break.

For that break, I went home to my then-still-married-parent's-couldn't-sell house. My sister Paige had moved into my room with the blue carpet stained with the cough syrup I had tried to serve my doll Amber. Dad moved his office into Paige's old room which didn't get as hot in the summer. Valerie stayed in her room, so dad's old office became my new bedroom. I read Germaine Greer's *Daddy, We Hardly Knew You* and waited for Hans to call. He did finally call. To say that he had been thinking and his So Cal girlfriend and he had talked, and he was going to London School of Economics next year to study abroad, and he probably couldn't see me in that way anymore. Was there another way to be seen by a man? I didn't think so.

That next semester, I didn't manage to do much but burn the whole of what I'd wanted to think was my barely growing forest down to the nubbins. I was still "Ler" to Hans and "Killer" to others. I pretended to believe that I was something stealth and mean. I could be the killer, not the killed. I tried to see if any of the guys I slept be enough like Hans to cook camas cakes for me and carry me across campus, but they were not Hans. Not at all. Just guys who liked to dance at shows and take me home where I'd slip out before light so Hans didn't see this even messier version of me.

Christian, Hans's roommate, had the smaller but private inside room. There, sitting on his bed, I could complain about Hans and the problem with So Cal and the fact he called most Reedies fucking hippies which they were but maybe so was I. And maybe Christian was too. Sitting on his bed, he calculated his chemistry equations with me. I read the first pages of Jeannette Winterson's *Sexing the Cherry* which would form the primary text of my thesis. On his bed, we debated the merits of English versus chemistry degrees, and whether chemistry could be art even if English were my major and vice-versa for Christian and I told him that at least I didn't have to wake up at 7:00 a.m. and he said, you know, children of alcoholics have demonstratively high alpha waves which makes them smart but also prone to alcoholism and anxiety. Alcohol balances out those over-reaching waves and I said, do you really think my lips are beautiful because I loved thinking maybe I was smart and he said, let me show you how beautiful those lips are and I opened mine and he opened his and how it turned out that two good lovers, proper pressure on mouth, on stomach, on hips, on pubic bone, shared a dorm room I will never know.

The next morning, when we awoke in his bed, he was late for class, and I was way too late to slip past Hans unnoticed. Worse, I told a friend where I'd been last night and she told someone else and that person told Christian's girlfriend, Leah. I already had a hard time with boundaries. I wasn't good at staying in my lane. I should have known better than to sleep with someone's boyfriend. Rebecca's ex was one thing, and still not good. Christian's non-ex was wrong. People do stupid things, in college. I get it. But when you've construed yourself as a victim, as the indirect object at the end of someone else's sentence since you were ten, you often fail to take responsibility as the subject of a sentence. The actor of actions. A bad actor at that.

By the end of the year, neither Hans nor Christian was speaking to me. At nights, instead of eating dinner with them at the dining hall, I walked between the Student Union and the health clinic in the rain wondering if someone would come and stop me before I got soaked. They did not. Like being in the back of Noah's VW Bus, I felt lost. Like I didn't adhere to anyone. I could spin right off the campus, maybe even off the planet, and no one would notice. I lay in my twin bed in my own dorm room across the hall from Christian and Hans's room. I played Fugazi too loudly. I acted out dramatically the last line of their song, Promises, "Touch your hand to the wall at night." The wall was cold.

Instead of dropping out of college, I came back the next semester vowing to spend as much time as possible outdoors. The nice thing about summer break is you can come back and, magically, the whole social scene is reset. Christian and Josh came over to Rebecca and my house with the orange carpet to watch the First Gulf War on TV. Josh brought his saxophone over sometimes to play Warpigs. Christian and I wrote a collaborative novel about an ornithologist. I had no boyfriends for the first time in my life but two friends who were boys. Sometimes, I had sex with Christian, after he and his girlfriend broke up for good. Josh was a virgin, and he wouldn't have sex with me although he would take LSD with me which is definitely a kind of intimacy.

Josh was the first male friend I didn't sleep with. Josh and Christian stayed late watching TV or writing our novel about ornithology, which I kept calling oralthology and made stories of birds with big beaks and big teeth. Both would sleep over in my queen size bed with me in the middle. There was no touching except the night I held Josh's hand. A couple of weeks later, he came to my house by himself. As he sat in my orange papasan chair and I sat on the floor, I tried to convince him that we should start dating.

"I really like trees," might as well have been what I told him.

"Right. Trees are great. But you've had a lot of trees in your life. Maybe you should take a break from loving trees."

"Everyone loves trees. But, you are the best tree I know. You play saxophone. You're a chemist. I love chemistry. You like birds with big beaks. You make me want to ride my bicycle instead of drive my car." I wanted him to pick me up, sweep me off my feet, and take me somewhere else, forever. But as you know, I had seen one too many episodes of *General Hospital*.

Josh sat forward, elbows on knees, not afraid of my cigarette or my request. "I am from Ohio. This tree thing, it's not really me. We haven't had trees for a while. I don't drink. Don't have sex. You're used to a western kind of cedar."

"Ohio. It was once all forest too."

"I'm going back east when I graduate from Reed. I'm going to start the forest over there."

It was clear I was not eastern forest material, even though he was my dear friend. And even though I threw my neediness upon him, he did not draw back. He continued to sleep over at my house with Christian on a weekend night. We ate everything but tomatoes together. Josh hated tomatoes. I had just learned, thanks to Renee, to like burritos. What really was the difference between having this tree for a boyfriend or having him for a friend? Boyfriends, I mistakenly thought, were something you could plant, and thus, keep.

One day I would get the hang of making friends and not try to date them. Christian and I still hooked up once in a while, but we did not become boyfriend and girlfriend. I gave off, "I need a whole forest vibe," to him as I had with Hans. But as I practically lived with him and Josh and Rebecca and her new boyfriend, Todd, for the first time since the babysitter, smoke began to clear. The ground I stood on felt not ashen, but loamy and rich. I made them laugh at my song about resin in the pipe they smoked weed in. When people laughed at my jokes, my whole nervous system sang.

That year, I went backpacking for the first time with Christian and Josh. With our backpacks filled with pesto and Campbell's Chicken Noodle soup, covered in black garbage bags to protect us from the rain, we hiked what felt like twenty miles but was probably six, up Mt. Bachelor, just outside of Bend. Josh and Christian hiked faster than me, but I kept up all right, despite my occasionally stopping to smoke and my insistence on singing Don McLean's "American Pie."

It takes a long time to boil water at 9,000 feet in 45-degree weather. By the time we'd cooked the noodles, the rain had watered down the pesto and the oxygen had browned the basil. We ate a few bites of crunchy pasta and buried the rest by the firepit which we had vowed not to use in our "leave no trace" promised hiking. I'm not sure if a pound of buried pesto pasta counts as "no trace" but it has disintegrated by now and I might even eat pesto again one day soon.

We slept in the tent together like we often slept in my bed at my house when it was too late for Josh or Christian to ride their bikes home: me in the middle, Christian and Josh on either side, none of us really touching. Maybe we held hands sometimes. We didn't hold hands in the tent because our hands had to stay inside our sleeping bags where there was some hope to keep them warm.

When we woke up in the morning, Josh's lips were blue. Snow covered our tent, our garbage-bag covered backpacks, the lake from which we had pumped and filtered water last night. Shivering and fireless, one night of camping seemed like enough time to spend although I could have stayed for familiarity. The broad-scape version of this place was familiar enough—like the canyons of Little Cottonwood and Big—green triangle and brown squares patched against the morning's gray sky. But here, maybe because it was just the three of us, camping in late October when no one else was anywhere near, that the rain droplets beading on the needles seemed to emanate from within the tree. The ground smoked its residual summer heat. The fog met that heat, commingling around our legs. Other shapes, not just triangles and squares, came into form—pudgy mushrooms, splayed pages of ferns, whales of fallen logs. Bark flaked. Wind ruffled. A leaf rose up to meet a snowflake. Everything listening to the other.

As we hiked back down the trail, snow turned into rain, which felt colder to me. Oregon's humidity is just thin enough to slip between nylon's tight weave but heavy enough to stick to every particle of your skin and your hair and your clothes. Snow is a solid—a movable substance that you can shape and store elsewhere. To air and water, you are the movable substance, and the rain and fog will move you out of the forest, into your car, and back indoors any way they are able.

7

Well-Fertilized Soil

Mt. Bachelor, where Josh and Christian and I camped, is on the drier side of the Cascades, near Bend, where it rains about the same amount as it does in Salt Lake City and Flagstaff, about eleven inches per year, and yet we emerged from our backpacking trip drenched. The garbage bags meant to serve as waterproof covers kept our clothes and sleeping bags dry did not work well at all. Josh's lips were still slightly blue when we got back to the car, but I liked the cold forest. Even when the trees were still, I could feel something happening. Little dots, coming together.

I had spent almost two years in the Pacific Northwest now. In Portland, my socks were never fully dry. I wore a waterproof coat instead of an umbrella because umbrellas are external to the self and coats are an extension your body and my body was Portland now. I felt each flick of a raindrop on the top of my head. Drop, drop, drop. I counted every dot. Here, my understanding of scarcity and abundance changed. In Utah, rain came in big monsoon storms or in the form of snow or not at all. In Oregon, rain came not only from the sky but from the ground, from the trees, from the mushrooms forming almost in front of your eyes. Abundance reigned.

With Josh and Christian, on that side, even the less wet side, I had begun to see what the rain makes happen. Giants of trees. Plethora of mushroom. Carpets of moss. A saturation that seemed like the moist soil continued to the next layer of basalt or granite or the lake of groundwater that received the inches of rain per year with open arms. What's one more inch, foot, acre? Each drop digs in, promises to come back out in some other way—a moss, a mushroom, a spring, a tree.

There was no good reason to start dating Drew. We had no friends in common. People had warned me away because of his promiscuous behavior. It was said that he had slept with over twenty women. But, unlike Josh, Christian, or Hans, he wouldn't think my sexual history was a flaw—he'd find it to be an asset. I could hide my past behind his history—we're just open-minded college students. What was Reed's unofficial motto? Anarchy, Communism, and Free Love. My past was to him, revolutionary.

Plus, we both had a thing for water. A thing for rain. It was Drew who read with me *Ancient Forests of the Pacific Northwest* where we learned about how the mycelium knit the hyphae between decaying logs and mycorrhizal fungi and both nourish and gain nourishment from living trees. It was Drew who bought the first copy of *All the Rain Promises and More*, David Aurora's field guide to mushroom hunting. It was Drew who drove my Jetta out through the Cascade and Coastal ranges as we gave up wanting to be famous writers and decided to be forest experts instead.

The second time we hung out, I gave Drew three hits of LSD. I don't remember why I gave him so many. I thought his tolerance must be as high as mine. We had already compared how many people we'd slept with, and the numbers matched at somewhere near twenty-two. He was trying to sleep with me. I presumed all our numbers matched.

When I first met him, he didn't seem my type. He was flamboyant, loved talking to strangers, had been a theater kid in high school. He did not know the bands Crass or Fugazi. I met him even before my freshman year began. Mom and I had stopped by Walden Books at the mall in downtown Portland before we unpacked my stuff on campus. Perhaps it was the book that he gave me that allowed me to dose him so fully.

"You have to read this book," the bookseller with black hair and pale skin insisted as he loped over to us.

"Do you work here?" My mom asked.

"This is my last day. I'm going back to school on Monday. I go to Reed College."

"Oh. That's funny. That's where my daughter is going too," my mom said to him. To me she whispered, "Say hello."

"*Geek Love.*" He handed me the book. "You have to read it. It's crazy. About a boy who is part frog. Arturo the Water Boy! Do you know what a geek is?"

I raised my eyebrows as if to say, yes? I'm looking at one.

"It's someone who bites the heads off of chickens."

Fast-forward two years: After I gave him those hits of acid, he turned so pale. His cheeks grew slack. He couldn't track movement with his eyeballs. I tried to give him one of my Diet Cokes but all he wanted was a cigarette. I only had Marlboro Lights 100 in the box. I gave him one although I knew he smoked Camels.

"We have to go to class," I told him. One of my short stories was going to be workshopped.

His skin was so white. Like paper white. I could have drawn on it. If he'd been having more fun, maybe I would have.

"I don't think I can make it," he said.

"You can't miss my workshop," I complained.

Drew loved my writing. Or said he did. It's a good way to get me to have sex with you. For every sentence I wrote, he wrote three of his own about what he liked in my story. If he left me to go it alone with only Lyle, the student in our class, who told me about my last story that "women don't eat ice cream in the hopes of getting pregnant," I would never forgive him. A week before, we had workshopped Drew's story called *The Inside Passage* about a cruise trip to Alaska from a young girl's point of view. I'd suggested the story was about discovering sexuality. Lyle said it was a perversion of Lolita with the dad as Vlad. We needed each other as protection against Lyle's feedback.

"You mean Humbert Humbert," Drew corrected.

"Do I?" Lyle chided.

From Drew's story, I remember the description of the glaciers—everything in the story had a crevasse the girl could fall into—her father's gaze, her own vagina, the gashes in the land itself. Drew knew things about bodies.

Too high, Drew didn't come to my workshop. My story was weird, according to the teacher. Lyle had written all over in black marker. I wouldn't go on to revise it. I didn't know what to do with a story except subject it to praise or criticism. Then, I either read the praise over and over, trying to force the news to sink in or with criticism, whereby I shrank into a tiny, never-going-to-write-ever-again ball of sorrow. After the workshop, I walked past Drew who was waiting for me in the library. I didn't stop. I went to the chemistry lab to tell Christian how bad things had gone, both with Drew and the workshop. He let me practice some stoichiometry with him while I waited for the LSD to wear off.

But then Drew kept calling me. He wanted to work on a project for our Women Poets class. We had started with Christina Rossetti, made our way through Elizabeth Bennett, then Marianne Moore, then Plath, and now Audre Lorde. He was the only guy in the class and anytime he spoke, the women in the class rolled their eyes because I think the idea of the class was to give room for women to talk. Drew did talk as much as the most loquacious of the women students and way more than I did. Professor Schreiber asked us to pair up for presentations. Only I would pair up with Drew. I invited him to come to my house to work on the project. After that evening, he never went home. Partly because he lived with a pig named Sophia as he squatted at his friend's apartment. Partly because it was the apex of the AIDS crisis and although we used condoms until we could be tested, the day of the test, we had sex on the orange carpet on the stairs up to Rebecca's studio/bedroom without condoms, so now we were glued to each other, sticky with awaited results.

Before Drew and I hooked up but during the Women and Poetry Seminar, some women from the class hosted a Take Back the Night March, and, before the march, a Speak Out where women could take the stage and tell their stories about sexual assault. Josh told me he was going to support the women he knew.

"Should I go?" I asked him.

"Do you want to go?"

"I don't know if I can tell my story. Does anyone need to listen to this?"

"I will be there." Josh promised.

Josh didn't know my story. No one knew at Reed. But, just as I had imagined when it happened, I assumed everyone had an inkling. Gossip travels like negative ions, clinging to whatever attractive surface it can. All human ears are magnets. They'll do anything to hear the metal of a story. I just said that I'd had sex very young. I didn't call it molestation or interference. I elided the abortion.

At the Speak Out, I did use the word "molestation" because that seemed less harsh than the word rape. Many other women told their stories. I wonder if I'd been resilient enough then to stay with the women and talk with them, if I would have leaped ahead a few years to getting where I needed to go—with women where we would go and tell our stories and listen to others. But I wasn't there yet. Instead, I climbed off the stage and Josh took my hand. He walked me back to my dorm room. He sat on the papasan. I sat on across from him like I did when I tried to convince him to be my boyfriend. I wanted to ask Josh if he thought differently about me, but he gave me the same expression with his big brown eyes and his smile that raised his bony cheekbones even higher.

I could have stuck with the matted humus floor of friends I'd been stitching, ripe with ferns and mosses, and underlayment of promising mycelia ready to support not just one tree but a whole forest—newly empowered, having told my story, engaged in therapy, spent most days with my two guy buddies, a best friend with whom I lived and another, Renee, who lived down the street in Reed house with her ferrets. I could have befriended the feminist women in the Women and Poets class and the women at the Speak Out. I could have told Drew it wasn't his turn to talk. I could have become a lesbian, but instead I followed that worn path into the basement of my dreams where weird things felt normal, therapy was trite and redundant, friends would leave you, and a man offered a vision that seemed like the only way to feel whole.

With Christian, Josh, Renee, Rebecca, and Todd, I'd begun to see myself as more than a girlfriend to a boy. I, who had always eaten any Mexican food with the beans, hamburger, cheese, and tortilla separate became a team-player who first tried burritos thanks to Renee's insistence. I was sometimes funny. I played They Might Be Giants and Tori Amos too loudly in Rebecca's and my duplex, dancing around like I was making music videos. I studied hard. For the first time since I was ten years old, I wasn't defining myself by who was having sex with me. Perhaps if I knew then what I know now—that I would be friends with Josh and Hans and Christian and Renee for the rest of my life, perhaps I wouldn't have wanted so desperately for them to date me, love me, have me. If I had known that each of them would in just a few years come to my wedding, lie on grass outside the venue, me in my white dress, they in their formal attire, with our heads touching so someone could take a picture of us in a perfect circle, maybe I wouldn't have sought out Drew's green promises.

My friends weren't drawn to Drew. He was theatrical. A bit of a know-it-all. He smiled weirdly when he thought he was being clever. When he turned twenty-four, he jumped on the table at the bar and read aloud from Dylan Thomas's poem, "Twenty-four years remind the tears of my eyes." He had graduated from Tigard High School, near that same Motel 6 where Derek and I had landed that first night in Portland. He kept with him his high school friends and, since my friends didn't want to hang out with us, I adopted his, forsaking my fledging forest for his native one.

I told Drew about the babysitter. I told him about my parents and how we'd tried to move to a different neighborhood but couldn't sell our house. I told him about Dr. Tony LePray and how my sisters, because of me, because of my parent's imminent divorce, because no non-Mormon really prospers in mostly Mormon public high schools in Salt Lake, were now caught in the whirlpool of group therapy from which they might never emerge.

The year of my abortion, my sisters had been eight years old. They were used to playing dolls with me. Then, something shifted. They continued to play with dolls. I stopped. My parents didn't directly tell them what happened. But my mom and dad tiptoed around me. They spent nights in their bedroom talking privately. My dad stopped building radios and popsicle stick sailboats with me. Mom drove me downtown to therapy twice a week. The twins had each other but it wasn't the same as having all of us devoted to their second-grade needs. My dad started drinking more—not just glasses of ice filled with chardonnay, but glasses of ice filled with vodka that we mistook for water.

Drew's previous girlfriend had been molested too. She too had gone through extensive therapy but had quit when she and Drew started dating. When she tried to kill herself, Drew knew he couldn't be her only resource for her mental health. But maybe he could be for mine? We didn't have an open relationship at the beginning like he and that girlfriend had, but we did entertain a threesome.

We invited a woman from my psych class into my room in the house we rented on Woodstock. We played truth or dare. She seemed willing but nervous. We stopped before we all took our clothes off, but we could have gone forward. I was a "we" now. It felt safe to imagine "open" relationships as long as the W and the E didn't split into Drew's own "I love women" in that way that some feminist-men say so they can try to sleep with all the women.

He was very well-practiced at sex. I thought, I must be pretty good at it by now too. Something shimmered between us that made us think we were different from other couples. All couples think that, but we thought we were beyond the rules. Like Hans and I had, Drew and I drove into the dark forests. We listened to the hard rain, listening to Bob Dylan sing about it, singing ourselves as streams sprung from to run alongside the road. We knew if we got out of the car, we would get soaked, maybe risk hypothermia. But sometimes, it didn't matter how cold we might get—it was worth his lips on mine, my nakedness covered by trees' slashing shadows and clouds digging low to the ground for me. Drew was willing to kneel in the thrumming ground while I lay back on a moss-covered log and tried to keep my eyes open to see if raindrops would fall in.

After, dry, back in the car, Drew said, "Therapists don't know everything. Maybe having sex young didn't fuck you up. Maybe it gave you a world view no one else has. And maybe it makes you extra good at sex."

To me, I saw sex as mostly performative, which did make me good at it. Like I was in the movie version of this sex scene. I could act

He continued, "Perhaps, you see sex as not a big deal. It's normal to have sex, let us normalize," he said on the stairs and on the beach and in the forest where his father had taught us to hunt for chanterelles in the coast range where we found golden caps whose undersides undulated as intricately as labial folds. We learned to cut the mushrooms off at the stem so the mycorrhizal fungi could continue reaching across the forest floor—he was into reproduction, just not the human baby kind. I admit that I wasn't honest with him or probably myself about the crater I still felt in my stomach—the way that my belly rung like open, empty bowl. He couldn't have known what the hollow felt like— empty, but also waiting. Fecund like a narrow valley, covered in moss, not trees, but with humus rich enough to one day support their roots. I don't know if there's a cure for empty uterus syndrome besides another pregnancy. Still, we fill our emptiness in any way we can, even if that way is not the most mentally sound.

Drew and I read a book together called *We've Had 100 Years of Psychotherapy and the World Is Getting Worse*. The premise of the book is summed up by the title. Therapy, they argue, might be the kind of bullshit that promotes the individual at the expense of the community. Is the world getting worse? In Dr. Tony LePray's office, the concern was with me, not with the world. How, if I was going to survive to adulthood, I must develop a kind of street smarts. No one ever considered that the smarts required by the streets be questioned. Why do the streets need to be this way? The kind of impulse that made me submit to the babysitter or wave enthusiastically at guys across the street in Manhattan was seen as the problem. The idealist, optimistic approach that we can change things is not street smart. It's not even book-smart. And yet, as we may heal as individuals in therapy, we aren't spending time knitting more tightly together our families and communities.[1] What if therapy had a communal aspect to it? What if every hour you spent getting yourself together in the therapist's office, you spent another hour getting the world together? If therapy is a kind of bullshit, then maybe spreading it around could lead to a more fecund relationship between self and world?

What I loved about Drew was the possible futures. Although polyamory might have been a part of his dream, not mine, we shared the dream of a collective existence. We weren't total hippies, but we were commune curious. I scrouged around the bottom floors of Powell's bookstore, buying used instruction manuals for gardening, rain harvesting, seed saving, canning food, staving off insects, building greenhouses and outhouses. This was the year I read Norman Rush's *Mating* about an anthropology student striving to finish her thesis as she visits a utopian community called Tsau in Botswana. Although the commune is matriarchal, the narrator falls for the one man, Nelson Denoon, who lives among them. The narrator pursues Denoon who is an emblem of utopic love. Utopia, like love, is elusive but Rush makes his narrator's pursuits seem almost attainable. The book questions how intimacy exists in an open-community, how does a man resist elevating himself to cult-level status even if a narrative pushes him there? And how does erotic love complicate notions of democracy, equality, and community? Utopia, we find, is in the details. My favorite detail is the story of how the outhouses are built. One is used to pee, the other to poop because uric acid inhibits poop from decomposing. You can have excellent compost, as long as it's urine free. The outhouses, according to the narrator, don't even smell badly.

    I could picture this communal future in ways I couldn't picture a future as a lawyer, an editor at a big publishing house in New York City, or a restaurant server—the futures most likely for an English major. In the Cascade Forest, possibly near the town delightfully called Sweetwater, we would install a waterwheel to power our mill. We'd grow wheat berries for the mill to grind for our bread. Carrots, artichokes, and lettuce we'd sow, but we'd also eat watercress that grew along the edges of streams where we'd also fish for trout. We would raise chickens, collect their eggs, and I'm sure one of the less-hypocritical women would catch a chicken and behead it for me so I could roast it and make mashed potatoes and gravy like my grandma did on Sunday nights. This wouldn't be the same as my grandma's life as she too collected vegetables from a garden and relied on fish from the streams to feed her family of ten. But here, we'd have more adults than children—people to contribute and work together. We would build, as in *Mating*, a collective of women with men, or one man, who loved women democratically. He would dig by outhouses with us and roast chickens with us. I could not then see how, like my matriarchal history (my great-great grandmothers were wives of polygamists), there was more than just a hint of polygamy than polyamory as the number of women Drew would invite to live on our compound grew.

    Communes weren't our only projects. We also planned to start a publishing company called Ziggurat. We posted posters with a picture of a rectangular stepped tower on every lamppost on Hawthorne Street. Sadly, we didn't not understand the difference between posters for bands and those for literary magazines. People did not flock to our temple, i.e., did not overwhelm our inbox with their literary submissions. We got exactly zero. We read *The Monkeywrench Gang* and studied *Earth First!* pamphlets, although we never spiked a tree or threw a cowl trap down a logging road. We even talked about having a baby. I don't know whether it was the projects themselves I loved or the idea of having someone to do the projects with, but being productive, as a forest is productive—building, growing, reaching, sowing and reaping, felt empowering, or, if not empowering, it felt like it organized my life. I wouldn't know until many years later how all of these projects would become a life of organizing. Drew did help me sow some of these seeds and spores.

When Drew, Rachel, and I moved into duplex on Cora Street, we grew a quarter-acre of vegetables in beds cared for by tenants who had lived there for twenty-seven years and had been kicked out by the new owners. All that work making soil so fertile that you could drop a lettuce seed on Monday and eat salad by Friday, handed off to a bunch of twenty-year-olds who knew better how to grow weed than artichokes. But we figured it out thanks to the instruction manuals from Powell's, Andy's garden-advice-giving parents, and our willingness to weed unwanted plants, grow cover crops to keep the ever-encroaching Bermuda and Kentucky grasses at bay. For a few months, we only had to go to the grocery store for beer and chicken. We weren't quite ready to adopt chickens, although I did buy a how-to-make-your-own beer guide.

As part of my job at the Oregon Winegrower's Association, I made brochures about wine regions and wrote newsletters about cover crops and phylloxera outbreaks. Is not a primary feature of utopia the ability to make your own beer and wine? In Oregon, it really seemed possible, as long as "we," Drew and I, would do it together. No one likes to shovel outhouses alone. From that good compost, we would grow our own mushrooms—those that can be domesticated—oyster, shiitake, portabella, cremini. The wild ones, we'd have to go into the forest and gather—but the forest wouldn't be far away because we'd have settled there. We'd understand all manner of soils, humus, and manures—even getting to know our own shit, intimately.

To plant a billion trees, we're going to need a lot of fertilizer. As Dr. Richard Houghton pointed out, it's important to plant trees in environments that are particularly suited to them. If you plant a ponderosa on the west side of the Cascades, it will be too wet and too warm for it to thrive. If you plant a Douglas fir in Flagstaff, it will probably survive but the ponderosas will outcompete it for sunlight. But as the climate changes, it becomes harder to predict what species will grow best where. As trees from the Southeast inch toward the Midwest, as trees scoot their root systems upward in elevation above the old limits of tree line, or move inland to survive rising seas, learning to trust barnacles in ways they differently trusted the nutrient deliveries of the mushroom's mycelia, what we thought we knew about trees and where they want to be and what they need to be themselves will have to be renegotiated.

We make a lot of bargains with nature. If we do this to you, dear nature, we'll make it up to you like this, as when, after years of logging and hunting in the park, Yellowstone's wolves were returned. The wolves hunted the elk and deer, which allowed some of the overeaten shrubbery to flourish which allowed creeks to flow in more organized crevices, which allowed trees to take root, which allowed mycorrhizal soil to return which helped the trees grow taller which led Yellowstone to a kind of rewilding.

Called a trophic cascade, the wolves instigated in Yellowstone a series of indirect interactions that control entire ecosystems. Trophic cascades occur when predators limit the density and behavior of their prey and thereby enhance survival of the next lower trophic level. Trophic cascades can work to restore native ecosystems as well as undo them. If humans kill too many predators, the number of prey animals increase, which can stress native plants, making way for invasive species that may overtax hydrological and other systems.

The story of Yellowstone is just one of the ways humans shape and then reshape the environment. We humans, as Whitman knew, contain multitudes. We produce food and cars, babies and microchips. Multitudinous, we also produce a lot of waste, nearly 2.6 trillion pounds of it per year—two pounds for every tree we plan to plant! And humans, animals that we are, produce 860 billion gallons of sewage a year—and that's just in the United States. But like Yellowstone, our imagination is gripped not only by wolves but by shaping our environments.

In Egypt, the sun hits the desert sand at 2,000 kilowatt per hour per square meter, which is good for photosynthesis but not so great for the sand itself.

That much heat kills bacteria and the mycorrhizae which spawn mushrooms. When soil is desertified, the mycelia that usually contribute nutrients to plant networks cannot grow. But in the town of Ismalia, in an attempt to un-desert the desert, to stop sand from blowing into destructive storms, a research group planted a combination of native and non-native trees. Researchers installed a drip-irrigation system that pumped water directly from Ismalia's sewer system to the area. The effluent not only supplied water but nutrients the trees need—just as mycorrhiza do in natural forests. If these were fruit trees, the fruit would be inedible but since they are just photosynthesizing, sand-holding down sand, they don't care where they get their phosphates and nitrogen. Thanks to human waste abundance, the generators of these nutrients won't run out any time soon.

Without these generous, generative microscopic organisms, land-based lifeforms wouldn't exist. Mushrooms are useful too! Humans know this. We grow shiitakes for our Miso soup. We replace Styrofoam shipping material with absorbent mushroom matter. Mushrooms can serve as batteries and as home insulation. Commercial mushrooms are grown in sterilized manure. Mushroom spores, the fruiting bodies of the mycelia spreading throughout a forest floor, delivering sugar and nutrients to trees, are inoculated in cow manure that has been cooked at high temperatures and is anaerobically exposed to healthful microorganisms, and then aerobically exposed to additional healthful ones, making mushrooms healthful additions to human diets.

But some humans are particularly good at recognizing abundance and inventing new uses for them. Plus, mushrooms are the consummate recyclers. While growing mushrooms on treated cow manure has been practiced for centuries, converting the abundant effluent produced by humans to food *for* cows is a new venture, patented and verified. Instead of growing mushrooms on cow manure, mushrooms are grown on human sewage. The cows are fed these mushrooms, which smell as delicious to the cows as they do to humans. Sewage is as abundantly available in the United States, where this practice began, as it is in Egypt. It's a more sustainable than growing alfalfa and the mushrooms produce lignin and cellulose for the cows. However, none of this helps decrease the amount of methane that cattle burp and fart and their shit accumulates exponentially. In 2019, *The Guardian* reported that by 2030 that the planet will be generating at least five billion tons of shit. Much of this shit ends up in our wastewaters. We can't even use the shit fast enough even as we spread it on fields to grow crops or to cultivate our domesticated mushrooms.

Drew was good at finding wild mushrooms. I too could find the silky orange caps set off against the velvet mosses, in those green, green Cascade forests and the forests of the ocean range, Drew reminded me to use my knife to cut the chanterelles at the base of the mushroom.

"If you pull the mushroom from the ground, you'll destroy the mycelia."

I had bought myself a knife for this purpose. Its hilt rested against the sheath until I had to en garde! and take that mushroom on. Mushroom hunting is hard. Even with the backdrop of so much green, finding the peeking caps push their tongues from between the lips of moss required persistence. One can get quickly obsessed, looking and finding—a little positive reinforcement—and then looking some more.

On a gentle slope, moss made a blanket of the earth. I don't remember who saw them first, but neither of us had seen them before. white chanterelles. Against that backdrop of green, they were not tricky to find. They revealed themselves like full moons. Drew started to gather them up. I followed. But if I could have said what I wanted to say, I might have said, I see it all—the invisible threads that connect moss to mushroom, mushroom to mycelia, mycelia to mycorrhizal fungi to plant hyphae, plant hyphae to tree roots, the pattern of tree roots redoubled in the pattern tree branches cutout against the sky.

"Why isn't this enough? Why can't we live like this, just you and me?" I wish I'd said aloud.

I imagined Drew responding "I am like a mushroom. Like a tree. There will never be another like me and everybody would like a taste of me."

"But will there be another couple like us? Look how I roasted you a chicken last night. I feed you like those fungi feed the hyphae." I rested my hands on my belly. From the vibrating earth to my stomach, I felt the round of my belly begin to resonate like a Tibetan singing bowl. The emptiness usually found there was replaced by a different kind of space, something magnetic and hopeful. I tried to explain it to Drew.

"Maybe we should have a baby," I suggested.

"You expect too much. I cannot be a whole forest to you. I need to take a chanterelle to everyone I know."

"But I don't know anyone but you. Or at least no one who loves chanterelles as you do."

"And yet, I have all the chanterelles I'll ever need, here in this basket."

The trees leaned into each other forming a tipi over me. The branches and pines thrummed against each other, a soprano kind of song. Then, Drew stood over me, blocking the light the pines and firs that laced through their branches. Drew, a singer, sang a song about arms being too short to box with God. His pitch, though on key, did not match the tune of the trees

Drew wanted me to take off my jeans but all the dew from the moss and the ferns made them difficult to remove. He tugged hard on them. He wanted me. I wanted my stomach to be a cup like the upturned lid of the chanterelle. I wanted the chanterelles to stay in the ground. I wanted nothing to change this little bit of forest with its mixture of Douglas fir and western red cedar. A watercress pushed up by a spring. An owl might have hooted, maybe even a spotted one, if I knew what one sounded like. If fantasy serves as a protective force, perhaps fantasy could protect this place from the forces of production or progress. We were deep in—maybe not Bull of the Woods Wilderness area deep, but still, an old growth thickness, like rich fabrics, layering over each other. I could like down in this bed. I did lie down. Moss held me up, the air, warm and wet, held me down. I could imagine this place never moving, my never leaving. This kind of place inspires imagination. Living under the shelter of a gigantic mushroom cap. Twisting plaits of moss into actual blankets over layers of decomposing root, forest animal excrement, pine needles, and mycelia. Making a magical forcefield of spider webs and cedar needles to reject intruders. You cannot make a clear cut or a field or a farm out of me, this grove would say.

But to be true to itself, this ancient forest would probably need to reject me and my intrusive knife. I came with extraction intensions. Could anyone leave these rare chanterelles behind? Drew bent over to cut another mushroom from its stem, leaving its mycelia intact. The green looked a little less bright, denuded of its contrasting white. But I learned late that it was bullshit—pulling the mushroom from its stem ruins the mycelia turns out not to be true. You don't destroy the mycelia if you pull the mushroom out of the ground, stem and all. The mycelia can survive even the most aggressive tug.

Later, Drew and I parked in the driveway in front of the house on Woodstock. Fighting, or at least talking animatedly about whether "progress" exists.

"How can you not believe humans have progressed as a species? Abolition. Civil rights. Women's rights," Drew asked.

"At some deeper point in the past, there was no slavery. Maybe we're just going around again to a time when matriarchal culture was the norm. Where skin color didn't mean anything."

"Technology? We are listening to music beamed to us from across the city. We just drove in a car, a machine invented only 100 years ago, five miles to dinner."

"So we can park in the driveway argue light of the dashboard? We could have hunted and gathered our food and argued by a campfire. It's different. But not necessarily better."

"You can't say it's not progress to send people to the moon."

"People have been on the moon all along." I said ridiculous stuff like this sometimes, to slip out of arguments I was losing. I did it with Rebecca when she and I argued whether there was anything like freedom of thought or if we were conditioned to think every idea that pretended to wander originally through our head or whether form mattered more than function or if art was an end to itself or could we use it for political ends?

"Do you think we should have just stayed in caves, drawing on the walls?"

"Listen." I copied his imperative. "We've always had art. And we had more animals around us to draw to boot. The Multnomah and Clackamas people who lived here didn't have to cut down the forest to eat roast chicken every night."

I've thought a lot about this argument, progress or no progress. Drew should have been on my side. He's the one who read along with me about the processes of succession forests—even as the trees grow tall, they eventually, hundreds of years later, they must fall. When they do fall, they become nurse logs, feeding the forest floor which feeds the saplings which will become the tall forest again, if we let them.

I suppose I do believe in anti-progress. Some days, I can imagine cave living to be quite pleasant. People chose their caves and built them up well—shaded in the summer, sun-focused in the winter. These days, people build their houses facing whatever direction the street tells them to. Is that progress or hubris or just convention? Was there something reactionary in me that made me not want to progress? Did I just want to tuck into the past, imperfect, but known? It wasn't so much that I was scared of an unknown future so much as I wasn't sure how the past would transform itself—into something rich and nutrient-filled or into shit. Or were those they same thing?

"You shouldn't romanticize Native Americans," Drew reminded me. But I did romanticize them. I thought of the blackberry and bison stew I'd made from a recipe Jeff Smith, *The Frugal Gourmet*, who was later accused of child molestation, that came from Indigenous peoples. Can you trust a child molester? Perhaps you can, about blackberries and bison. Salmon smoked on racks. Mushroom cornucopia. If I ever had to live off the land, this would be the land, I thought. But I had conjured another fantasy, I knew, as we sat in the driveway, the heater warming our skin damp from the proximity of clouds, dashboard lights cutting through my bullshit. I should have known better than to imagine I could live a different life from the car-driving one I lived. I couldn't even imagine polyamory. And Multnomah and Clackamas which were once integrated forests flush with life, cycling through successive growth, deepening the rich humus on the forest floor, are now just the names of counties in Oregon.

Renaming is everything. What environmentalists call devastation, lumber companies call harvesting. What some call clearcutting, others call making way for the next thing. The process of harvesting trees destroys everything in its wake. Tractors and bulldozers dig up the soil as well as tree roots. The trucks crush nurse logs. Banana slugs become the mucus they seem to be. The mycelium, exposed to the sun, burns in the heat of 1,000 kilowatts per hour. Egypt is calling. It wants its desert back. In an old growth forest, not only on the ground but high up in the canopy where humans rarely visit, another world of microorganisms and insects live, feeding the tree, as well as mammals and birds, from above. Soil exists in this mirror image. That sky forest in the trees, knocked down by bulldozers, falls to the ground, is rubbed out by the cat tracks that roll back and forth across square acres of 500 years of growth. Which system is progress? The growth of the trees or their decimation of them?

It couldn't last, Drew and I, fantasizing we were going to be famous writers, we both planned on publishing in *The Paris Review,* soon! And also live off the mushroom-fecund land. Believing we were different from other couples and could manage open-relationships equitably. Thinking we could imagine something deeper about psychology and trauma and the best way out is through. Where did we think we were going? We'd read Derrida. We knew there was no "out" of this psychological, cultural system to go.

But it wasn't my brain—it was the body that took the blows. Drew left me when the sex ran out. As a believer in non-progress, in non-linearity, I figured that there were vicissitudes in desire. We didn't have to have sex every day, did we? I imagined the notion, the sometimes great one, that we could live an unconventional, maybe even open relationship, was just a step on the succession of our growth, a part of the process—a bit of a deciduous tree on the way to some old growth cathedral. Then, we'd collapse and start over again.

If our apartment, the one we rented together with our cat named Phaedra, had been a forest instead of a duplex, our relationship would have ended like this:

Listen. Paul Simon's "The Obvious Child" playing in the background.

"Why am I not enough?" Why indeed deny the obvious child. No one person is enough.

"I'm leaving you for all the women who want me," Drew said.

"I want you. I just don't want to have sex right now."

"For you, it's all or nothing. Those women. They mean a lot to me. You yourself said, we shouldn't take possessively from the forest. Plus. You only make chicken for dinner. You get so mad when you just cook the same thing over and over and I don't want to come home and eat chicken."

"I meant we shouldn't take greedily from the forest. I roasted you an entire chicken," I said as I wedged my boot between a rivulet in the bark. I found two handholds and pulled myself up to a branch, but I couldn't stay on that one—only the next higher branch could hold my resting weight.

"I cannot eat chicken for the rest of my life. I need something else. I'm going to move to Hawai'i. Or to Singapore with Rashimi."

He walked up to me, put his hand on my stomach, and said, "I could have conjured a baby there."

"Look. You did say we could have a baby. You changed your mind about that. But no. Don't conjure. I can't have a baby upside down. It's contraindicated." I said as I edged myself onto the strong-enough branch, my knees pinching its curve.

"We were going to have a baby but now I realize that babies are a bad idea. They are the antithesis of progress. I am going to become something else."

"Once a tree, always a tree," I said as I swung down like I used to in grade school before the babysitter, before I wore make-up, before I needed a man-like creature to navigate the path for me.

"I would like to be a bird. A bird without any babies," Drew may have said.

"You can't have sex with a bird," I said as I hung from my knees, my hair swinging back and forth along the ground. Maybe I could convince some mycelia to nourish me through my hyphae like hair. I am of you. "I am of you," I said aloud to Drew.

"We couldn't have a baby. You're only twenty-one."

I'm twenty-four now. My dad will die in two years. You and I will actually succeed in getting back together and then falling apart. You will tell me I'm fucked up and that I need to deal with my father issues, and I will say that sounds a lot like psychotherapy to me. You'll say let's quit smoking and I'll say OK and then I'll say fuck that and I think that maybe you leave me finally for the final time because I'm too flexible. Watch me rise up and grab this branch. I can throw myself from this tree like a gymnast. Is it sexy or do I look like a pre-teen—short, square, smoking behind your back while I wonder where my doll Amber wen?

The world looked upside down from there, but whether that was before or after the leap, no one could have said.

After he moved out of our duplex, I went upside down anyway. I hadn't seen Josh, Christian, Hans, or even Rebecca in months. I'd been incorporated into Drew's friend forest and when he left, he took the trees, the humus, the chanterelles with him. I stayed home with the cat and the frozen chicken. I lost my mind. I drove by Drew's apartment. I walked by his work. I managed to find myself at the same gay bar watching the same drag show. I over-identified with Bonnie Tyler's "Total Eclipse of the Heart" and bit Drew's ear when the man in the blue gown and long eyelashes sang, "Turn around, Bright Eyes." I lost twenty pounds. I drank gin martinis without vermouth or olives.

It felt like a fire, but it was just a clearcut. In some ways, clearcuts are worse. The damage is fully intentional. The mycorrhizal soil is displaced. All the little sinews connecting soil to plant to sky are broken. But there was enough bullshit in that relationship, enough writing, enough paper, enough arguments, enough theories, that it substituted for some of that ground work.

And then the forest planters came. Renee, finding me on the couch with a glass of gin, pulled a chicken from the freezer and said, "I'm going to thaw this. And then cook it. And you're going to eat it." She roasted the chicken whole, pulled the meat from the bone, and fed me piece by piece like I was a little bird myself.

Renee took me to the river. She stepped into the water, then kneeled, then lay flat on her stomach and started pulling herself upstream by pulling on the rocks. It looked easy enough to do. I followed suit. We called it grappling—climbing up a river rock by rock. A fully textured kind of swimming.

Drew, no enemy, now friend, said to me, "At least you have your art." Maybe that was a continuation of a bit of bullshit, a minstrel poet wandering from town to town, asking with so much sincerity, "What is your art?" But I pose the question about everyone I know, as bullshitty as it sounds. I remember to ask myself every day. "What is your art?" Questions become nutrients to feed fungal soil which feeds you back. Grow back, little mycelia, grow.

After the break-up, my sisters came from Salt Lake to stay with me for a month. Reed gave me a scholarship to create a dance performance based on my poetry. Double art! We choreographed poems to Peter Gabriel's music from the movie *Passion*. Oh, and also to an Enya song. We wore green leotards and mirrored each other's movements like we were triplets instead of I the oldest and they the twins.

I volunteered at the homeless shelter with Josh. He and I listened to men tell stories about Portland's Chinatown and where the word Shanghai came from—barstools in Old Town with trap doors. Men fell through to the docks and were sent to work on slow boats to China. I went to a therapist who asked me to shape my body into my emotions. She said, "What does your body look like when it's sad?" I wrapped myself into a ball. "What does it look like when you're happy?" I lifted my leg high in an arabesque, raised myself up onto the toes of my left foot and stretched as tall as a branch I could swing upon.

"You should quit smoking," she said to me. And, for the first time, I thought maybe I could quit for good. If you want to be a forest, you have to stop burning yourself all the way down.

8

Reseeding

I didn't quit smoking right when the therapist in Portland suggested. Instead, I moved back to Salt Lake. The same city wherein I had smoked those early cigarettes with Noah in the driveway of his house on Chadbourne. I had smoked through many houses by the time I returned—the house on Woodstock where Drew and I lived with Renee, Becky, and Lee. The house where Drew and I lived alone with the cat Phaedra. The house on Cora where Drew, Rachel, and I left because the landlord sold the lot where we'd grown our vegetables. I vowed never to rent after that, and, with help from my dad, bought a house in Portland where, various people lived with me—Rachel, Drew, Rhett, Renee, Mike, my sister Paige, and Jonathan—and we grew lime trees and tomatoes in the greenhouse and harvested figs from the backyard.

Leaving Portland was hard. After Drew and I broke up for the last time, I spent less time looking at the affirming cooperative behavior of trees, at least exclusively. Growing so much food in that quarter-acre made me believe in something like self-sufficiency. Or communal sufficiency. I couldn't run the greenhouse without my roommates who sprayed tobacco juice on the plants to keep the aphids away, watered the lime trees, picked the fruit. I didn't know how to grow tomatoes until Renee, who planted tomatoes in every yard she lived in like a Johnny Tomatoseed, taught me how. The last time Drew and I broke up, I wasn't left with a barren wasteland. I had friends. We shared things. It was the polyamorous life Drew might have been looking for, but just with friends, not with sex. With my roommate Rachel, who cooked chicken fourteen different kinds of ways, we hosted dinner and parties feeding dozens of people at a time. I had learned to appreciate things that grew horizontally in the ways of pumpkin vines and cabbage. Everybody loves trees, but there are other ways to grow. Verticality isn't the only way forward.

We bought a two-bedroom, one bath, finished basement, in the Avenues on G Street together—my sisters seeming to say, "You want roots? We will give you roots!" I might have stayed in that house forever if I hadn't wanted this one other thing: a job that would help me have a writing life. I believed in things that don't leave: trees, houses, boyfriends willing to become husbands. Salt Lake held the promise of all three. Utah men are a different breed from Oregon men. They are the marrying type, but, in Utah, marrying often means giving up a lot of what makes a community-minded, ambitious, writerly woman. Most women in Utah take their husband's last name when they marry. A lot give up their jobs. Their community, even if they're not LDS, is meant to be their family, not a gaggle of writers getting doctoral degrees in writing.

Trees are different in Utah too. Oregon has plenty of kinds of trees—they're not all Douglas fir, but the interplay between forests and mushrooms felt primeval—as wild and foreign as the *Land of the Lost* where Hans and I pretended while we hunted for camas, focused my attention. In Utah, Douglas firs proliferate in the mountains—the triangle shape of the evergreen inverse to the steep V of the canyon. But there too grow aspens in northern Utah's mountains like Little and Big Cottonwood near where I grew up, and most of the other mountains, even in southern Utah.

Pando, considered to be the world's largest organism, is a giant collective of aspen trees, which grows in Fish Lake National Forest marking the beginning of the end of northern Utah or the beginning of the beginning of southern Utah. Stretching over hundreds of acres, aspens fan across hills, down valleys, up near the tree line—not a single tree at all but a blanketing of trees. A tree is such a lonely word, normally, in the scheme of things—a lightning rod or challenge for loggers or in which birds upon a singular branch nest. No one thinks of a lone tree as family but a single aspen fares as well as the whole group fares. Aspen trees mirror mycelia in that they connect in networks underground, some grouping sensing some trees' needs from over five miles away, sending the nutrients if they can. This family, thanks to the ability to share resources, adapts quickly but even so can't quite keep up the pace of the cows eating their shoots and suckers, the elk inking their winter longing in the white bark with their antlers?, the warming air confusing their response times—should our leaves turn to speckled yellow Post-it notes now? Now? Do we turn now?

Black cottonwood *Populus trichocarpa,* cousins to quaking aspen *Populus tremuloides,* don't communicate with each other. Perhaps because they don't live close enough to each other. They don't share root systems. Cottonwood trees grow across the state, which is how you can find hidden rivers. Bright green leaves, ribboning along seasonal streams canopy in such abundantly green, it makes you think there might be enough water in this state for all these immigrant people. You are probably wrong to imagine abundance enough, but to see these trees, their glassy sheen, draws your eye to the shiny flash as you drive through ribbons of limestone and red of southern Utah or the gray-green grasses of northern Utah. Wherever there is even a hint of water, cottonwoods capitalize on a potential future that seems impossible to me: Such huge trees. So little water. Their fat rivulets of bark, crusty and thick, support wide, embracing branches with leaves reaching out into the bright blue desert skies, scrub the air for extra molecules of moisture. The trees press their roots deep into the ground to drink from invisible streams. These gigantic, arching, reaching trees amaze me for their ability to survive in parched environments.

But look. There's a problem. Cottonwoods grow as fast and tall as weeds. Their branches are not oak-strong, nor are they like ponderosa pines, which bend with the wind. The cottonwood tree's branches grow up fast and they lose them just as quick. In the summer, limbs fall from them like leaves—but heavy, dangerous leaves. In the wind, they break like bones. I love cottonwoods but they're hard, like Utah, to trust. The dominant religion that dominates the legislature that dominates women's right to choose is always visible and always felt. It's dangerous for women to walk under the heavy branches of deeply ingrained male supremacy. Now that I had begun to understand how to make a forest, I didn't want a cottonwood. I wanted a space for trees to grow old together. Maybe I was more like Drew than I thought. And yet, I suspected there was a kind of tree that could stand forest-hood, even, or perhaps especially, if it meant sharing our roots.

It wasn't as hard to come back to Salt Lake as I thought it would be. That's where the fire of the molestation had burned my forest so hot, I had nothing but this ceramic bowl of a uterus and a mind that ran mashups of soap operas and punk rock songs. My dad and mom had divorced, taking the mycelia one way, the hyphae another and my dad couldn't really survive without the nutritive sustenance she had garnered for him for twenty years. My dad had died two years before I returned to Utah. He had a hard ending that was even hard to hear through the electrons spinning through the phone lines. We connected only through that thin and spotty cord. "Nik. I always knew I would die at fifty," he would call to tell me at 3:00 a.m., from where his vodka-addled mind thought was 3:00 p.m. "Nik, I've won all the awards I am going to win." I think I understood more than others how the carrot of winning a prize was a key to staying alive. I also liked to win. Carrots worked on me better than sticks. Dad's carrots had all been eaten. His skin turned more yellow with cirrhosis than orange with beta-carotene. Still, I keep boxes of his awards in my attic. I knew where he really lived.

My sisters, though, were in Salt Lake and made space for me to come home. Paige grew seedlings in the breakfast nook at her house. Valerie had just returned from New York where she'd danced and lived for a year. We hadn't been the three of us living in the same city for a long time. The ground we'd fortified as kids remained soft. It was easy to plant myself back with them. And, we'd all moved out of the suburbs of Salt Lake to downtown where, although the architecture of the church loomed large, the university on the hill added some weight to balance the scales. Fifty-thousand people studying across hundreds of disciplines and majors splintered and cracked and the Olympics were coming, further fracturing the church's singular stranglehold on some laws. For example, by 2002, you could order a drink in a bar without buying a club membership. The Salt Lake I had left was not the Salt Lake to which I returned. In fact, the ground felt much more pliable.

As I started graduate school, my mom started dating Carl, a retired dentist who lived in Ogden, an hour north of SLC. The distance between the two cities was just enough for me to start to see the babysitter story from a different perspective. Perhaps it wasn't only my shattered ego that allowed the toxic substance in the form of the babysitter to make his way into my developing forest.

The story my mom and I told each other was this: I had tested into the Gifted Program when I was in second grade, third grade, and fifth grade but for the fourth grade Gifted and Talented program, the district implemented a new test that I did not pass. Mom believed that it crushed my ego, blew a hole in my nine-year-old-girl-tough confidence. She and I, when we try to understand why the babysitter targeted me, we agree on this answer. We have decided that the gold star of Gifted and Talented would have worked as a shield, protecting me from overzealous boys and my own attention-seeking ways.

It mattered because if you couldn't be Mormon, at least you could be smart. In the 1980s, grouping students according to their "intelligence" looked more like grouping kids into their social class and social status. My dad's job at Christensen Diamond, his grandfather's company where they built diamond drill bits, and his next job at Terra Tek, searching for oil in sandy soils gave us a little of the social class, because of the lack of religion and the habits of drinking, gave of little of the status. Being smart mattered in our family. Intelligence was the ingredient that turned diamond drill bits into smooth, black gold. When my family, after the babysitter, attended therapy together, one of the rules the psychologist gave my dad was to not use the word "stupid" against me, my sisters or my mom. I don't think he thought we were dumb. We just did stupid things and should try harder to match his savvy, white man IQ.

All my friends were gifted. All my friends were talented. That year, as I stayed in the regular classroom, I watched as the gifted and talented students climbed aboard the bus to visit the Utah History Museum, Hansen Planetarium, Ballet West performances. I looked around at the other regular kids sitting at their desks. Had they spent the first years of elementary school looking out the window wondering what they did wrong to miss out on these field trips?

I have pored over the internet to see if I could find the test they gave us in third grade. I remember a piece of paper with five circles across and eight circles down. We were told to be creative and make something of these circles. I am pretty sure that I drew sunglasses and turned the rest into a bunch of grapes. I do not know the correct answers although I did find on the web when I googled "gifted and talented circle draw test" an image of circles one drawn into a watermelon, another an earth, another an orange? I'm not sure if these are the "correct" answers or not. I'm pretty sure sunglasses and grapes would give watermelon and oranges a run for their money. Or maybe not? What do I know? I am not circly gifted. But if smart guys from Reed wanted to sleep with me, wasn't that a kind of gold star of its own? What if I had been so fucking gifted and talented that I'd talked my way in and around an abusive situation until my getting pregnant finally put a stop to it? Good job, brain.

My mom told me that Carl didn't think anyone would marry me. He'd told her that men don't marry smart women. Was this a compliment? Did this explain why he never married my own smart mother? Or is that just another story to explain why, at twenty-six, I was still unmarried? An odd thing for a girl from Utah, but one I had attributed more to my having gone down a wrong, unmarriable path than to the fact that I had been admitted to and attended a liberal arts college in Portland, Oregon—despite my inconsistent testing skills.

Salt Lake City's mountain valley cradled the trauma of my dad's death, the dominant culture that had made me feel outcast, the assumptions of people like Carl, and the story that my mom attributes to why I was susceptible to the babysitter's whims. From that cradle, a tree-seeker grew. There's a saying about why people make choices that run against their best interests, "Why do trees love the axe? Because the handle is made of wood, and thus, the trees thought it was one of them." If Salt Lake was the cradle, and I'd gone to Portland to study the bargains made between trees and mycorrhizal fungi, perhaps the wooden cradle could be reshaped into something that no longer stunted my growth. The memories of the babysitter were born here too, although those go with me everywhere. Could I shape them into something better than rotten wood?

The babysitter, the babysitter, the babysitter. But I was tired of thinking about him and what effect he had on me, my family, my future. I didn't want Salt Lake to be forever defined by him. I wanted to come home to my mom and sisters. In the Avenues, just a couple of minutes from the university where I studied writing, I lived in a little house on a plot of land that grew mostly Kentucky bluegrass that sucked up too much of Salt Lake's limited water, which I killed by covering the grass with a layer of newspaper, a layer of peatmoss, a layer of soil, and turned it into a vegetable garden. Unlike the house where

Paige and Valerie and I grew up, I had no fruit trees—just box elders, a kind of maple, a potentially invasive species which are impossible to kill, no matter how little you water them. For now, I'd keep these trees. My succession forest wasn't ancient yet. It was still a baby and those quick, growing deciduous trees pave the way for hearty cedars and firs. I just had to trust the process would roll me into its humus, ferns, Douglas firs, and fungi and wait a thousand years. Or one. A year after I started grad school, I met my actual, non-soap-opera imagined, would-be husband, Erik.

Erik with the long, swooping hair. Erik, nearly a foot taller than I. Erik who looked like Matt Damon in *Saving Private Ryan*. Erik who also saw Fugazi at the Speedway Café and the Indian Center. Erik who made too many jokes about corn and digestion. About the way I operated, or failed to operate, the gas pump, the gas grill, the gas lawnmower. Basically, anything related to me and engines was fair game for his "OE—Operator Error" joke box. Erik who wore ripped shirts even to dinners with my mother. Erik who shaved only once a month. Erik who sometimes looked more like Brad Pitt than Matt Damon. Erik who made me ski down black diamonds and hike up mountains with the word "horn" somewhere in there. Erik with horn jokes. Erik who lay me down on wet mosses and red dirt and on the banks of creeks. Erik who didn't think having babies was a bad thing. Erik who had a Jesus-y vibe, in that he would shovel your sidewalks for you but probably wouldn't accept an invitation to your house for dinner. Erik who talked so low and under his breath that every time I laughed at his joking, my mom asked, "What was he saying?" He was probably teasing me about the gas grill, and how I may burn my eyebrows off as he did when he was fifteen and lit the barbecue and then we could be twins and then could beat the twins, my sisters, at their own game. Erik, stubborn as an oak, thin as a willow, as down to earth as earth itself, loamy, quiet but resonant. Erik who said he would sue me for copyright infringement if I used any of his jokes in my book. Erik, who hiked with me in Oregon, Utah, and Arizona and could tell when a forest was old enough to be of use—when roots and mycorrhizal fungi balanced water and microbial soil to lift a mushroom from the mycelia. Erik, who was on the main floor, called me, where I was upstairs working, to say he was leaving for work. I said, "I was just down there. You could have given me a hug." He said, "Come back down again and give me a hug." I said, "Come up here and give me a hug." He said, "I don't think you know how hugs work." Erik, a very exacting carpenter, who knew if you make one wrong step, the whole wooden structure—be it cabinet or dining table or tree farm, is bent and weak. A forest is a whole structure. Better to plant a billion forests than a billion trees.

Rebecca and Todd, having helped make what forests they could between each other and with me, brought Erik and me together one cold January night in Salt Lake. Todd played in a band called Fistful who played the kind of punk rock where you could actually decipher the notes and the lyrics. They also occasionally covered Pat Benatar's "Heartbreaker." I danced, not caring who was watching, until I saw who was watching and then I cared. I showed Erik my trick of taking off my bra without taking off my shirt. It's acrobatics like this that have make me goofy, although, apparently, some guys think it's quite hot. Erik took me home and we watched Harold and Maude while we made out on the floor. I made him go home before we had sex. I was working on looking for trees that could withstand fire.

Erik's dad and my dad had died around the same time. His parents had divorced when he was only five. He'd lost his best friend to leukemia. He had a glimpse of what a burn scarred wood looked like. He did not look away from mine.

Later, I told Erik about the babysitter. I feel like some forewarning was necessary. I might be perennially "fucked up," I warned. He nodded teasingly, "Maybe." His bright blue eyes narrowed. "I'm sorry, Nik." He took it seriously, more seriously than I had for many years. He said, "I want to kill him," which no one besides my mom had expressed before. "You can't kill him," I said. "It's my territory. If someone should kill him, it should be me."

He said, "That seems right."

I wasn't going to kill anyone, but it was nice that someone recognized that it was my right, no one else's. For the first time after telling someone, I didn't feel like they were looking through my skin, at my rotten and ashen insides. Erik looked at me. I looked right back. Then, after a reasonable amount of time, he stopped being so serious. He told me about corn. "People can't digest corn. They just poop it out." I had no idea why he thought to tell me about it at that moment. But I laughed. Every time we eat corn, I look at him and roll my eyes and laugh.

Erik took me to Greenstreet for our first official date even though we'd been together for three days straight since the San Raphael Swell camping trip that Rebecca had invited me to join and Emily, Bek's friend and Erik's cousin, had invited him. They were unsubtle in their arrangements. Erik smoked my cigarettes. I hiked alone into the hills behind the campsite. He followed. Under a yellow moon, our faces streaked with red dust, he kissed me. We came back to the house on G Street. He seemed to like both me and the house, for he did not leave—except to go on our official date to the bar.

We sat outside on the patio. I ordered a Cape Cod. Erik ordered a Sierra Nevada.

I lit a cigarette. So did he. I smoked Camel Lights instead of Marlboro Lights 100 in the box by then. He smoked Winstons. Sometimes, I'd take one of his.

"Listen," I said. "We can do this, but the sex has to be weird."

"What do you mean, weird?"

I knew what I meant but it was hard to convey. Place had something to do with it.

"It's already weird in one way. Like when we were at Ken's Lake after the swell and we let our hair get wet in the waterfall. And then when we were at your parent's property in Torrey, by Sand Creek, when we barely got dressed when the guy walking and reading the newspaper walked by. Like when we first had sex. At the San Raphael Swell with the moon as big as an egg."

But place wasn't the only thing I meant by weird. Maybe I was trying to scare him off. Maybe I just wanted to say I wanted "weird." I thought about Noah and the four-lane highway, the weirdness of garments, the weirdness of power, the power of pretending. Is playing out fantasy just a kind of hiding out? Is "weird" just a way to buy some time before you figure out exactly what you mean by sex and weird and I?

Erik nodded while I struggled to explain what I meant. He listened as I vowed the situation with the babysitter had no lasting impact. I told him about the Take Back the Night March and Josh. I told him about Drew and how he theorized many things about me and sex and weird.

"Maybe," I said, "'weird' is not the word I meant."

Perhaps, if I had asked this, I would have understood what I meant:

"What is sex for?"

"Having fun. Making babies."

"How many babies can we have?"

"Twelve."

"We're not Mormons."

"We can start a commune. Babies in the woods. Lots of goats."

"What if I need you to look me in the eye when we have sex?" I could have asked.

"I'll do it."

"What if I need you to pretend you're a Mormon bishop wanting to correct my wayward ways?"

"I'll correct you."

"What if I need you to be a police officer who has to punish me for driving too quickly? What if you make me open the back door, put my face against the vinyl, and make it clear that I should drive more slowly."

"I can punish you."

"What if you were my professor and I wrote a story in which you featured as a professor who, after reading the story I wrote about the professor who laid me over his desk, laid me across his desk, would you teach me?"

"I would teach you."

"What if you were my lawyer? Would you take my case? Would you give me a deal if I raised up my skirt?"

"I would give you a bargain," Erik could have said.

Erik studied to be a filmmaker in college. When we first met, he was a carpenter. Both talents require very precise, straightforward, thoughtful movement. He could have wanted to shape me like Drew had tried but he did not. For someone who loves straight lines so much, he didn't seem to mind mine skewed. Perhaps it's because he had an art beyond meticulous editing and woodworking. He played guitar. He jammed. He followed notes he made up in his head rather than on the page.

Perhaps weird didn't have to be interior thoughts and explicit fantasy. Perhaps weird could be weird outdoors. We had weird places—or at least outdoor places. In the waterfall at Ken's Lake, under the moon at the San Rafael Swell, in the mangroves by the sea turtles and in the sand by Hug Point, next to

Carcass Creek, under the chairlift at Alta, in the dark on Walnut Canyon Road. And, if I didn't want to have sex, indoors or out, Erik never complained, never coerced, never even rolled his eyes. Perhaps that is the weirdest sex of all.

We planned our wedding a year after we met. Our families had generational roots in Salt Lake. Even if we'd left the church, we dragged mycelia behind us like tin cans dangling from behind the car driving away, "Just Married" scarred into its paint with shaving cream. It's as if our ancestors had been amending the soil just for us. Our great-grandparents even shared a last name: Christensen, although, we were assured we weren't actually related. Well, no more than most people born and raised in Utah are.

We were so committed to the idea of family and history that we resourced our entire wedding from Salt Lake City stores where our grandmothers shopped like Feldhorn Buchman's and ZCMI. We didn't get married down the road at the LDS Temple, but we got married up the road a bit in Memory Grove where both my grandmother and great-aunt had been married in the late 1930s. We were "of" Salt Lake and expected to stay there.

For the wedding, on a budget, Erik and I shopped at thrift stores for bowls in which we'd decorate our tables with fruit instead of flowers. I thought of my belly, that empty bowl, and wondered if twelve children would be enough to fill it. In the end, we settled for two kids, the first, hard to come by, the second, easy as pie, and three dogs and eight cats so far. I am working on getting the goats.

It wasn't all going to be perfect. If Erik would have touched my stomach, after I explained my meager sense of self and sex, maybe we would have been prepared for ways this simple falling in love narrative fractured. This is not to say we are not still married and not still in love. But it wasn't *voila*—a perfectly balanced ecosystem. I am ambitious. Erik is ambitious. I like a lot of people to come to my house for dinner. Erik prefers just me and the kids. In retrospect, we should have known that in a real forest, things fall apart—and that falling apart, like a fallen log becomes a resource for many other forest plants and creatures, is a good thing.

It caught us by surprise, when things sometimes went wrong. Perhaps if I said these words, "Also, these baby times are an equal adventure. Another billion baby stories waiting to happen," maybe we would have taken the raising of kids a little less seriously. I had been clear about the how many kinds of people we could be at once, that we could tell more stories at once, I tried to say that I believe everything happens all at once at the same time and that punishment and bargains and correction and teaching were ways to lighten this heavy story. Perhaps I did say enough. Knowing what to say takes a lot of practice. Knowing when to stop talking takes even more. Trees are known for their collaborations and communications, but they're competitive too. The key is to keep the rest of the forest involved and healthy. We fall apart. Then, we sprout weird fungi from the inside of our decaying trees. It's called a succession forest. A succession marriage? A kind of success.

9

Vertical Trees, Horizontal Forests

Graduate school was the first place where I didn't feel desperate to glom onto a particular person. I mean, I did glom onto Julie Paegle at first, who was beautiful and erudite and beloved by everyone in the department. But she was elusive and I knew my habit of believing in the one-true-tree. I found a different kind of ecosystem than I had known before. Competitive, but truly supportive. The kind of support that felt like, if I didn't win it, I'm glad you won it kind of support. So many people who I still am in touch with: Steve, who told me "Suffering looks good on you." Lynn took me to yoga and on hikes and drank red wine into the night with me. When we see each other a few times a year, we do not look or act older. We still go on hikes and drink red wine. Margot, with her thick, long hair, who had gone to PhD school after working for a few years as a consultant in Manhattan and who edited *Bending Genres*, edition one and two with me, Matt and Jenae, who were Erik and my closest couple friends and who taught me to make duxelles of mushroom for beef Wellington even as I thought I knew all the ways to cook the mushroom. Peter, who said, every time he saw Erik and me together, "You will have beautiful children" in his highly flexed New York accent. Jenn and Dave, other good couple friends. Jenn taught me to cross-country ski on the snow of liberty park and Dave, who asked me who my favorite poets were, and I, not knowing any, said, "you and Julie." Eric who skateboarded down Emigration canyon and taught me to love Presidents of the United States' song, "Peaches," Jeff, who read my novel and said it was good and who sat with me at our friend Jane's funeral. David whose booming laugh told me that he didn't love poetry much, but he loved mine. And, of course, Julie, who wrote pounds of comments on my poems and my novels and made me think I was a real writer and who, once, when I asked if I were fat (she was vey thin and beautiful), said, "No. You are the perfect shape. Strong shoulder, cute boobs, and just a rounded bump of a tummy." I always felt pregnant around her. These were people with whom I shared the same sustenance. Our books were our trees. We shared them unequivocally. Mycelia hyphae connecting with the tips of tree roots, sending nutrients up the veins of trees, turning sunlight into cellulose, dreams into paper. In grad school, we loved trees as everyone did, but we also used a lot of paper writing our papers, theses, and dissertations. I hope we saved a tree by writing the trees, but writers are usually terrible saviors.

Let me nerd out for a minute to explain how the subject I chose for my dissertation, "Immanence and the Meaning Within," and mycelia became the metaphor I live by. The year after I got married, I took my PhD Qualifying Exams. I had only been in the doctoral program for one and a half years, although I'd finished my MFA a couple of years before. Most PhD students took their quals after year three, but I was nervous. This would be the final test of my giftedness and talent. Maybe I wanted to fail—confirm that a shattered ego leads to some kind of victimhood. Or perhaps if I took the exams early, I could blame my failure on my foolish impatience. Perhaps if I hadn't been so hurried to take them, I would have been better prepared for how, no matter the results, my confidence was the real subject of the test. The orals came first—a three-hour long Q&A. Then came the written in exam in which I had seventy-two hours to write a thirty-page paper that answered the question: "How do the particular formal and metrical choices made by the authors of the following poems serve their meaning in George Herbert's 'The Window,' Dickinson's poem 502, 'At least—to pray—is left—is left—,' in Gerard Manley Hopkins' 'The Windhover,' and Marianne Moore's 'The Jerboa.'"

My job was to look at how the form of the poem, the meter, helped constitute the meaning of the poem. Working with these measuring tools which you can find on the Academy of America Poets' website:

Iamb: a metrical foot containing two syllables, the first of which is unstressed and the latter of which is stressed (e.g., "today").
Trochee: a metrical foot containing two syllables, the first of which is stressed and the second of which is unstressed (e.g., "matter").
Spondee: a less common metrical foot in which two consecutive syllables are stressed (e.g., "heartbreak.").
Three Syllables
Anapest: a metrical foot containing three syllables, the first two of which are unstressed and the last of which is stressed (e.g., "unaware").
Dactyl: a metrical foot containing three syllables, the first stressed and the following two unstressed (e.g., "Waverly").

I was to count the syllables, the stresses, the line breaks to show how poetry's sonic math conveys its potential meaning.

A jerboa is a rodent that jumps over hills like an iamb. Dickinson knocks in spondees on the chamber of her walls praying to Jesus-in-the-air. Herbert's voice bounces off the church windows in dactyls. Hopkins's falcon threads "daylight's dauphin, dapple-dawn-drawn" sky to gold-vermilion soil in anapest. As you try to escape the bonds of mortal life, you climb the rungs of meter, knocking against the walls of church rooms, something to knock against, until a break in the meter allows an escape through the church windows leading you directly to Jesus's high throne. Hopkins, who sensed God lived in the soil as much as the sky, didn't need to do as much knocking as Herbert. This argument made sense to me at the time but most of my religious background had been formed by the soundtrack to *Jesus Christ Superstar* so I'm not entirely sure I represented the full idea of sin and transubstantiation in my rendering. I knocked on wood, turned in my exam, and hoped I got it right.

At the end of the year, there was a party thrown not for me, but I had completed my exam on December 7th, and the Winter Break Party hosted by the English Department was held on December 10th, so the date felt correlated to my success if not causal. The party was held at the Cottonwood Club, where I had spent a large part of my childhood. My parents joined the club so my sisters and I could swim in the outdoor pool while they sipped gin and tonics—then only legal at places called "clubs."

The Winter Break Party was held in the Cottonwood Club's dining room—a formal space reserved for weddings and holidays and big parties, encased in windows that looked out over the creek, through the branches of cottonwood, to the little lake. This is the room where my dad had tried to teach me to waltz. The same room where I had returned to the buffet eight times, grabbing three oysters each time and no one stopped me once. My dad approved of having an otter as a daughter. My Aunt Brooke married her husband in this room. I had dreamed of getting married here, outdoors, on the bridge that curved over the creek which ran from Big Cottonwood Canyon on whose snow my sisters and I had skied. I thought of that creek and this room as my family's. Or at least it had been before my dad died.

At the end-of-the-semester party we grad students, David, Lynn, Margot, Steve, Peter, David, Jenn, Julie, dressed in Poet Black instead of Funeral Black, jumped to Gloria Gaynor's "I Will Survive" on the same small dance floor where dad and I had waltzed. I wore high-heeled cowboy boots so I could only dance so long. I took a break. Sitting between two of my favorite profs, Kathryn Stockton, gender theory scholar, and Barry Weller, a classics scholar. Barry had refereed my exams. I gulped a gin and tonic, too fast. They were talking about the new dean.

"He came from the sciences," Kathryn said.

"Perhaps he'll know how to raise money then," Barry said.

"Do you ever want to be a dean?" I asked both. I didn't know how deanships worked. I assumed that serving as dean would be a desirable promotion but both Kathryn and Barry looked at me like I'd just swallowed my whole drink in one sip. Which I had.

I had interrupted the flow of conversation. Academics are not the best at small talk. I felt guilty for making it awkward. I tried to think of something to talk about that didn't involve deans.

"Kathryn. Did Barry tell you I passed my exams?" I turned to look at him, puppy dog needy. "I did OK, didn't I?"

Barry looked back at me with a blank face. "The Herbert scansion was really off."

I felt like he had slapped me. I hadn't expected him to say anything except, "You passed!" I had thought I had done well. Barry wasn't known for coddling grad students, but he didn't publicly shame them. Had I even truly passed? I had received a note from the chair of my committee that I had. But perhaps it had not been unanimous? Even in my tall boots, I shrunk. Rather than asking what I could have done better or standing up for myself or quoting the chair of my committee who said I had done well, I took my short legs and ran blindly out the oak door into the night. The branches of cottonwood trees, stripped of leaves and cotton, smacking me in the face.

For the PhD exams, I had chosen forty historical, forty contemporary and forty theory books to read and absorb and, supposedly, understand. I compiled my books around the idea that nature could be separated neither from God nor man. In what was a not-fully-realized version of Donna Harraway's idea of *Staying with the Trouble*, I relied on Charles Altieri's book *Enlarging the Temple* to explain how I believed poetry to work. The more poems, the more stories, the more voices there are in the world, the more possible personal connections. I argued that words illuminate the stuff of the world, inviting readerly people to pay more attention to every object's brightness. Altieri took the title of his book from a W. S. Merwin's poem that reads, "if you find you no longer believe, enlarge the temple."

If you stay with the trouble, be it climate change or personal trauma, details you didn't see reveal themselves. It's not that the trouble is necessarily fixable—it's that by staying and looking, you may find some of the complex connections between the things of the world. How do you enlarge the temple? You look at it closely, through a microscope, through a telescope, upside down and, if you're gentle, inside out.

As I read through my 120 books, I stuck a Post-it Note wherever a poem or a theory buzzed with the ideas of indwelling, inscape, or instress—the idea that inside the word, the thing, and inside the thing, the word. William Carlos Williams's edict that one should write "No ideas about the thing but the thing itself" mirrors Hopkins's inscape. What we need to see already exists. We just need to look harder. Just listen to all the stories of all the beings of the universe, the poets say. Our attention is all we can give the universe. "Attention, taken to its highest degree, is the same thing as prayer. It presupposes faith and love," Simone Weil wrote. Bright green pine needles sparking chlorophyll toward the sun make a different sound than duff-colored pine needles, fallen to the forest floor. Those make a sound even the microbes can hear. But still, if you're patient enough, you can hear that slow stretching into something next.

Interconnection is, to me, a way of imagining what others mean by God. It turns some kinds of Christian thought on its head. If the divine is inside everyone and everything, then reaching out and beyond ourselves, transcending this world isn't necessary to reach God. As opposed to transcendence, immanence means that God exists inside of things.[1] Transcendence is a thing I'm not great at. I like to dig around in the mud and the permafrost, the mushrooms and the snow. I'm not good at catapulting from those experiences into seeing the world as if from above. Sometimes, I would like to see the forest for the trees, but I'm distracted by roots and bark.

Immanence is not about "escape" as much as "inscape." Don't transcend up and out of this world but touch more actively the things of the world, like mycelia touch the microorganisms they bring to trees' roots. The poet Gerard Manley Hopkins coined words like indwell, instress, and inscape to explain his approach to language. Inscape was the essence of a being. The instress of that being—be it a tulip, a hawk, or a golden grove—is the relationship between how that being sends that essence into the world and how the observer embraces it.[2] Immanence translates to me as the physical form inscape—that which we don't see that makes everything thing possible: fungi, microorganisms, hyphae—these strands and beings that pulsate energy, chemical exchange, breath.

If I combine what I've learned about mycorrhizal fungi and their relationship to trees with what I tried to understand about Hopkins, I understand more clearly these non-hierarchal relationships. I imagine underneath the forest floor, the mycelia pushing and pulling different nutrients from different microbes in the soil, communicating needs from one side of the forest to another. Hopkins understood the things of the world as communicators themselves—their inner essence communicated to an observer. Humans are finally beginning to understand. other creatures speak to each other. The London School of Economics started a new school to study animal sentience. But even in the plant world, trees communicate via electrical impulses. Researchers have found that during a solar eclipse, spruce trees synchronized their electrical signals with each other. When they attached electrodes to the stumps of trees, even the stumps re-aligned with the other trees, suggesting not only that they too communicated, but that they were still alive. It wasn't God that imbued things from above with spirit. The things themselves shuffled meaning from one being to the next on a level playing field.

Robin Wall Kimmerer, famous for her book *Braiding Sweetgrass: Indigenous Wisdom, Scientific Knowledge, and the Teaching of Plants*, wrote an essay Speaking Nature, about language and how we use it determines our world view.

> It's no wonder that our [Potawatomi] language was forbidden. The language we speak is an affront to the ears of the colonist in every way, because it is a language that challenges the fundamental tenets of Western thinking— that humans alone are possessed of rights and all the rest of the living world exists for human use. Those whom my ancestors called relatives were renamed *natural resources*. In contrast to verb-based Potawatomi, the English language is made up primarily of nouns, somehow appropriate for a culture so obsessed with things.

She asked her Potawatomi elder and medicine man if there was a word that undermined the hierarchy implicit in the pronouns we use. One that might level the playing field a bit. Might even make us a little hesitant to use everything we see on the planet as a resource to improve our human, urban and suburban lives.

> So I asked him if there was a word in our language that captured the simple but miraculous state of just being. And of course there is. "*Aakibmaadiziiwin*," he said, "means 'a being of the earth.'" I sighed with relief and gratitude for the existence of that word. However, those beautiful syllables would not slide easily into English to take the place of the pronoun *it*. But I wondered about that first sound, the one that came to me as I walked over the land. With full recognition and celebration of its Potawatomi roots, might we hear a new pronoun at the beginning of the word, from the "aaki" part that means land? *Ki* to signify a being of the living earth. Not *he* or *she*, but *ki*.

So that when the robin warbles on a summer morning, we can say, "Ki is singing up the sun." Ki runs through the branches on squirrel feet, ki howls at the moon, ki's branches sway in the pine-scented breeze, all alive in our language as in our world.[3]

By calling animals and plants "it," we necessarily subjugate them to a lower status. She suggests that we use the word "ki" to refer to all animate beings.

The cat's cradle is divine. The mycelia underneath the forest floor are illuminated with godliness. The quaking yellow leaves quaking in the wind flicker notes of God. Just like the Eucharist, God is in the thing. But unlike the Eucharist, no priest must bless it. It's not unique to the house of God—the room of the world is imbued with spirit. Perhaps this kind of thinking, inside-the-details, makes it harder to destroy things. If you destroy the tiny things, you destroy the divine.

In poetry, you have all the tools, sound, and sight, to at least rhyme with the world, to imagine into that inscape and instress. Hopkins countenanced that it could happen. His fantasy equaled his imagination equaled his belief. In his poem *The Windhover*, the bird flies as the syllables fly, the falcon is Christ himself rising up into the heavens and then coming back down.

> In his ecstasy! then off, off forth on swing,
> As a skate's heel sweeps smooth on a bow-bend: the hurl and gliding
> Rebuffed the big wind.

How, when like when you're walking in the forest where the trail lines a field, something cracks from the top of a snag and dives into the winter straw, you say these next lines from *The Windhover*,

> Brute beauty and valour and act, oh, air, pride, plume, here
> Buckle!"

Just like sheet metal, the sky has bent in on itself. It's brutal and valiant and all the words that wouldn't, unless you were here to see all the contradictory details, go together. When that bird takes flight, to say "off, off forth on swing" aloud to it reminds you that no matter how fully bi-pedal your movements are these days, when you were a kid, you spent a lot of time pumping back and forth on the swing sets in playgrounds and on the tire swing that hung from your grandparents' willow tree. And, even at that moment, standing affront to the open space, the forest protects your back from the wind but your face takes it. The wind falters but still weaves its way through your hair, which is just a different kind of flying.

What was also a kind of flying but in a horrified-by-shame kind of way was the way I fled the Cottonwood Club. Erik followed me to the car. He didn't know what Barry had said and even if he had, he would have thought, "So you didn't get the meter right on one of the poems?" And "You're crying, like you might die?" I didn't explain. I just cried. And smoked cigarette after cigarette. When we got home, I didn't go inside. Instead, I took off down the sidewalk in my boots that were too still tight and too tall.

Snow fell in big bells under the streetlights of the Avenues. I made it half a mile before my ankles finally gave out. Or maybe the ice had caught up with the concrete but either way, I fell down. Instead of getting up, I sat on the edge of my coat, looking at the snow as it zoomed at me like stars through warp drive. This felt deeply unlike flying. I smoked another cigarette. And then another. I was used to the burn. Maybe even looking forward to its familiarity.

What had cracked? This thin veneer of confidence. I painted it on as thickly as I could. With my classmates in poetry, fiction, nonfiction workshop I took their positive feedback in layers. More workshops, more layers. A publication. A fellowship. A supportive letter of recommendation. A passing grade on my PhD exams. This was supposed to have been it. This was how I was going to make it. I had, I thought, with writing and with approval from writerly friends and professors, recovered and repaired, restored and replanted that patch of burned up land I called my childhood. I painted in all the colors, even in Hopkins's gold vermilion, but is a painted forest just another fantasy I told myself? Had my PhD just become another episode of *General Hospital*? Was I still as dumb as the kid who didn't get into the third grade gifted and talented?

In wondering why Barry's comments buckled me in two, I hadn't considered that the place where it happened stirred me like a bird caught indoors. The Cottonwood Club held both my pre and postlapsarian memories. I had said my dad was done but I wasn't done with my dad. It's one thing to dance to "I Will Survive" on the same dance floor you used to practice waltzing with him.

It's another to realize that the wood of the dance floor is parquet, rolled out for just the occasion. No matter how much you pretend you can handle the collision of stories, without a solid floor, you won't be able to stand up for very long.

Years before: At the Cottonwood Club, tufts of white fell into the swimming pool. Not snow but the faux-cotton that falls from the cottonwood trees that overhang the deck. I held onto the shoulders of my friend Kelly—the friend I first told about the babysitter—as she swam like a dolphin. We rose up from the water, fluffy seed pods flying into our noses. My mom and dad sat on the pool deck, sipping their drinks, pulling out the occasional cotton fluff from their glasses. The branches caught a gust of wind. Kelly and I took shelter underwater, returning to our dolphin cave. My parents' heads remained vulnerable to the cracking and breaking of a tree whose mass expanded so quickly that the bond between the cell structures was weak, stretching across too vast an area. Cottonwoods growing so high so fast are like rocket ships trying to escape. Where are you going to go, trees? Your roots are committed to this planet. As Derrida wrote and Jim Morrison titled his book, no one here gets out alive. "Here" is the only place you can be.

When the chair of my committee, Donald Revell, emailed me that I had passed my exams he wrote that "You have found and built a house," I had believed him. The knocking on the windows and the chamber doors from the poems were like a house—maybe even a church with an altar that I was trying to get inside. But perhaps I wasn't supposed to be building a house. Barry made me feel bad. Like I'd abused the trees for wood. Maybe I was supposed to stay outdoors. Perhaps I should have moved into the wilderness where the gods of W. S. Merwin lay. In the soil. In the mycelia. Inside the hyphae where the rhyme is. The happenings in the world in the dirt next to the sidewalk, the ants, leaves, grass, and snow, have their own stories to tell.

Eventually, I realized I had to get off the sidewalk and out of the weather. I'd smoked half a pack of cigarettes. Houses exist for a reason and Erik was waiting for me in ours on G Street. I would explain about Herbert, and he would remind me he does not care about scansion, and I will realize that whatever walls of confidence I'd built with grad school letters weren't going to hold up in a big wind of doubt. I'd need more structures. I'd need more trees. I walked home scanning the sidewalk in a kind of meter that felt right, if a little slow and bobbled, to my feet. Eventually, I would visit Pando considered the largest organism in the world, which grows near Erik's parents southern Utah cabin, and walk for miles under lettered aspen leaves. Maybe Erik and I lie down between their roots, and they would hold their lovers in a woody cat's cradle and I could imagine different rhymes and different measures.

10

Breathing Old Growth

I quit smoking when Erik and I were trying to get pregnant. Mostly. If our friend Dave was around, we'd bum a lot of Camel Lights. We owe Dave a lot of cigarettes although he long since quit smoking. In the twentieth century, all English majors smoked. In the twenty-first century, only a few of us were left. By the time the Olympics arrived in Salt Lake in 2002, I'd given the smoke up for the flooding effects of red wine. Donald Revell had told our poetry class one night, you have to quit either drinking or smoking by the time you turn thirty. He was the poetry man. Who was I to disobey?

When I finally did get pregnant, I had to give up wine too. And sushi. And deli meats although I didn't eat those very often in the first place. I bucked against the rules. Who are you to tell me what to do with my body? But, again, I obeyed, because I wanted to have a big healthy baby. And yet, no matter how good I had been, Zoë was born almost two months early. I blame myself. Did I eat soft cheese? Did I pee too often? Not enough? Did wishing for a baby make my body give into the wish, but then give up?

Hanging in this hammock of questions, though, I felt stable. Balanced. I liked thinking about my body as a source for creation, not building up, rather than the beating up my body image for not being thin enough or sexy enough or strong enough. But then, my actual body, as diligent as I'd been avoiding wine and sushi, failed me. Failed her. I wondered how I had gone wrong this time. I went into labor when at thirty-two-and-a-half weeks pregnant, and though the doctors and nurses tried to stave off the contractions, I gave birth a day and a half after my water broke. Because she was born early, she was at great risk for RSV—a respiratory virus that can lead to pneumonia quickly. She was born just shy of the two-month preterm birth cut off to receive the vaccine. The insurance didn't cover it and it was $6,000 each for a series of shots. Zoë grew so fast and drank so much breastmilk that they let her out of the NICU just three weeks after she was born—they'd threatened she would have to stay the entire 7.5 weeks, until her projected due date. We thought she'd be OK.

Erik and I believe she caught RSV on the way to New York, where I had gone to give a job talk. Zoë wouldn't drink from a bottle, so she and Erik accompanied me on the flight to and from Rochester. I didn't get the job. Zoë did get the virus. The alveoli sacs in her lungs thickened and stiffened until one of her lungs collapsed. Breathing, which is automatic to both most humans and this planet and usually quiet, became loud, full of measurements, warnings, and alarms. It was my fault—job seeking with a preemie. I wonder if I would ever know whether I got my priorities straight or not. That's one problem with living with a fantasy-driven brain. You don't know if your projections are based on reality or imagination. To have gut instinct, you have to have time as a child to learn to trust your gut.

Two years later, I was on my way to a meeting at the university in Michigan where I had just begun my teaching job when Erik called me from the office of our pediatrician, Dr. Roberts.

"We are driving to the hospital. The doctor almost ordered an ambulance for Zoë. I told him I could drive there fast."

It was my first department meeting. Erik and I had taken our baby and uprooted ourselves from our easy Salt Lake life so I could take a tenure track position. We had no family to help. No friends, yet. This job was all we had and I couldn't miss the faculty meeting. That morning, Zoë, two years old, had, upon wakening, started coughing. Erik would have to take her to the doctor's without me for albuterol to treat the RSV.

"He wants you to go the hospital?"

"The ER."

We had been here before. We'd been trapped in Primary Children's in Utah for eight days when Zoë was eight months old, the respiratory therapists snaking tubes through her nose into her chest to draw out mucus that collected in the alveoli sacs of her lungs. The suctioning made her cry harder. She made more mucus. For six days, they suctioned her lungs through her nose every four hours. On the seventh day, finally they gave her more fluids as I had been begging for. She went home twenty-four hours later.

"Did you tell them we'll have her drink more juice?"

"He tested her oxygen in the office. It was 93 percent." At Primary Children's her o-sats dipped to 91, sometimes even 89 percent. Above 95 percent is considered fine, but that 2 percent difference makes doctors panic.

I told the chair of the department I couldn't make the meeting. I turned away from campus, back toward town to meet Erik and Zoë at the hospital.

What I found was alarming. Zoë had been strapped down to a crib mattress. They were trying to start an IV.

"Don't do that!" I insisted to the nurse. Had I ever said those words before? I should have practiced them earlier. Perhaps every day since I was born. But sexual interference mixes up your understanding where your rights end and other's might begin. "Just wait a minute. Her o-sats will go up if she calms down."

The nurse looked at me warily but paused, needle in hand.

Zoë saw me and started to relax a bit. I stroked her naked chest and curled my fingers into her hair. Her o-sats rose to 95 percent. The nurse left and I thought, "Phew, we can go home."

But instead of being let go, the nurse brought a doctor in.

"You will not let the nurse insert an IV?" she asked.

"No, no. She's fine! Watch. Her o-sats go right up. She needs some juice. Apple juice. She just gets upset and her oxygen levels drop."

"We need to follow procedures, ma'am. She'll need an IV and to be put on oxygen."

Zoë's o-sats rose to 97 percent.

"No, see. She just needs to move around. If you give her an IV, she can't cough. She'll get worse—the mucus settles. We've done this before. She needs to cough on her own. To drink fluids. To not get upset." Maybe I was overthinking this. One legacy of rape culture is that everything can seem like a violation. Am I overcompensating? Undercompensating? I cannot be sure, but I know my child like I know my own body.

"Are you saying you are denying treatment?"

Was I saying that? I knew from the eight days in Primary's and from the other times she contracted RSV that she needed fluids, albuterol treatments, and the chance to move her body. We had albuterol at home.

"I guess I am saying that."

"You'll have to sign this paper that you're leaving the hospital against medical advice."

I relied on facts and experience to make this decision but maybe I was wrong. I would like to say my gut told me to take my daughter and go home but what did my gut know? I flip through *The Body Keeps the Score* to look for passages that show that survivors of sexual abuse have a hard time with reality. It's hard to make decisions when you are not sure the ground upon which you're standing actually is ground, that your gut may not be the most accurate gut. I found phrases like "How do people learn what's safe and not safe?" and "I was amazed to discover how many of my patients told me they could not feel whole areas of their bodies. Sometimes, I'd ask them to close their eyes and tell me what I had put into their outstretched hands. Whether it was a car key, a quarter, or a can opener, they often could not even guess what they were holding—their sensory perceptions simply weren't working."

Dr. Van der Kolk confirmed that people with traumatic histories might not be reliable experiencers of reality.

I did know. I was certain. Trauma or not, I'd held this baby for two years now. I knew what a sniffle meant. A sneeze. A cough. Retracted breathing. If I could have counted more than one rib, I would have been as worried as the doctor.

Her o-sats were up to 98 percent.

I looked at Erik. "Let's take her home."

I signed the paper that said against medical advice I won't sue you if my child dies.

For someone who doesn't trust her gut feelings, I had no problem signing the paper. I didn't have guts. I had facts. Ninety-eight percent oxygen is normal. Let's go home.

It's not like 98 percent of the trees are gone. Just 98 percent of the old growth forests that is. The surge in population growth demanded more fuel. Japan's population increased to 50,000,000 by 1910. Trees grow everywhere. In Brooklyn. In walled gardens in China. In the Congo. Even places that were once denuded of trees now again have trees. After reaching its minimum area in the 1830s, the forest area in France has doubled since the mid-nineteenth century. The reasons for this positive trend include agricultural abandonment, the development of alternative energy sources and the implementation of massive reforestation programs. The UK's supply of timber was depleted during the First and Second World Wars, when imports were difficult, and the forested area bottomed out at under 5 percent of Britain's land surface in 1919. That year, the Forestry Commission was established to produce a strategic reserve of timber. There are more woods and trees in the UK today than at any time in the last 100 years. But England remains one of the least wooded countries in Europe. And they keep losing ancient woodland—ecologically the most valuable resource.

Forests built the world's economies, our geopolitics, our wars, and our cities. Japan codified in the words *fukoku kyohei* ("rich country, strong army") what industrializing countries understood. That to build a centralized government anchored in a well-organized tax base to create an up-to-date, steam-powered navy and a large, national army required mining and manufacturing facilities; establishment of railroad and telegraph systems, and appropriate training of the general populace to function in this new world has a massive impact on woodlands. Most obviously, it called for a vast increase in the use of both timber—for ships, buildings, vehicles, railroad ties, telegraph poles, and mine timbers—and fuel wood—especially for steam power and industrial smelting. That demand for fuel was also increased by a new surge in population growth, which, in Japan alone, increased the population to 50,000,000 people by 1910.[1] Woodlands, wildlands, forests exchanged for roads,

By 1910, the amount of forest land in the United States had significantly decreased, with estimates suggesting that only around 34 percent of the total land area remained forested, indicating a large reduction in old growth forests compared to pre-European settlement levels due to extensive logging practices. One hundred years later, we've planted some trees in occasional places but the amount of contiguous, un-logged forest is small. In Europe, only 3 percent of ancient forest remains, 3 percent in Canada, 18 percent in the United States and only 35 percent in the Amazon.

The Amazon rainforest was once called the lungs of the planet. So much of that forest has been decimated that we do not think of it that way anymore. Ranching, mining, illegal logging, fires, and urban development have shrunk the forest by 17 percent. When 25 percent of the forest has been logged, burned, clear-cut, scientists predict that the rainforest will reach the tipping point, where "rainforest" will turn to savanna lands. Thirty percent of the world's biodiversity lives in the Amazon. Researchers continue to discover species, even though known species disappear by the thousands every year. Once the climate cycle of the rainforest changes from wet to dry, not only will most of the forest-dwelling creatures die out, the forest that once served as lungs will now serve as skin—100 percent in need of touch, care, moisturizer. Is it possible to imagine a different ending for the Amazon?

Getting pregnant with Erik should have been 100 percent easy. I'd been pregnant before. I'd been holding this empty bowl in my hands since I was eleven years old. I had strummed the rim so meditatively, I'd worn the edges. I'd soften the edges of the bowl like a cervix softens during ovulation. Sex and pregnancy had been intermingled in my mind for so long but in my body sex and pregnancy had been disambiguated from the beginning: yes sex, no pregnancy. Perhaps my body was confused even though my mind had no doubts. The red dots on the toilet paper were a betrayal. If I could imagine a fetus, dream of one, feel the near-quickening sensation, why couldn't my body obey?

The capacity to imagine should bring that reality to fruition, shouldn't it? Gerard Manley Hopkins and W. S. Merwin had made me believe. I had made myself believe that the story you tell is the story you live. But I remember in high school when a friend of Rebecca and mine really wanted Rebecca to fall in love with him. We read all kinds of books, like Fritjof Capra's *The Turning Point* and *Gödel, Escher, and Bach* about the collective unconscious and shifting paradigms. Jim wanted to shift Rebecca's paradigm and make her fall in love with him. I wanted to shift my egg to the left, Erik's sperm to the right, and create a baby. I had dreams that I had given birth to a girl I named Amber. I talked to myself on the toilet, whispering to my toilet paper, stay white stay white, as though my eggs and the pulp of trees could collude on my behalf. I picked my cat named Box up and carried him around, sang him songs about Fancy Feast, patted his back to burp him. I envisioned a baby in my arms, on my breast, against my belly but these visions were nothing but unpalpable air. Fantasy, it turns out, does not fix everything. Although, often, the consultation with a fertility doctor sometimes does. This question of when to follow one's imagination and when to seek out physical resources may be my greatest imbalance—perhaps even a mental instability.

Still, I pictured that baby in her onesie, swinging on the swings, eating the white rhizomes of grass while crawling on a picnic blanket at the park, resting her head on my shoulder, making whooshing sounds from the baby seat on my bicycle, handing her to my mom who she gives big hugs to, to my mother-in-law, whose hair she strokes, to lay her between Erik and me in our bed, squeezing all three of us between our dog and four cats, picking raspberries, drinking lemonade. I wanted my body to make more body, to thicken like the loamy forest floor, for the layers of matter to warm, to coax the seed from its cone, to excite the cells to burgeon, to make this fantasy a reality.

When I finally did get pregnant, my sense of body autonomy changed. I didn't give up my body, but I stretched it wide. I shared that body with her. Did she want that grilled cheese for lunch or did I? The effort of replicating cells to make an 8-pound creature out of a microscopic zygote exhausted me. I fell asleep sitting up once, the plate that held my grilled cheese empty on my lap. The way my hip muscles loosened in their joints made me feel like a marionette being steered by someone with enormous hands. People tried to put their hand on my stomach to feel the baby. I didn't mind. Touch my stomach. It's a kind of blessing. We welcome this baby into our world. The skin, muscle, fat that provided a barrier between that baby and that community wasn't really mine anymore. I think I had known that if I'd been forced to give birth when I was eleven, whatever agency I'd had would be gone. Agency was be given over to a baby or an adoption and "alternative" high school for wayward girls, and an early, unexamined marriage. Giving birth made it even more clear—the "I" wasn't mind, it was body and it was making the decisions, turning itself inside out, back-bending, the head throwing, the hands pressing the hips open. This time, I had the choice to let it.

My choice to direct my own body was ended by the Supreme Court when they overturned Roe v Wade. Suddenly, my life felt illegal. My body felt illegal. My body turned ex post facto under surveillance, imprisoned by fiat. I was now owned by the state—my fate, any woman's fate, any transperson's, any person's fate, really, was now orchestrated by people who knew nothing about me or my friends or family or community. The decision had already been made. I would be permanently pregnant forever, everyone's hand on my stomach, in my vagina, speculum to cervix. Whatever deviant path the babysitter may have put me on, my mother had tried to set straight by calling the Women's Clinic, by arranging the abortion, by getting the babysitter's parents to pay half, getting me a therapist, telling me that I could tell my story, would not have happened if then had been now. Utah's legislature has banned abortion. Only an injunction by a judge keeps women's options open for now.

Turning abortion laws over to the states isn't about giving state's rights. It's about curtailing rights. Reproductive choice is a gateway drug to taking away other rights like due process or the right of free speech or to freely assembly. Once one slash in the fabric that humans have bodily autonomy means no one can be sure of their rights, the whole tapestry falls apart. It's all or nothing. If in Texas I have six-weeks of rights, in Arizona, fifteen weeks, in New York, forty, then I am not the same person in every state. If depending on where my daughter is or where my friend lives, I can or cannot help her, my rights are curtailed, thus, my rights are curtailed everywhere. Perhaps stated more plainly—where one woman has no rights to decide her body's fate, I also have absolute zero say about my own.

They say you can't be a little bit pregnant, but, when abortion was legal across all fifty states, maybe you could. When considering an abortion, you're in a state of limbo. And, every pregnancy you carry, carries its memories into your next. And memories of your last. When I was pregnant with Zoë, I drove by the Utah Women's Clinic on my way home, the only place in Utah that performed abortions. Place is a portkey to memory. As I slowed my car, I was teleported back to my bedroom in the house on the other end of the Salt Lake Valley, where my mom, twenty-two years earlier, opened my bedroom door and asked me, "Are you pregnant?"

"Are you pregnant?" she asked again. Was she just guessing? How did she know? Maybe she had noticed fewer tampons were missing from the bathroom cupboard. Maybe she had emptied the bathroom garbage fewer times than usual. Maybe she could just tell by the mother in her seeing the mother in me although even typing that makes me want to throw up.

Psychologists distinguish between traumatic revisiting and healthful reclamation of memories. When something—a coat, a stuffed animal, a smell—triggers someone recovering from trauma unexpectedly, their body reacts. The heart palpitates. Skin chills. Teeth coat themselves fuzzy. When a memory is coached, invited, participated in, the memory becomes a story.

"The act of telling itself changes the tale," Dr. Van der Kolk writes in *The Body Keeps the Score*. To me, memory doesn't only hold trauma, it also holds transformative power. Our job is to sit down with what we remember and turn it into something else. Van der Kolk concurs, in a way: "The mind cannot help but make meaning out of what it knows, and the meaning we make of our lives changes how and what we remember." Each memory forms its own potential meaning like the hyphae that make up mycelia that, unfurled, reaches out toward some need—meaning, a reader, understanding—a little tree-root, looking for something only the fungi can give it—selenium, perhaps.

To make meaning out of abortion risks giving abortion more weight than other medical procedures. We don't endeavor to give meaning to hip replacement surgery. We do place "blame" on people for some diseases, like liver cirrhosis and lung cancer, but that's just mean, not meaningful. Abortion though, it does trip through the mind. When I broke my wrist, I totally forgot I'd had surgery on it. I never forget the abortion. It has grown filaments that stretch into my current beliefs about who I am—a person a little toughened by that experience. I eschew sentimentality. Erik kisses me on my head every day, which is sweet. I need it. But I don't reciprocate. With Zoë, I wanted to make sure she was strong—that she could handle the shittiness of life—without having to have experienced it firsthand. The abortion story I told myself reached into my motherhood, making me say things to my kids like "When you're driving, assume everyone is trying to kill you." And "Wear a condom. Wear two." And "if any of your friends gets pregnant and needs someone to talk to, I'm that person." But this toughness has tender spots that I don't like to touch—the image of my mom in the waiting room, sitting on a chair, staring so hard at the door that when I finally appear, she can't see me, newly vacuumed. I was all door to her now. Shut. The light that swung above my head on the surgical table that later reminded me of the table on which Sibyl was abused in the movie about multiple personalities with Sally Field. The image of the exterior bricks painted gray as if they wanted to make the Women's Clinic disappear. In 2024, they would succeed. I wanted to make my story of the Women's Clinic disappear. It took writing the essay for the *Times* to show me how my story would always be my story. How I should share it. How it opened the door, for my mom, and for others, to share theirs.

In Flagstaff, I live in a climate snow globe—a bubble unique from southern Arizona—although the snow falls less and less. I know it's bad when the monsoon storms fail to show up in July. I know it's bad when it snows only twenty-three inches all winter. I know it's bad when the fires start in April instead of June. Bad that they start at all. I also know it's good when it snows 147 inches one year. I know it's weird when the monsoon storms start in May instead of July. But I can objectively observe the climate suffering consequences, at least for now. I can measure facts with my own eyes. They inform my gut that this is bad, but not as bad as it could be. I haven't felt the effects on my body yet—except when it's sixty-five degrees in February when it should be thirty.

    I know it's bad when fires burn in humid South Carolina in March. I know it's bad when fires burn in New York State, in the Boreal Forest in Canada, in the tundra of Alaska. I know it's bad when the forests burn in the rainforest. I know it's bad that the rainforest is disappearing. Other people know it too. In Pará, Brazil, for over thirty years, José "Zé Cláudio" Ribeiro da Silva and Maria do Espírito Santo campaigned against ranchers who used burned swaths of rainforest to raise cattle. They worked with cattle ranchers and local rubber tappers who tapped native trees to pull sap to process into rubber. Brazil used to be the only place where rubber trees grew. Before petroleum products took over the plasticization of the planet, Brazil's forests were safe. The Industrial Revolution needed them. But then a British man gathered seeds of the Brazilian rubber tree and took them to Asia where rubber trees now outgrow those from Brazil. The trees, worth less, succumbed to a different economy: People who love to ranch cows, or love to eat them, needed more space to grow alfalfa. The rainforest seemed overgrown to these ranchers. Clear it, even of the rubber trees, they said, to make space for meat.

In 1997, José and Maria helped succeed in petitioning the federal government to create the Praia Alta-Piranheira agro-forestry settlement, eighty-four square miles of public land so this portion of the Amazon didn't fall the way the rest of Pará was falling—trees burning, activists getting shot. This was a kind of compromise. Some growing of cow-based-meat in the fertile soil to the left. Some rubber tapping, regular old tree growing to the right. A lot of the forest left alone to forest as a forest does.

But the settlement didn't stop activists taking the brunt of their activism on their bodies. In 2011, José Rodrigues Moreira allegedly hired Lindonjonson Silva Rocha and Alberto Lopes do Nascimento to kill the husband-and-wife activists after the pair opposed Moreira's efforts to evict three families from his land. Moreira also effectively had their killers killed, since Silva Rocha and Naxcimento were sentenced to forty-three and forty-five years in jail respectively. José Rodrigues Moreira was acquitted of charges that he commissioned the death of Silva and Santo. The ultimate denial of bodily autonomy.

Whose rainforest is this? Is it Moreira's? The landowner, rancher says it's his. He bought it and he bought the cattle who roam. Is it the rubber tappers who kept the trees alive traditionally and capitalistically—drawing good money? Is it José "Zé Cláudio" Ribeiro da Silva's and Maria do Espírito Santo's who worked to protect the land? No. It's not theirs anymore. They are dead. Is it all of ours? The description of the rainforest of the lungs of the planet has become a cliché but really, what kind of sane person chops down the alveoli sacs in the lungs that keep a body alive?

After we return from the hospital in Michigan, as I lay with this two-year-old pulled close into my arms, as I counted her breaths, slow, easy, not congested, I ask whose child is this? Who owns this child's body? Is she mine, the doctor's? My mother's? If she is the world's child, was I right to take her home to protect her from suffering? Was making Zoë stay in the hospital worth not being in trouble with the doctor? What if the doctor had been right? Had I taken autonomy too far? Ask the rainforest. What does it prefer? It probably prefers everyone leave it alone, but no one asks it. I couldn't ask Zoë. I had to make that decision for her based on what I thought my body knew, but my body nor my mind can never be 100 percent certain about anything.

The planet still hosts many trees. In Brooklyn, Detroit, London. We plant them everywhere we go, Johnny Appleseed Johnny Appleseed. But the tree, planted between squares of concrete, or even the swaths of ground replanted in the boreal forests of Canada, the ponderosa pine forests of Northern Arizona, the forests in the Rockies and Cascades, are checker boards of forest, cut into squares by roads and agriculture, fires and logging. The forest systems that are uninterrupted by humans are rare. "Our World in Data" reports that intact old growth is nearly gone and that many trees that populate most industrialized countries aren't part of an ecosystem.

> But we should be cautious here: it's often not the case that the 'positives' of regrowing on planting one hectare of forest offset the 'losses' of one hectare of deforestation. Cutting down one hectare of rich tropical rainforest cannot be completely offset by the creation of on hectare of plantation forest in a temperate country.
>
> This is especially true when we consider how that forest is grown or used. In some temperate countries—such as in the United Kingdom—a large part of forested area is in the form of single and non-native species plantations, which doesn't have the same biodiversity benefits as natural regrowth.[2]

Bruce Hungate and I, as we met over coffee to try to wrap our minds around the executive orders coming down from the white House and how we were going to write against them, were discussing how forests in 2023 had contributed to rather than reduced greenhouse gases. The fires in Canadian had negated whatever work the rest of the world's forests had absorbed. We were bemoaning the lack of snow this year. Was the slowing jet stream to be faulted? Or should we blame the poor little girl, La Niña, even though she has been working the weather system for centuries and never has Flagstaff had zero snow in January. I told him about Elizabeth Rush's *Quickening* a book made of braided stories, like this one—about her pregnancy and her trip to Antarctica where she saw the Thwaites glacier one of the largest glaciers in the world, begin to break apart. Also, it turns out we're missing clouds. Earth used to reflect more light, and thus, heat, back into space—called the albedo effect. But now, the seas rise with dark water. Even the trees, our supposed saviors, are not doing their part. Bruce tells me of a study where, at least in the north, if we cut down all the trees, it would lead to less warming—the snow would do more to reflect light/heat than the trees do to absorb CO_2.

> These latitude-band experiments thus suggest that projects in the tropics promoting afforestation are likely to slow down global warming, but such projects would offer only little to no climate benefits when implemented in temperate regions and would be counterproductive, from a climate-perspective, at higher latitudes.[3]

We're planting trees in these temperate zones while still cutting them down where they do the most good—in the tropics. Of course, this model only works if the temperate regions receive regular amounts of snowfall.

Bruce has lived in Flagstaff longer than I. He has a longer snow memory and doesn't remember anything like this year. I moved here in 2008. In 2010, the second year we lived in Flagstaff, it snowed 110 inches in January. It kept snowing and snowing. So much snow. Roofs caved in. Schools closed. It felt like a disaster. On April 1, the *Arizona Daily Sun* ran an article that our governor, Jan Brewer, who was foisted upon us because Obama took AZ governor Janet Napolitano to be Secretary of Homeland Security, planned to seed clouds so it would always snow that much in Flagstaff so Phoenix could rely on rain instead of Colorado River water. Not realizing the date, I complained to the chair of our department. "How could we live every year with that much snow?"

Research released this week noted that in 2023, the hottest year on record (the article didn't include 2024, which will probably, when all the data is in register even warmer), fewer low clouds collected in the atmosphere. Like the ice sheets that reflect the sun, clouds help cool the atmosphere by reflecting sunlight back into space. But a warming climate makes it more difficult for clouds to coalesce. Plus, there's the question of availability of condensation nuclei particles for water vapor to coalesce around. Bob Berwyn from Inside Climate News writes, "Global warming itself is driving the loss of clouds by diffusing distinct layers of the atmosphere that promote the formation and persistence of low-elevation marine clouds." With fewer clouds, more warming. With more warming, fewer clouds. Although it's called a positive feedback loop, it is actually a pretty negative situation. The hope that the southwest, or anywhere, would be wetter, is evaporating quickly.

I would give a lot for the wetter climate model to have been true, but now I feel that I acted like my kids acted when they wanted a snow day from school. Put a spoon under your pillow, wear your pajamas inside out, and drop an ice cube in your toilet bowl and pray and pray and pray for snow. I look outside at the towering ponderosas. They don't know yet how much snow there is not. They will by fire season. It's enough to make we want to call Jan Brewer and ask her exactly how this cloud seeding thing works—except, from what I can tell researching it, cloud seeding during drought is another hope that, like spoons under our pillows, doesn't have much basis in reality.

Perhaps, like leaving against medical advice, we should take an all or nothing approach. Doing so might lead to less warming if we cut all the trees down. At least in places where it continues to snow. Instead of dark, green trees absorbing heat, the snow reflects more light, which would lead to less warming. Maybe, when the rainforest turns to savanna, we can paint the savanna white, or grow white grass, the color of the rhizome that grows underground. Without photosynthesis I don't know what we'll breathe and eat but the earth could become a big white marble instead of this greenish one, cooling our tree pocked, burning planet down.

Having the scarlet letter Against Medical Advice on your medical documents burns to the bone. Erik and I opened the letter from Dr. Robert's office. "Due to your unwillingness to cooperate with established medical procedures and hospital policies, we regret to inform you that we can no longer provide medical services to your family." They had gone all or nothing. Obey or we will deny you care. Now, we were in Michigan, far away from home, without family, friends, or even a pediatrician.

I called the doctor's office. They had to let me explain. And they did—I told them about the oxygen saturation levels. I told them how upset and mucus-generating Zoë had been. I told them that when we got home, she drank a gallon of apple juice and coughed and I nebulized her lungs and she was fine.

Thanks to facts that supported the decision to leave the hospital—her o-sats were in the high 90s, the ER doctor had not read her full history, that the albuterol we used at home was the same they used in the hospital, Dr. Roberts let us come back to his practice, but only after I fought against what felt like an intractable force. Doctors, like ranchers, are so certain they are correct. Their paternalistic authority they show over their patients, over their cattle, over their knowledge-base, over their land, makes them really hard to talk to. I'm lucky Dr. Roberts let me tell him my version of the story. I'd like to tell the ranchers that the number of cattle outweigh the number of trees—we're going to tip the planet sideways with our love of beef and then try to tip it back with our love of trees.

She wasn't cured from her RSV but she wasn't hospitalized for it again. Until she started first grade, whenever Zoë she caught a cold, I slid the nebulizer machine out from under the bed, dribbled albuterol into the dispenser, and plugged in the machine for it to diffuse the medicine into her lungs. Four times a day and then a fifth right before she went to bed, I sat on the floor of her bedroom and the round rug with a lamb knit into its middle. I pulled Zoë into my lap, fit the dinosaured-for-kids mask over her nose and mouth, stretched the elastic around her big head, careful not to pull her hair, and turned the nebulizer filled with albuterol to hum. She didn't resist. It must be nice to feel the alveoli expand with the intake of the medicine. The oxygen must feel like relief itself. I sang all the verses of "Frog Went a' Courtin." Sometimes, all the verses to "American Tune." She lay in the crook of my arm, her gigantic head heavy, breathing in that specialized, medicated air, converting oxygen to carbon dioxide through her blood and lungs, exhaling into one of those unprotected forests.

11

Bodily Infestations

Michigan had plenty of forests. Most of them were fourth or fifth growth. The two springs we spent there, Erik and I tried to forage for mushrooms. Morels sprung in the April, usually on burned land as their mycelia relishes that chemistry, but our brains could not organize around a non-autumnal harvest. There were so many trees that you couldn't rise above them to get a view. You had to make decisions on the ground, which may have led to my short-sightedness with Zoë's doctor. It might have also led to us leaving for a mountain town as soon as I could get a different job. In Flagstaff, we found metaphorical loamy soil—we brought uprooted roots and found some mycorrhizal partners. There's a saying for academics who are forced to choose the job market "to bloom where you are planted." The saying usually refers to people who want to live in big cities living in small towns but Flagstaff was the perfect size. Big enough to sustain one's human social needs. Small enough to live in the middle of the forest and feel like you were living in the middle of a forest. But all towns of any size have human-sized problems. Like stunted trees in a tree farm, humans in close quarters can't see what they are doing to each other.

I took it with a grain of salt. I put it in perspective. I balanced what might have happened with what we knew as facts. One day, Max's daycare moved next door to Rosemary's dad's house because he had just had surgery she said. She needed to be close she said. Could she still care for six children, ages one, Max's age, to five? The five-year-old was Zoë's close friend. A year younger than Zoë who just started kindergarten, this friend still needed daycare.

We all needed daycare. NAU didn't provide a childcare center on campus. A future-colleague emailed me before we left Michigan, "You should get on the daycare list now. The options in Flagstaff are so limited." I did what she said. I found a preschool for Zoë at the Ark Preschool five months before we left Michigan. We weren't religious and the school was, but we took what we had been told we could get. Later, after Max was born, finding childcare for infants seemed nearly impossible. We just needed a couple of days a week. Erik and I could swing the in-betweens.

Enter Rosemary—one of the best-regarded home daycare providers in Flagstaff. She had dozens of references. She invited Erik and me to her house to tea. She described how she took the kids up, toddlers and all, to the ski resort every Friday. Dressed in their ski gear, she drove her Suburban to the Snow Bowl, windows down, so she didn't have to outfit the kids. Skis on the ground, no need for poles, to the Hart Prairie lift the kids shuffled. She fed the children whole foods and allowed minimal screen time. In the summer, the backyard held its own playground, nicer even than the one Zoë had enjoyed at the Ark Preschool. Both my friend Okim and I signed our kids up. Did I have a gut feeling that this was a bad idea? I thought I had facts: References. Longevity. I could at least rely on Okim's gut.

I imagine a perfect community—one where people help each other out. Flagstaff is close to perfect. We fill sandbags for houses in the flood zone after the Pipeline Fire. We post on the Next Door app, "Watch out for the javelinas on Country Club and Mount Pleasant." We carpool kids from soccer to basketball to dance to piano. If you have surgery, a friend puts a meal train together. If you lose your cat, half of the people living in Flagstaff will share your Missing Cat post and text you to see if you found him—the other half will go out looking for him.

Stitching myself into this community was healing. It would be healing at both the transitive and the intransitive sentence level. I heal the world. I heal. In high school, I hadn't been a joiner. In college, I'd reached out to Hans, Christian, Josh, Renee, and Rebecca to create a safety network, but it was smallish, that group. In grad school, that web of connection grew. By the time, I got to Flagstaff, I became an energy mentor, joined sustainability programs, gave talks at the Ecology Teach-in. I wrote letters to the governor asking him to restore funding to higher education and public education. I campaigned for ballot initiatives to increase teacher salaries and to limit giving vouchers to parents for private and home school. This felt like part of my job—bridging the university community to the local. It felt solid and real.

Like the mycelium under the forest floor, public schools form a basis for community. They provide nutrients for the structures, like the trees and the Safeway, to grow tall above ground. Public schools are where we hold holiday bazaars, where we meet strangers who become our friends as we wait outside the door for the bell to ring to pick up our kids. The climate scientists I work with use the metaphor community to describe an ecosystem. Every part—mycelia, microorganisms, water, xylem, light, soil, insects, webs, and moss—make up that community. If you take the moss away, the water, the trees, is it still an ecosystem? Charter schools and vouchers cut big swaths out of the community forest. The tensile strength of the threads is forced to stretch and threaten to break as they try to reach across a checkerboarded system. It is at Sinagua public middle school, not charter schools, that wildfire evacuees take shelter.

A perfect forest can stave off bark beetles. When you and your compatriots are thriving, bark beetles can only get a foot in the door, they can't wrench it open. A nibble here or there, the tree can stand. The bark can heal over. The cambium, softer, more susceptible to injury than bark, with enough nutrients and water running through its cellulose, can repel the insect. But as climate changes and droughts persist, the bark beetle has more leverage. It can not only wrench open the door to feed itself, but it can also keep the door open for all its cousins. Eggs are laid. The babies, when hatched, devour. Everyone is munching on the cambium now. Cellulose service is interrupted. What the ground giveth, the beetle taketh away. The needles cannot photosynthesize without water.

In canyons throughout the west, forests are striped. Brown, green, brown, green. A different pattern than the checkerboard pattern Hans and I witnessed in the clearcut forests of Oregon. Streaks of dead. Alive. Dead. Alive. 85,000 square miles have been affected in the United States, 65,000 square miles in Canada. Europe's and Russia's forests have not escaped. Global warming affects the whole globe. It just doesn't get cold enough in places where it once did to kill the insects off. A researcher at the University of Utah noted that one infestation was so intense, when the beetles ran out of trees, they started attacking telephone poles. Southern pine beetles die when temperatures go down to fourteen below zero. But as the global temperature ratchets up, the latitude where fourteen degrees Fahrenheit climbs about forty feet per year. The beetles climb north. They survive warm winters. The trees, although they too move north, cannot outrun the bugs.[1]

In a perfect society, teenage boys wouldn't molest younger girls. Why do they do it? The daycare owner's son took a five-year-old into the bathroom. He pulled down her pants and touched her vagina. Why did he do it? Opportunity? Sure. An overly sexualized media culture? Yes. A patriarchal, male supremacist culture that says boys can get away with almost anything? Also yes. But nothing quite explains why he would hurt a five-year-old. Could he have possibly think she would like it? The twistedness here is as unfathomable as boys who shoot AR-15s into kindergartens and boys who grow into men to torture prisoners. It's hard to compare broken social ecosystems with broken natural ones because we have evidence of a formerly well-balanced, harmonious forest—everything has a role to play that serves the greater ecosystem. Whatever human history has been recorded, there are few moments where the balance of humans had everything they needed and nothing they didn't. But perhaps imbalance is where stories are made. There are stories where Indigenous cultures lived with the land instead of draining its resources. These stories are hard to hear above the drones of cities, the stamping feet of cattle, the revving of chainsaws.

And yet, hope for a utopic version of the world drives me to this question: What went wrong for this daycare owner's son, what went wrong for the babysitter, that made him think, well, this really won't be so bad for her. Or maybe physical need—for both power and sex, trumped every thought about the five-year-old. Or the ten-year-old. If I had had the tools to say what I felt, if I had told the babysitter a story about myself, maybe he would have seen me as a real person instead of a tool for his desire. What if, in this situation, we shouted are ages, "I am ten and I still play with dolls and feed my horse grass under the fender of its front tire and I drag my stuffed animals around by string around their necks because my parents won't get me a real dog." What if she had said, "I'm five I'm five I'm five. I barely can write my first name. My story is that I am five." The first thing we should be taught as children is to tell our stories, even if they just begin with our names and our ages. If our culture valued stories as much as we value desire, maybe we could listen more attentively, like the trees do.

The DA pressed charges against both the son and the daycare center owner. He, for sexual abuse of a minor, she, for child endangerment. She had tried to protect the children, she claimed. That's why she moved the day care over to her father's house. Next door. One parent said he'd seen the son over at his grandfather's house. Another said she'd seen daycare kids back at the original house. The five-year-old was asked to tell the DA what happened. The DA, when addressing the parents of the kids in a conference room at the courthouse said, "She will be OK. My daughter was also molested when she was a child. She's OK now. She's a doctor."

When people say you can't see the forest for the trees, they mean that you are dumb. You will not be attending the Gifted and Talented program anytime soon. To be able to look at the big picture, to see the whole system, to understand the ecologies, the cogs and wheels, the pulleys and levers—to see the whole forest is to be able to extrapolate meaning. In telling the babysitter story in so many ways, I am trying to remake the forest. I have forsaken a single narrative for the love of many trees, for the microscopic network below the forest floor. I can see and I can feel, sometimes even at the same time, but mostly, I just want to look and see what happens if I lift this limb, if I dig this patch, if I upturn that mushroom.

 Children also love trees. They make fantastical use of them. Kids climb trees like pirate ships. They gather unique sticks for swords and for shovels. They pull at the bark to see if this ponderosa smells like vanilla or like butterscotch. They use a tree for a backstop. For a pull-up bar. They sit in the shade of a secret tree. They swing from their branches by ropes into swimming holes and at their grandparent's house, in the warm round of a halved tire. When forests burn, kids' stories burn too.

The five-year-old told her story to her parents, to the DA, which didn't prevent her molestation, but it might have prevented others. She told her story and the boy spent some time in a juvenile correctional facility, was on probation until he turned eighteen, had to commit to all kinds of counseling, and perform community service with other formerly incarcerated people. I am glad he was forced to work with others. Maybe he worked cleaning up garbage. Maybe he filled sandbags. Maybe he cleaned the public toilets at the public parks. I hope that whatever he did, he didn't have to do it alone. I hope he had to listen to his fellow community servants tell their stories. I hope he heard them hard.

I imagine asking Rosemary's son as I arrived to pick Max up, questions about what he could have been thinking. She listed the games Max played, even though he was strapped into a highchair. I'm at the table. The daycare center owner is there. The son is there. Max is not.

"She'll remember this forever," I tell them.

"We all remember everything forever," they tell me in unison like a Greek Chorus.

Listen. This could become her main narrative. The one she never forgets. Every bad thing that happens to her in the future, she'll think, see, this is what I deserve, or, how come bad things keep happening to me? Or, when good things happen, she'll move past them immediately. She'll say, "I don't deserve this."

"But what about me? This is my bad thing, too," says the daycare center owner.

"But what about me? This is my bad thing, too," says the son.

Yes, that's the problem. You, too, will think bad things keep happening to you. But remember what part of speech you are in the sentence. You abused the girl. The girl is the object of the sentence. You, both of you, are the subject. You do and get to keep doing. Even if a lot of that doing is community service. Bad things don't happen to you. You drove the bad thing.

I think of William Carlos Williams—"the pure products of America/ go crazy." Is anything purer than people being born of so many riches than wanting more? Anything more American than using natural resources around us—trees, children—as products of our own?

Max has no recollection of his time at the daycare center. And, he was a boy, which matters in this situation mainly because the girl abused was a girl. And I am a girl. But being a girl is no prophylactic. In Illinois, the DA uncovered 1,997 instances of abuse in the six Catholic dioceses. Illinois began investigating the Catholic Church in 2018 after Pennsylvania uncovered 1,000 instances of sex abuse by the church there.[2] Molestation happens to all kinds of children, boys, girls, rich, poor, Black, white. It happens because it's easy. Just as pine beetles kill trees, the patriarchal climate allows adults to molest young people. How to change the climate? Change the ease. Find ways to empower children. Make it clear they have a voice. Let them write. Heck, let them vote. Perhaps the single biggest difference between us and trees is that while we have the capacity to defend ourselves, trees have don't have a say in how to bring the snow back.

Maybe we can beat the infestations at the numbers game. In India, teams of volunteers plant a million trees a day. In Ethiopia, volunteers planted 350 million trees in twelve hours. But in Brazil's Amazon rainforest, they cut a million trees a day. Humans like to pretend they're very good at balance, but they measure weight in proportion to their own mass. Trees know nothing about pounds. Microorganisms couldn't care less about ounces.

It might seem that adding carbon dioxide to the atmosphere would be good for trees. Trees respire CO_2—hence planting more trees will reduce the amount of CO_2, one of the main gases contributing to the greenhouse effect. But climate change is bad for forests. A warming environment leads to deeper droughts and drier vegetation, which lead to an increase in the extent, intensity, and frequency of wildfires. Drought also forces trees to close their stomata, the pores that let in carbon dioxide, meaning at higher temperatures, they sink less carbon. When trees die, they probably won't come back. Some forests will be replaced by shrubland. When trees are exposed to a drought or wildfire, they can become less resilient to pests and pathogens. This phenomenon is already evident in the western United States where pest populations are causing massive tree die-offs, with the bark beetle alone destroying 45 million acres of forest in recent years. Burning fossil fuels not only emits CO_2 pollution, but also nitrous oxide gas, which eventually rains down on forests as nitrogen pollution. Mycorrhizal fungi are extremely sensitive to this nitrogen pollution and thus, mycorrhizae are disappearing.³ At some point, as the rate of decomposition increases, forests begin to exhaust more carbon than they take in. What used to be a carbon sink is now a source.

By digging up and burning plant matter that has been cooked and mashed underground for hundreds of millions of years, humans have shifted a balance we barely understand. The tidy relationship between mycorrhizal fungi and the trees' outstretched roots intertwining with hyphae, sharing nutrients back and forth, feeding tree and mushroom, are such intricate machinations we are just beginning to get to know. The chemical interactions in the soil as carbon tries to manage nitrogen, oxygen mitigating enzymes are steps on the ladder of a stoichiometry we have just started to climb. Planting a billion trees might be helpful to an extent but if the trees are planted into drought conditions, without the support of dynamic soil and enriching mycorrhizal fungi, it's not a long-lived forest—it's a park or maybe a garden that won't outlast the slightest change in wind or temperature or precipitation.

We've upset the balance: A warmer climate invites insects into forests, the trees, drought-stressed, can't stave off the pests' voracious appetites. Bark beetles roost in the skin of Douglas fir. Whole swaths of Colorado, Idaho, and Montana forests have turned dead-brown from the bark beetle's insatiability. The forests are striped like the US flag but in brown and green instead of red and white: A column of dead trees lined up next to a column of perfectly healthy ones. Scientists study why some trees can forestall the beetle and why some fall prey.

Back east, the tree situation is not any better. Moises Valequez-Manoff wrote for *The New York Times* an article called, "Can Humans Help Trees Outrun Climate Change," where he highlighted arborists' attempts to move trees to different forests. Since trees can't literally run, climate adapters relocate the trees from the south, which are used to warmer conditions, to the north. Diversifying forests helps combat the insects. Finding plants and fungi which support tree roots helps them defy pests too. But since trees can live centuries and environments are changing so quickly that even these moved trees may not be able to adapt in fifty years, let alone 100. Researchers continue to search for ways to make forests more resilient to climatic upheaval, but they do know a single solution won't be enough, and the resources, time, and space to make it happen may not be enough either. These great uncertainties can prompt "analysis paralysis," according to Marai Janowaik, deputy director of the Forest Service's Northern Institute of Climate Science, "but we can't keep waiting until we know everything."

Psychologists and therapists can't wait until they know everything to try to help you. As they help reintegrate a person with their trauma, to metaphorically replant the traumatized mind with healthy forests, they offer as many treatments as they can find. An ecology of treatments might include drugs and talk-therapy, EDMR, cognitive behavior therapy, and yoga.

A fully connected ecosystem is what I'm looking for. Even if I could get rid of those two devastating years, I wouldn't, necessarily. That story has become mine—who would I be without it? I wish it hadn't happened, but once it did, I'm not able to eradicate it. We are only the stories we write about ourselves. Writing is rarely catharsis. The word cathartic comes from Latinized form of Greek katharsis "purging, cleansing." But excising a part of yourself can be a kind self-annihilation. How can you save yourself if you have to reject yourself. Perhaps "revise the self" is a better take.

Writing is not a paregoric. There is no throwing up one's story, tossing it out of oneself, flushing it down the toilet. This story is part of my body and even cutting off a limb won't make it go away. But in writing—telling it from this wide braid of climate change inside this church of multiplicity—there is integration. It is not *the* story. This story is one of many stories about me. The path I supposedly went down, I may well have gone down, but I wandered down a bunch of other paths as well.

To tell the story is to make something of it. "If you find you no longer believe, enlarge the temple," Merwin writes. The more I see in the story, the more ground I have to stand on. To make art is to make a place to stand—every word a microbe keeping the soil alive.

My brother-in-law, Marshall, works for the Forest Service in Boise, Idaho where he directs crews to fires across the west but, before that, he worked in Montana where he deployed a defense against the bark beetle as it encroached upon the Douglas fir forests. Marshall and his crew took an individualized approach. Instead of a one-size-fits-all solution that may include raining down pesticides or offering the trees to timber companies at a low price, the crew set out armed with pheromone patches which they attached tree-by-tree-by-tree. Beetles communicate via these pheromones, saying come-hither when they've found a tree vulnerable to attack, sending different "the-inn-is-full" pheromones when the tree can sustain no more beetles. Scientists have isolated the chemicals that act as those repelling, inn-is-full pheromones. To manage both the pine beetle and the Douglas fir beetle, Forest Service workers attach patches to trees, signaling to the bark beetles that this tree is unsustainable to the beetle, allowing the tree to remain sustainable to itself.

Marshall walked up and down hillsides. At every tree, he patted the bark where the patch would go. Then, he took his hammer and his tiny nail and affixed the patch to the tree. The tree didn't mind. It was just a little pinch, like a COVID-19 vaccination. It knows the sting not only saves its individual self but the forest as a whole.

Communication is key. I should have told my mom what happened the night the babysitter unrolled my tube top and lay down upon me while MASH ran in the background. I went over to his house without coercion. I met him in his backyard. I didn't know what I was doing but I did indeed unravel the fabric of my family and maybe even the social fabric of the neighborhood and my parents' friend group. I thought what happened with the babysitter made me special, but really, it just made me toxic. I thought I was the one and only.

What if I could say what I should have said now?

"Mom."

Maybe I wouldn't even have to had to say the words: "The babysitter is touching me. The babysitter is not OK. The babysitter should not babysit."

Maybe just the tone of my voice or the tilt of my head or whatever signal I had sent to her to tell her I was pregnant would have been enough. Maybe I would just have to say my name. Or his. I didn't know what the consequences would be for speaking up. I could get in trouble. I could lose my friend. I could lose this dismaying, unwanted, but still noted, kind of attention. Maybe if I'd said something then, I wouldn't have to have these conversations with myself now.

What would a tree say to this? In a forest, if you're singled out, it's not for any good—someone has tagged you as special either to cut you down or save you from an imminent beetle attack. It's the tree that doesn't call attention to itself that survives both the bark beetle and the axe. And yet the individual tree is necessary—it pulls or pushes nutrients into the mycelia in the forest floor. It joins up with the others to inhale the garbage the humans put into the sky. Neither the individual or the collective is more important than the other. My mom would say, "Nik, I should have protected you better." She doesn't blame me for the babysitter any more than the forest blames the tree for the bark beetle. This is where we are at, says the mother, says the forest. We have to work with what we've got.

Max brought the green tape measure from the pink sewing basket I still own that my mom gave to me when I left for college. The tape measure is sixty inches long. Max pulled the tip to his eyebrow.

"See, mom, I'm at least five feet tall."

At least an inch of it was stuck under his toes. Still, there was five-foot hope.

"Everett's as tall as you. Are you sure you're five-three?" Max asked me. Everett is Max's best friend. Just two days ago, he stood next to me and said, "I think I'm taller than you."

Max put down the measuring tape and picked up the basketball which I kept telling him to stop hitting against the wall. He didn't.

Then, I really yelled, "Stop bouncing the ball against the wall," and he did stop. As I cut onions for tacos, without measuring tape or ball, Max grew bored enough to pull himself up on a barstool to watch me cook from the counter.

"When did you start smoking?" he asked out of nowhere, which is his M.O.

"When I was fourteen. Maybe thirteen. Maybe twelve."

"Twelve!" Max was twelve. He couldn't imagine smoking at his age. At any age, I hoped. We had been talking the day before about condoms and consent. He has a girlfriend and while, again, I hoped neither of us could imagine him having sex at twelve, I wanted to prepare him early and often.

"How much did you smoke?"

"I don't know. Maybe half a pack a day?" A glimmer of hope. At least for Max. If cigarettes stunted my growth, the genes Max inherited may be taller ones than my height might show, giving hope to his basketball dreams.

"How much is half a pack?" I nodded in approval that he didn't know how many cigarettes were in a pack.

"Ten." I smoked more than ten.

"Ten." He repeated. "Is that how much Paige smokes?" In Portland, my sister and I smoked in Portland in the greenhouse. By then, I had quit smoking Marlboro Lights and smoked Camel Lights like everyone else.

"Paige smokes less than that now. Like one cigarette a day."

"Why did you start smoking?"

I looked at my bottle of wine. Was there enough to get through this conversation? And worse, when would he start asking questions about the wine?

"You've read parts of my books. You know I had a kind of messed up childhood. I was molested by the teenager across the street." I didn't soften the words. I tried not to flinch. If my kids are my forest people, I needed them to know what kind of forest this was and where the matches lay.

"You were molested?"

"He had sex with me when I was four years younger than he was. He wasn't that much older. It wasn't like he was an uncle or anything."

"Jesus, Mom, why are you telling me this?"

"I don't know. This *Roe v. Wade* overturning has really fucked me up. Or maybe unfucked me up. I don't feel like I should hide anything anymore. If I don't speak up. Max. Your friends. Your girlfriends. Zoë. To find out your body is not really your own. Are you OK? I'm sorry if I'm being too blunt."

"Yeah, I'm OK."

"Do you know why I'm telling you this?"

"Yes. Do we have to go to another "protest"?"

"Yes. October 9th. Want to make a sign?"

"I want to play basketball."

"I have to tell you one more thing."

"What?" He did not sound curious. He sounded like he did not want to know one more thing.

"I had an abortion."

"Really?" he asked. I did surprise him a little.

"Yes. Me and almost everyone I know. So."

"Like who?"

I was about to start listing off names when I thought better of it.

"It's their story to tell. Not mine. But listen. Guys are part of it too. Do you want to have to tell someone's parents that you got someone pregnant? Please wear a condom."

"You're really not going to tell me who?"

"I told you about me. That's enough. But I do wish people would talk about it like they talk about getting their appendix out."

"Who got their appendix out?"

I said, "They'll tell you their appendix or their abortion story when they can. Thanks for listening to mine."

"Sure, mom."

He slid off the stool, pulled on his shoes, and took his basketball out the back door where he would play basketball in the cul-de-sac for an hour. I would stay here, blinking at the onion and tomatoes wondering if this counted as staying with the trouble or just causing trouble. I could hear his dribbled echo. Perhaps basketball is a kind of art.

12

Fires That Burn Too Hot

I met Bruce Talawyma when he performed a Hopi welcoming ceremony and I presented a poem on how the university is like a ponderosa pine because I cannot quit with tree metaphors. Later, he invited me and my friend Beya to the Hopi dances in July. Beya and I drove toward Winslow, stopped at the Grand Falls where the Little Colorado flows like chocolate, and then went on to the mesas. Watching the dances, we sweated through our shirts. We'd forgotten to bring hats. In Flagstaff in July, it's cool but in northeast Arizona, on the mesas, the sun caught us out. We tried to hide under eaves of houses and under the umbrellas of people who'd come prepared. The dance was a harvest one and baskets of corn, watermelon, strawberries were handed to families of the dancers. I could see the Kroger stickers on the cartons of fruit. It made me feel a sense of community that we all shopped at the same grocery chain, maybe the same store even as we lived two hours apart.

Between dances, we followed a path taking us to an overhang. Paths paved half in brick, half in tamped dirt led down to something green.

A woman who introduced herself as Marie asked us not to take any pictures of people but said, "you can take pictures of any of the plants you want." She told us she worked in Winslow, about forty minutes away, but came for the dances.

"July's dance was how I met my husband thirty-two years ago."

At the edge of the spring, about halfway down, kids threw rocks into the water. The edges of a pool had been built up, again, half brick, half dirt, and some concrete. It was an amalgam of building materials, rocks, concrete, mud, patched and pasted for hundreds of years. The water in the spring looked clean, if also rock laden due to the kids' good throwing arms.

Another 300 feet down, we reached the terraces. Levels of plants—beans, corn, tomatoes, squash and also strawberry plants, not bearing fruit yet, hence the containers of strawberries bearing Kroger stickers at the dance.

In the middle, the leaves of the trees fold like the leaves of fruit trees do, like paragraph breaks looking for a new way in. This green, so bright against red sand, against blue sky. Instead of by sprinkler, the tree is irrigated by the spring just a terrace above, the water carried by gardeners who test the roots for rot, check the bark for beetles, and talk to the trees about their needs. How anything grew in this sand made no sense to me. Beach sand, red as sunset, it looked like. Where are the mycorrhizal fungi, the microorganisms in the soil, the nurse logs dissolving into nutrients for the next generation of trees?

There are other ways of growing a forest—ones only Hopi people know, words I don't have the skill to say so instead I will say, I don't know how the red sand has sustained these trees for centuries. The Hopi are one of the few communities to have survived US Treaty making. Perhaps they knew the promise of treaties was as thin and flammable as the paper it was written on.

We don't need to use trees only for paper. Grass can be turned to pulp. A grass fiber company in Germany called Creapaper combines the long fibers of grass to the short fibers of recycled paper, to make soft fiber—a fair substitute for toilet paper. Isn't there a real kind of shame in cutting down trees for toilet paper? Isn't that perhaps the definition of shame? Unlike paper, hemp is shame free. There is nothing you can do to hurt its feelings or to make it feel bad.

You can turn hemp into clothing, oil, milkshakes, airplanes, fuel, even paper. Hemp is adaptable, taking up far less growing space than trees and far less water than bamboo or cottonwoods—which farmers also quick-grow to turn into paper. Hemp will wrap you like a blanket, carry you like a sling, drape you in the shawl of its love. Hemp has no meat. No slag. No sharp edges to cut you like paper or cheatgrass. Hemp is never hot. Even in the sun, it turns its mirrored leaves out, reflecting what it cannot take in. Hemp grows so easily it's hard to capitalize, which is probably why the United States banned the growing of it early on.

At first, the news reported a man living in his truck committed arson in a part of the Coconino National Forest right next to Flagstaff. A white pickup with

Louisiana plates had been spotted in the forest where the fire began. I asked Beya's husband, who flies helicopters to fight fires, how they would be able to know if it was arson or not. He said, "Fire investigators do incredible work, figuring these things out."

He was right. Just a few hours later the investigators concluded the man hadn't intentionally set the fire. Instead, he had been camping in the forest and not wanting to litter, burned the toilet paper he used the day before and stowed the paper under a rock. The paper smoldered overnight and, the next day, when the wind came up, sparks flew toward the trees who were suffering from the dry needles on the forest floor. At first, the fire burned only one acre of forest, but wind plus mega-drought plus ashamed-to-litter toilet paper turned the acre to thousand, then three, then four thousand acres, then five. The fire edged closer and closer to town. Fire fighters began to evacuate people. They set up a shelter at Sinagua Middle School but fortunately, few people needed it. Thanks to a bit of rain, the fire didn't cross the highway or leap into the crown of a wildly dry batch of trees. They called this 5,000-acre burn, the third wildfire that year, the Pipeline Fire, but you can Google Toilet Paper Fire and find the same results.

You can make toilet paper from other things: from trash you can combine short fibers of old paper, from lawn clippings you can stitch paper using the long fibers of grass, crosshatch the core of papyrus plants. It's work, to make art. It's also work to cut down a tree but to take a life-giving tree and pulping it into bleached sludge is more like making excrement than art. To take a being that provides multiple services, something that supports soil and birds, forms mushrooms, stores carbon, that come back from the fire dead, as my friend, the eco-science researcher George Koch said of the redwood fires, "to rebuild a crown of vigorous green foliage after losing everything," flattening it into single-colored reams and rolls of paper is the definition of anti-art, a definition of death.

Is all true art a kind of recycling? To make art is to transform something from the muck of your mind, the crud of your past, the gunk of experience, the rubbish of shame and layering it in horizontal then vertical layers until the surface shines smooth and bright, silvering into an image or a mirror, shimmering in duplicate, triplicate, four, all the prismatic, luminescent edges, corners, planes, faces, nuances of this ever-expanding world.

What if you don't have an art or lost your art along the way? What if your third or fourth growth single-species "forest" has never been terribly resilient. Suffering from drought and pestilence, the lack of diversity makes it primed for infestation. The sticks of pine planted so close together, they rub their itchy bark against each other like matches. What if the trees across the way can't sense your nutrient needs, or worse, what if the mycelia in the forest can't understand your call? If you don't have the energy to grow toward the light, you can't photosynthesize. If you can't photosynthesize, you can't store any carbon in your core. Your roots, loosened, become further unanchored in every wind. When the fires come, the flames lap at your thin bark. We can't save all the trees. But by amending the soil, adding to the diversity of kinds of trees, changing the story, we can save some of them.

When the forest researchers George Koch and Andrew Richardson presented their study of the CZU Lightning Complex Fire, ghost trees filled their laptop screens. Shreds of bark hung from black branches like hair. Ash stirred—clouds of burned cellulose, bark, squirrel, mushroom, needle, microbe, bear rise up with potential lift but then fall back, too heavy to rise above the charred cornices, turrets, naves of what had been a cathedral. Standing in the middle of all that emptiness, that goneness, the smell of all that potential energy flattened in one big kinetic burst.

In a healthy forest, you could press your needs into the soil where the mycelia might carry the message down through its web, searching out what it could find and borrow from neighboring trees. But in this seemingly dead forest, you press your feet, maybe even your hands, into that ash and nothing comes up but more ash. If you stand in the trouble too long with too many questions and the questions, like ash, will bury you.

How do you stay with the trouble long enough to see the bright green nubs start to form on what looked like permanently dead trees without getting buried? How do you resist the burning in the first place? You could tell some funny stories. You could tell some sad ones. The more stories you tell, the more likely the ground under your feet starts to tickle with responsiveness. Tell me another story, it says. I'm alive under here. Inside the tree, the decades-old carbon says, tell another story. I'm alive in here, says those crazy would-be green shoots. Keep talking. Stories awaken. But not everyone who is at risk of burning it all down is lucky enough to be born into an old growth forest. Some of us were born into second and third growth forests. Some of us were born into clear cuts. How do you resist the burning?

It could go this way: You do everything you can to put the campfire out. You layer sand on top of ashes. You set stones on top of sand. You drain butter-smeared cooler-water on top of the stones. As you drive away, one tiny ember slips away, floats and lands on a dry twig that sits on a pile of dry grass beneath a drought-thirsty tree. But the ember, tiny, struggling, is crushed by the pressure of a rising barometer. Humidity lies down upon the spark, blankets its explosive potential. A single raindrop falls. Ember dies out.

But it could also go this way: You don't do crap to put out the fire. You let it die down. You throw the last bits of beer carton, along with empty beer cans, in a pit. The wind comes up. The cardboard warms, the B from the Bud and L from the Light start to curl. The embers gear up. The fire stokes itself—spark begets spark. You don't have to be at the place of agency to be at the place of change. The man who tucked his toilet paper under a rock had driven away hours ago. The group of teens drinking beer in the forest in late November took off long ago. In 2010, the Schultz fire began as an unattended fire. An entire face of a mountain shines moon-like, thirteen years later. In 1977, the Radio Fire, also began as a teenager's abandoned campfire, came within a few feet of town. In 2019, the Museum Fire started when an excavator, working for a company hired to thin the trees to prevent calamitous fire, struck a rock and fired a spark. From my home on the far side of Mount Elden and the Peaks where the fires usually burn, I saw the orange flames peeking through smoke, like a shy sun revealed briefly on a cloudy day. In April of 2022, the Tunnel Fire burned over 20,000 acres. Thirty homes were lost. The cause of the fire is still under investigation but the idea of a fire that size happening in the winter surprised even the most climate-jaded. Not yet not yet, they said. And then the guy with the toilet paper started the next fire, almost in exactly the same place, called the Pipeline Fire just a few months later. Did you know, like all trauma-scorched places, an already-burned forest can burn again?

When I think of dying, how isn't as important as *how long it will take*. I say that I would like to die by being eaten by a mountain lion but that could take a while. Do I want to hear the tearing of my flesh, the masticating of the cat, the gnashing of my bones? Probably not. Probably, I want to die like most people: in my sleep, quickly and painlessly. How dull! How very human. It's hubris to think a mountain lion would take the time to kill me. I'm not a threat. I'm full of toxins like wine and old smoke. My two dogs and I have run in the forest every day for the past fourteen years. I've seen elk and deer and rabbits. Perhaps a mountain lion has seen me, but he is not death. He's just a forest creature, wishing I would get out of his way. Death is the soft ash at the feet. A skybound tree laid flat—flakes of char.

My friends and I texted play-by-play about the Museum Fire. In Flagstaff, everyone knows someone who knows someone who knows more about the fire than you do. Beya's husband, Brian, worked fire from his helicopter. Lindsey's friend who volunteered at the look-out tower kept her up-to-date. Shamah knew a firefighter in town. Lawrence drove out to Doney Park to see what highway 89 out of town looked like. Angie's dad lived in Phoenix and kept us up-to-date on what the local news reported. Erik kept his eye on the alerts. I didn't have a person in fire, per se, but I did have Lindsey, Shamah, Angie, Lawrence, Erik, Brian, and Beya, who had her ear to the police scanner, to keep me updated. And my eyes, who could see the flames even though they were at least ten miles away.

The first reports said five acres at noon that Sunday but by 2:30 it had grown to 100. By 4:30, 200 acres. By morning, 1,000. By then, the fire was a mile outside of the far north side of town. Erik and I watched from our upstairs window as tankers the size of DC-10s followed spotter planes over Mount Elden, dumping bright red fire retardant on the southwest side of the mountain. The fire wrapped itself around hills, sneaking away from the front the fire fighters had predicted. Instead, it reached for homes on the northeast side where the Schultz fire had burned nine years before—Timberline, Christmas Tree Estates, the KOA campground set for evacuation. But the fire also poured down the canyon toward Buffalo Park, Upper Greenlaw, Swiss Manor, where a lot of our friends live. Seeing smoke Erik and I had become used to. Seeing the orange tongues of flames was new and strange. A helicopter swung a Bambi bucket over the flames, pitching water from Lake Mary on those tongues. They seemed to speak against the helicopter—don't try to shut us up. We have things to say. Or, rather, yell.

The fire came seemingly, suddenly, out of nowhere. No one has tracked that causal ember to its final effect. Is such a tracing ever possible? Even helpful? Does the reason the fire happened matter if the forest is gone? If in this book I'm tracing how I (so far) survived an early devastation, overcame the suggestion that my life-path was set in stone, then perhaps the single "why?" isn't helpful but the multitudes whys might be. How did you make it to a life in Flagstaff, teaching two courses a semester, writing books, and having mostly well-adjusted children? A planting. A telling. A making of something. But what if you have no art with which to tell your story? What if you don't know where to order trees and mycorrhizal spores? What if the clear cut of your birth is too full of bitumen and tar to absorb any of those spores? What if you have no means to reach the soil? What if you haven't even inherited or been handed a shovel with which to dig?

On a Sunday, the fire started. On Wednesday, as the fire in Flagstaff grew, my aunt Michelle in West Valley City was diagnosed with both cervical and lung cancer. By Friday, she had killed herself. Did her death come upon her as quickly as the fire had come upon this mountain town? Or had it been smoldering for years, just blowing up now, after an insurmountable amount of bad news?

Aunt Michelle was my mom's half-sister, born in Salt Lake when my step-grandpa and my grandma married for his second, her third time. My mom and her sister, Audie and Sue, left their grandmother behind in that house they had owned in Evanston to the new house on 15th East. Michelle, born when my mom was twelve, was the supposed reason for this reconstructed family but there was too much detritus from the past: past marriages, affairs, my grandfather imprisoned in Huntsville, and his subsequent return to Evanston after being released where he found my grandma at the IGA grocery store where she worked the checkout lane and asked her for money, not love. When she said no, he hijacked a cab driver with a knife and made him take him to a bar in Ogden. The police found him there and shot him. This was not Michelle's dad. This was my mom's dad. After my mom's dad died, the family built a new life in Salt Lake, duct-taped together with the promise of a bigger city, a bigger back yard, and closer proximity to the Mormon church.

Gardening is easier in Salt Lake than in Evanston. Salt Lake sits at 4,400 feet above sea level instead of the 7,000 like Evanston, and Flagstaff for that matter. My grandparents grew tomatoes and carrots. Grandpa sprayed the fruit trees. My mom and grandmas canned cherries, made plum jam, and pickled cucumbers all summer long. Planning for the future is how families stay together. "We have all these peaches to eat next winter." Maybe it's how we stay alive. "We can't die until we've eaten all the jars of pickles," we say to ourselves. Shelle put up plum jam with Grandma. She watered the tomatoes and sprayed them with Miracle-Gro like my grandparents taught her.

The house on 15th East was red brick, three-bedroom, one bath, no garage although there was a carport. My step-grandpa, who we just called Grandpa, drove buses for Greyhound. My grandma waitressed at Dee's Family Restaurant. My mom and her sisters had two dresses each—one for school and one for church. The living situation was better than in Evanston where bathwater was handed down like other family's hand down heirlooms—the eldest took the first of the turns. The youngest took the final bath in the same water that had washed twelve previous bodies. My mom and aunts told the bath story at least once a year. Shelle, born in Utah, had avoided this bathing ritual. I thought she should have been relieved to miss this grungy baptism but when they talked about it, Shelle looked like she thought she'd missed out.

Shelle, as we called her, was born to my grandma later in life and my grandpa even later in his, never fully assimilated into the family. She was different. She drove a Brat, the truck's answer to the El Camino. She didn't graduate from high school, although she passed her GED exam. She worked at Patrick Dry Goods, packaging mainly dishtowels. Occasionally, she embroidered images of cats on them and gave them to my mom and aunts for Christmas. She lived away from home for a couple years in an apartment building next door to my Aunt Sue whose husband owned the complex. She moved back home when my great-grandma left Evanston so she could provide full-time care for her and for her parents. Great-grandma and grandpa, who were close in age, sat close enough to each other on the couch to share an afghan, one losing their hearing, the other losing their sight.

My mom and her sisters left home as soon as they could. Aunt Audie and Sue left for marriage, my mom for college, each of them for her own bathroom. Maybe once her sisters left, the house felt expansive. Grandpa built her a deck off Aunt Shelle's room, installed a sliding door so she could slip outside to smoke. After Grandpa died, Grandma let her smoke inside as long as she exhaled up the chimney. She went through phases of drinking, first beer, then nothing, then cranberry vodkas. Even though Grandma was LDS and didn't smoke or drink, she only worried about Shelle's health. She didn't make her quit. Even though they fought like a married couple, Grandma was indebted to her. She needed someone to watch *Wheel of Fortune* and *Jeopardy* with. She needed someone to feed the cat Otis his half a can of tuna and then make them tuna fish sandwiches with the other. Grandma kept an open sleeve of Saltines on her counter. Shelle spread them with butter and carried them out on a plate as hors d'oeuvres.

When Grandma died from complications of diabetes, the daughters inherited the house equally but Sue and Audie and my mom gave Michelle half of the proceeds because she'd lived there most of her life. Because she took care of their mom. And grandma. And stepdad. Although Michelle had tried to keep the house up, the kitchen still smelled like tuna. There were saltine crackers in the cushions of the couch. The single never-updated bathroom, pink ceramic toilet and sink, smelled like grandma. It was time to let someone else take over the care. The cherry tree died a while ago. No one had planted tomatoes for years.

Michelle had to move out of Grandma's house and move on. She was fifty-eight years old. She had enough money to put a down payment on a small house further west or to rent an apartment. Instead, she started dating a guy for the first time ever. She moved into his trailer. Partly because of his cerebral palsy, partly because of his sense that someone should take care of him, and partly because Shelle was used to taking care of people, she cooked and cleaned and watched *Wheel of Fortune* and *Jeopardy* for him like she did for Grandma.

Once, fire was the right thing for the forests. Those low-burning, not-too-hot fires burned the detritus, left the canopy and its strange world alone, left the mycorrhizal fungi untouched. But every year, more neighborhoods in Flagstaff are told to prepare to evacuate. This fire, the Museum Fire, the one I watched from the windows of my house, sometimes from the driveway, from the porch, was declared first priority in the country because it grew closer and closer to town. A mile from town is not far when fire can move 6.7 miles a minute. This fire could have run up a hill, over a ridge, or gone around the back of Dookʼoʼoosłíí́d, and scalloped along Highway 89 where Lawrence had reported traffic was starting to back up as people tried to leave town.

City authorities changed neighborhoods closest to the Peaks from "Ready" to "Set" status, meaning don't just think about evacuating. Pack your cars. Book a hotel room or find out where the closest shelter might be. Those who live on the outskirts of town should find a trailer for their horses. If they can't find a trailer, be sure to unlock the barn doors. Even those of us just on "ready" status packed our photo albums and birth certificates into boxes and put them in the trunk of the car. Flagstaff felt strangely calm, even under these orders. Most of us went to work. Max's summer camp still ran although the Museum Fire canceled my friend Gretchen's son's Discovery Camp.

But streets looked like war zones when I drove closer to the fire to pick Max up. Barricades patrolled by the National Guard stood between road and fire. Volunteers scooped sandbags for potential post-fire flooding. Firefighters in helmets drove in the back of trucks. The bright green Hot Shot buses lined Highway 180 that leads past those forest roads and will take you to the Grand Canyon—if and when they take those barricades down.

It sounded a bit like a war zone too. The double-bladed military helicopters dropped their water bombs. The DC 10 tanker dropped its fire retardant. We, an ever-turning group of friends and neighbors, sat on each other's porches and witnessed what we could.

I wondered if I could see anything the firefighters couldn't see from my balcony. Vultures flew in gyres over unburned ponderosa pines. Can their wheeling keep the fire at bay from at least that one section of forest? The shelters asked for donations of Gatorade for the firefighters. I broke my embargo on Gatorade—their bottles made of so much plastic—and took a case to Sinagua, where also my son goes to school. I think of the substances in Gatorade. The substances in fire retardant. What happens to mine tailings when they go up in smoke? We put so much stuff onto the surface of the world. When it burns, how much of that stuff do we inhale? I think of ash and burned fur. How many animals did I inhale? What is the price for breathing the remains of the victims of human-caused climate change? How much fire and its products are becoming a part of us?

I see a man set down a flame.
I hear a woman die.
These people trouble me. I trouble me. I could let go. I could let myself go. I could, I think, let other people go.
I watch the deer step high through the snow. They look for grass, trees, any kind of forage. Their system of living, like the trees, feels more substantial, sustainable, than that of the mountain lion I pretend I want to meet, than that of the human that I love. Predators, as much as I love their forward-staring eyes and their lone-wolf status, I feel they, most of them, favor individualism at the expense of the joys of collaboration. Wolves are actually an exception. They are not loners. Wolves live in communities, packs of families and friends.
Humans, because of their communities, their communalism, their communication skills, built the world we live in now. But strangely, it's a world of fences and roads, cars where individuals listen to their individual music and their individual phones.
I don't think humans are a good thing for the planet. Does this make me a would-be murderer? A genocidal monster? If I understand a suicide, does that make it plain that my heart had already turned away from the hope of humans getting out of this alive? Do I sometimes wish they wouldn't? Could the humans evaporate and leave what's left of the trees to the deer and the wolves, the soil and the weirdness of fungi?
But then, my Aunt Sue just texted me to thank me for the night at my cousin Tim's house. We'd all gone up after Aunt Shelle's funeral. Tim and Camille have restored a house on the Emigration river to its midcentury modern architecture and the windows bend round against the sharp V of the canyon's wall. Tim poured me a glass of wine from the bar in the living room. I sat in the Z shaped chair, chrome legs, yellow upholstery. I should have worn my bell bottoms.

Aunt Sue, mom to Tim and Tim's brother Trev, whom I love but who is so far politically to the right that he doesn't hang out with our family anymore, sat next to me and reminded me she had breastfed me when I was a baby.

"If your mom had to run errands, she'd drop you off with me. If you were hungry, I fed you. You and Trevor were so close in age. If I dropped him off, your mom fed him. It always made Trev so mad when I brought it up with him."

"I think it's great," I told her. "Think of how much more good bacteria I have in my gut thanks to you. That's probably why I rarely get sick. My immune system has your milk to thank, in part. Plus, in what world wouldn't you feed a hungry baby?"

Aunt Sue gets sad. She texts to tell me she misses Trevor, who once climbed trees with me, who doesn't see her, because he went Trump and she stayed sane. She misses her sisters, two of whom are now gone. My mom is busy with her boyfriend Bill. But my mom gets sad too. My sisters get sad. I get sad. We call when we can. As much as I find the situation humans have gotten us in abhorrent, I would save anyone who was sad, if I could. The abstraction of suicide I imagine as a way to re-balance ecosystems is just mental acrobatics. An easy fantasy. The reality of suicide is that I wish I could have been there to ask them if they could tell another story, would they change their mind?

After my grandma died, Shelle became uprooted from the only life she had known—her family and the house on 15th East. It's not that my aunts and mom didn't call or see her—they did. They invited Shelle to lunch and bought her drinks and made sure she had enough money, and that Steve was being at least half kind to her. But they didn't visit the mobile home very often. It was hard to get a sense of what was really going on inside the trailer. *Wheel of Fortune*, definitely. *Jeopardy*, sure. But what do two unemployed people do all day, trapped together inside a small space, with very few resources to get them out of there?

Still, Shelle's sisters didn't give up on her. She lost her teeth. Aunt Audie paid for dentures. Her eyelids thick and heavy over her eyes, drooping with ptosis, making it hard for her to see. Aunt Sue paid for an eyelift. My mom invited her to stay with her for two months after she fell down, bruising her face and suffering a concussion. Or at least she said she fell. She insisted. "Steve has cerebral palsy," she said. "He doesn't have the strength to hit me." Not with his hands, maybe. But his crutch is heavy and made of metal. For those two months, my mom helped her walk up and down the stairs from the guest bedroom to the TV room so they could watch *Jeopardy* together.

Shelle tried to reestablish her life, but she had prepared no good soil and that Steve had layered no leaf rot, no fungi, no microbes for her to flourish. Her sisters never abandoned her, but they couldn't sustain her fully. Not only did they have to devote resources to other people too, but they also didn't know what she needed. Shelle quit calling. She stopped going to birthday parties. She canceled dinner invitations. My aunts called her to join them for drinks—she didn't call them back. Sometimes, Steve the boyfriend answered the phone, accusing them of not helping enough. But what is enough when the forest is already so dry? It's possible this area has been in drought since the day she was born.

Trees suffering from drought try to form a tricky balance. By closing their stoma, they lose less moisture into the air but in closing the stoma, they have less ability to photosynthesize. If they photosynthesize less, they have reduced capacity to draw nutrients from the soil and the mycorrhizal substrate.[1] If you are stressed or traumatized, it doesn't matter how many nutrients you are offered—you just do not have the energy to keep the system balanced.

If there's never enough water, tethering yourself to those underground nutrients is a lot of work. When you get tired, it takes too much to draw in what you need. Shelle became untethered from the other trees. If a fire, like cancer, came near, she had few inner or outer resources to withstand the burning.

Pyro-cumulus clouds are made from the force and heat of a forest fire as the heat of the fire causes updrafts, making big, puffy, dark gray clouds. These clouds become weather systems of their own, making firefighting more difficult. The air cools as it rises, making poofier, taller clouds. As the fire burns the vegetation below, water from the plants evaporates. Water droplets condense and stick to particles like smoke and ash, turning the clouds gray, thickening the air. The clouds pile up, pulling oxygen through the fire, enlarging the fire in order to enlarge the clouds. The biggest reflection of the fire on the ground is the chemical explosions of air molecules in the sky. The clouds tumble as the fire spins below. In wet climates, these clouds might actually release rain, putting a damper on the fire but in the west, the air is too dry. The water in the clouds, even if it falls, disappears before it hits the ground. This could be an example of fire creating its own limits, but in the west, it cannot succeed in putting itself out with its own smoke-clouds. There is not enough ambient moisture to make it rain.

In the past ten years, drought and climate have contributed to not only the number of fires but the size of them. Fire managers battle for resources, for firefighters to fight, for water, for air support, for help but, as with the Dixie Fire of 2021, which severely burned parts of Lake Tahoe, all the fighting in the world can't put out fires that burn so hot and so fast. In the before-times, letting the fire burn was cleansing. Now, with the intensifying droughts and rising climate temperatures, if you let it go, you may not be able to turn it back.

Maybe my mom's half-sister thought, "I have been thirsty for so long. I don't have the energy to keep the fire at bay." She had nothing left to fight the conflagration of bad news and bad luck: no job, no home, no money, no mom. The fire started on a Wednesday with the bad news of cancer and, by Friday, so soon, the fire was out of control.

If my aunt did get up to get a drink of water, I imagine she went to the bathroom sink. Looking into the mirror, she said, "Let go. Just let go." I've said that before to my mirror, my face as cracked as a dry lakebed. Who isn't thirsty most of the time? Was there a moment where she could have doused her own fire? At what point did she come to realize there wasn't enough water left in the world to extinguish that fire? Or maybe she just let the fire burn all those questions out.

Everything is always burning. Lie on the forest floor, next to a Douglas fir that has fallen. It has a name, "nurse." Here, this tree feeds everything around it—mushrooms and plants, slugs and even its still standing sister-tree. On the ground, horizontal, it slowly burns down into a red-brown humus—ashy, in its way. Decomposition smells like doused fire. For microbes, a slow burn is better than a fast one.

Microbial scientists who study the Amazon, the largest contiguous rainforest in the world, to discover what happens when the rainforest is bulldozed or burned to raise cattle research how burning the forest affects microbial life. The number of microbes and their systems far outnumber what the scientists can map, but they have found trends that show what happens when trees, plants, insects, and animals are removed from the forest. Digging down ten centimeters, they measure the number of microbes and determine that there are far fewer microbes and less diversity among those microbes compared to intact rainforest. Recent research shows, the more microbes in soil, the more carbon it can store.

Microbes don't make it to be the mascot for the World Wildlife Fund or the Sierra Club or the Center for Biodiversity but microorganisms are as much us as we are ourselves. We are about 50 percent our DNA and 50 percent colonized by bacteria. We are a planet unto ourselves and our selves, those microbes, can also be found in, on, with, beside, other parts of the planet. Imagine your fingernail in the middle of the Amazon rainforest. You are literally there. Or at least parts of you, gleaming and teeming around in the soil.

Abundance for its own sake is one of the solutions I've been looking for. As I quoted Donna Haraway, the danger of the single narrative is that it will beg only a single solution. And a single solution follows the traits of a single anything—a thing alone, like an individual human or a flame, eventually dies out. Communities continue past that individual death. Ecosystems go on. Microorganisms, in their abundance, conspired together to evolve into trees, wolves, mushrooms, and humans. There's a lot of them. Pound by pound, they beat human mass by billions. If our work is to create art to expand the available universe, we could begin by writing an ode to each microbe.

I'm surprised I haven't burned to the ground with the way my ears turn so hot when I screw up. My sensitivity to shame doesn't pair well with my inability to keep my mouth shut. Once I realized that telling stories is my way to build community, I angered almost everyone. I feel like I'm standing up for Max when Erik yells at him for eating in his room again or for Zoë when she jammed the futon into the trim he'd just painted. Stop being so angry, I yell. He yells back, stop yelling and now I'm ashamed for yelling, for telling him to stop, for the fact we're doing all this yelling in front of the children I thought I was protecting from their future shame but really, it's just crumbs and scratched walls.

From the cross-country coach accosting me at Zoë's race for writing a newspaper column decrying the charter school Zoë attended for one year, to the Associate Dean filing a complaint with my dean for writing about her friend who went to Mexico to heal her breast cancer with bees (this wasn't the part she was mad about), from my friend Lindsey asking me to not write about her in my *Dear Ducey* column to my publishing the essay about the abortion I had at age eleven in *The New York Times*, I spend most of my days burning, my ears burn. My cheeks. Shame mixed up with who-are-you-to-tell-me-what-to-do redness. My face is permanently red from the flushing of my cheeks and the wine I gulp to try to cool it down.

And yet I don't quit making a mess. I keep writing. I don't believe in recovery; I believe in adding layers. I'm not going back over the same territory. I'm making new territory. These trees are new ones although the mycorrhizal fungi-filled soil has never burned so hot to kill it. The world is still full of drought. Detritus builds up under the canopy of the trees. The air is dry. Forests are primed to ignite. But monsoon storms are coming. They've skipped a couple of years so far, in this new century of new climate. I keep my eye on the horizon for clouds to build. I refresh the weather app every few minutes to see the future.

Reagan Wytsalucy grew up near Gallup, New Mexico. Her father, who grew up near Shonto, AZ, helped his parents herd sheep as a kid. He grew up to own a number of McDonald's franchises across Navajo lands. Reagan, who doesn't speak Navajo but wanted to learn more about her culture, transferred from BYU in Provo, Utah to Utah State in Logan where she could study with agricultural scientists and historians. She knew the story of Kit Carson and the forced Long Walk from what is now called Canyon de Chelly to Fort Sumner/Bosque Redondo in New Mexico.

In 1864 Kit Carson set fire to homes, crops, and orchards to prevent to Navajo from returning. Where the soldiers destroyed peach trees the Diné had tended for three centuries, not even stumps remained. Soldiers reported, gloated, they had burned over 3,000 trees. Other soldiers cut down 500 of what Captain John Thompsin called "500 of the best peach trees I have ever seen in the country, each one bearing fruit."[2] Some Diné took off for the mountains to hide in the canyons. One man, Chief Hoskininni, an ancestor of Wytsalucy, took peach seeds with him as he evaded capture.

In most parts of Canyon de Chelly, tamarisks—water-sucking invasive species—mark their impossible green against the red cliffs and red ruins. Although the original peach trees are gone, new trees have been replanted. Replanting is different from recovering. Recovering suggests going back and lying down, pulling the blankets up, and going back to sleep—a restful but backwards motion. Replanting isn't forward necessarily, but bi-directional, upward and downward. Roots are beloved for a reason. Before Kit Carson, Diné tended the peaches rubbed peach seeds with the fat from churro lambs to give both the seed and the soil sustenance. When the Diné returned from Bosque Redondo, Hopi offered them peach seeds on their way back. They added those seeds to the ones Chief Hoskininni had saved. They gathered their sheep, slaughtered a few, rubbed the seeds with churro fat and planted the seeds again.

To build bodies in semi-arid climates requires a wide network. Like the mycelia, that underground web of fungi, where the tiny hyphae exchange nutrients with trees, sheep fat and crenellated seed wind their own weave, the rendered grease interlaced between the peach pit's rivulets. A ram's horn marks each row.

Wytsalucy, in her studies at Utah State, where she stayed to pursue a Master's degree, discovered that many of the seeds had been salvaged. And although many Diné returned to Canyon de Chelly, others took different paths to different communities. Those seeds were planted too. Wytsalucy, her father, and two horticulturists traveled across Arizona and New Mexico, tracking lost seeds and orchards.

It took three years for Wytsalucy to receive her first peach seeds, handed to her by an 85-year-old woman in Canyon de Chelly, a lush collection of gorges in northeastern Arizona in the Navajo nation. Encouraged by that first success, Wystalucy kept knocking on doors all over the Four Corners area. Eventually, she tracked down eight more orchards.

Genetic analyses show that these peaches are significantly different from modern cultivars. According to Wytsalucy, that persisted despite the US government's efforts to provide new peach trees to Native people in the late nineteenth century. Instead, many of the elders kept the seeds from the government and the traditional peaches separate from each other—they didn't want them to mix.

Many of the peaches Wytsalucy tracked down in the Four Corners area are currently growing wild, without any human interference. They're smaller than modern cultivars, about the size of a large apricot. The skins are mostly green with a slight red tint. As for how they taste, says Wytsalucy, "they have a tart peel and are very sweet inside," and "a muskmelon flavor." Nutritional analyses show that they are higher in calories and have more calcium, fiber, carbohydrates, and total fat than standard peaches.[3]

Now, Wytsalucy works with communities across Navajo lands to study those old peach varietals. By diving into the story of the tree, Wytsalucy found ways to reach her community—this community, in many ways dispersed and facture, but one that has found a way to connect over thousands of square miles, state borders, treaty-defined borders, missing fruit, revivified seeds. Wytsalucy, every time she discovers a new orchard, she is writing an ode for the descendants of the peach trees that Kit Carson burned in Canyon de Chelly. This is not an effort of recovery but layers of discovery.

Julie, my beautiful friend from grad school died on September 11th, 2021. She left suicide notes and though I can't imagine one was for me—I didn't see her often enough—I can wish she wrote me to explain. Suicide makes wishers of us all. Wish that we'd been there. Wish we'd done something. Wish we'd known. I understand wanting to give up. I understand wanting to burn it all down. David Foster Wallace wrote that for some, the choice is between jumping out a window of a burning building or staying inside the building as it burns—the results are the same, either way.

The hardest thing about Julie dying was that I didn't know she was dying at all. Although when I last saw her in person, before COVID-19, she dissembled.

She was like a wobbly bike tire. None of her stories about her friends at work, her health, her dogs, rang quite true. She acted like she was playing the part of Julie rather than Julie herself.

When Julie died, I didn't know she had stopped writing poems. She stopped playing the cello. She stopped singing songs. She stopped doing impressions of her mother's Argentine accent and her father's Latvian one. Julie was a gifted poet. If I had known she had stopped making art, I would have worried.

She seemed OK when she Zoomed into my class to talk about the formalism in her book of poems, *torch song tango choir*. Her crown of sonnets is fifteen poems about building up—the Equity Building in New York, an acrobat's pyramid in Argentina, and falling down—Eva Peron, the World Trade Center Towers. The poems themselves follow the cadence of a tango. You could dance to her poems. Julie was not only beautiful and smart, but funny too.

She texted me after the class, "I can't believe we talked about my boobs!" she said.

I told her, "My students love boobs!"

I don't remember how the subject of boobs came up in the middle of a discussion about forms in poetry—perhaps the dip and spin of the sonnet mirrors the rise and fall of breasts. Julie was a regular friend and a regular person. Like me, she was the eldest of two sisters. Like me, her father drank although, unlike my dad, her dad quit before he died of it. When I first met her, she was nursing her mom back to health after being treated for breast cancer. She took care of both of her grandparents as they aged. She took in dog after dog after dog. She and I sent poems about wolves and whales and emus to each other.

I'm pro-abortion. There are enough humans on the planet. I'm pro-euthanasia. I believe suicide can be an act of free will. But in a video recording of a reading Julie gave here in Flagstaff in 2017, I watched her perform a beauty and grace so generous, so big-heartedly that was as if she was asking the audience to come up onto the stage into the poem, that she could protect them inside there, I realize there's no such thing as free will. Everything touches and presses and affects everything next to it. Unlike Aunt Shelle, Julie had an art. She reached out into the world. But like Aunt

Shelle, the connections between give and take were misfiring. But whereas Shelle's mycelia desiccated, Julie, whose brain chemistry had been affected by something we don't know, maybe genetics, maybe her stark recognition of how thin the line is between substance and ash, pushed her art, whatever carbon stores she had, into the soil. The soil tried to give back, but the pathways got routed the wrong way.

When Julie read in Arizona, she read poems about sky islands, mountains which rise above deserts, creating ecosystems so different from the ones below they seem to be completely separate parts of earth. Julie delighted in the abundance of life at these high elevations. To list is to celebrate every species that lives in those surprising places. In an interview in Sand Creek Review, to a question about what it means to her to be part of this "controversy" themed edition, she answered,

> In the *Iliad*, Achilles chooses to go to war in Troy, even though it will mean an early and unnatural death, because the heroic manner of his death will ensure his name lives forever. So in conventional epic economies, martial, masculine sacrifice is explicitly compensated. But what of all the women, children, animals, other life forms, wilds and wildernesses, whose lives and freedoms are sacrificed at the altars of dominion and greed? What is their compensation? I wanted to explore the unsung victims of humanity's worst impulses—greed, fear, power—to show that if we are to bequeath to our children futures worth having, we must not squander their futures during our collective present. Can we turn from the apocalypses we have set in motion? Can we reign in our excesses? Can we face our own fears without inciting fear in others?

Before she died, she called me about the fires burning in the mountains near Angelus Oaks, where she lived. She described the trees "as if a full color rendering of a black-and-white film, it's only colors, black and white." She called me about the fires every day. She wrote odes to animals threatened by the fires. Fires burned in Tucson too. She wrote odes for the species there, in the sky island. She was a species to me. She was in danger. She was endangered. She stopped writing. Art, if not always nutrient giving, usually provides fire-protective bark. But as we've seen, some fires burn too hot.

My friends from grad school, Steve, Dave, Margot, Lynn, and Matt, met in Dorr County Wisconsin in the middle of December to mourn Julie's death. That's what I needed: no forest blooming, no fires, nothing but Lake Michigan, pushing its freezing tongues at me, and stopping before they got to my ear to tell me where I had gone wrong.

"I think she couldn't live without her family," I told my friends. She and her sisters were so close, they exchanged houses and dogs and kids, for at least a week or two at a time when they all lived in Salt Lake. Maybe she couldn't live without her family, even though she had Steve (her husband) and the kids. Maybe when she moved to Angelus Oaks she thought, oh, yay! Forest! But the forest she needed was a bank of trees along the Big Cottonwood river that flowed behind her childhood home. Maybe some of us can survive transplanting but not all trees can make it in soils not their own. Common tree species such as Douglas fir, western red cedar, and maple would not survive without the help of mycorrhizae. Coming from a land of cottonwoods, Douglas fir, and Gambel oak, perhaps the bristle cone pines were too foreign for her.

Suicide takes a level of certainty I don't think I'll ever possess. A certainty that window-jumping and building-burning aren't actually the same thing—grief seems to be the nature of the twenty-first century. But I'm not great at decision-making. The ground shifts underneath me. Since the babysitter? Since before? Is it possible that insecurity and shame might be what keeps me from choosing to end it all—even though shame burns so hard in me I want to die then and there—because shame and insecurity make you wonder, well, is that really how the situation is? How would I know for sure? I'm not even sure I'm supposed to be here. And I wait until an hour later or the next day and really, whatever the "it" was is usually something else.

I envy people who are certain about things. Who can recover the past without fantastical story-making, or recover from a traumatic incident with grace, can let rejection roll of their back they are so confident in their art. Those who can make life or death decisions. These people seem like species unto themselves. But as long as this typing machine keeps taking my questions, I don't think I will ever stop asking them, which is one kind of way to not die.

13

Trees Are Not the Only Fruit

Tony LePray, my post-babysitter psychologist, told my mom I was very book-smart but not street smart. Since I'd recently failed the gifted and talented test, I didn't quite believe him about the book-smart comment, but I didn't believe him about the street smarts comment either. What did he know about streets? He was a psychologist. Had he been to see *The Massacre Guys* at the Indian Center? What kind of piercings did he boast? (I just had regular piercings but sometimes stuck safety pins through my earholes. Very street.)

But perhaps he did have a point. I wouldn't quite say I lack street smarts so much as I mistake what I think I can do for what I can actually do, or what I'm doing for what I think I'm doing. If fantasy runs half of your life, decision-making is a fifty-fifty gamble that things will turn our OK in reality.

I don't do a very good job of staying in my lane—hence the way the essays braid themselves between topics and stories—sometimes because I don't see the white lines indicating whose lane is whose. And sometimes because I think white lines are bullshit. Do you think mycelia in the forest care about lines? They just reach out! Here's some nutrients! Suck it up! But then again, maybe sometimes the trees are like, I don't want your salmon nutrients. I'm a vegetarian tree! A little pushback on the laneless mycelia could be a fecund area for further research. Picky ponderosas. Fickle firs.

The gap between what I think I can do and what I can actually do is fundamentally street-based. In New York, my sister Valerie and my friend

Renee, walked through Alphabet City, 2007. Three guys from across the street waved at me. I waved back. "Do you want to go to a party?" They asked. I shrugged. Maybe. I like parties. They walked toward us. Renee and Valerie shushed me and dragged me down the street. "Do you want to get killed?"

"I just waved hello."

"Do not wave hello in NYC."

In 2025, NYC is a different place and waving is mostly safe now, but I still don't do it because my worry that Renee and Valerie will call me street dumb is one way I've been trained to try to be quiet and don't get raped. A good lane to stay in, but also a lane that prohibits me from going to whatever party those guys were throwing.

During monsoon season, I ran in the forest with the dogs. Years ago, monsoon season was predictable. According to my next-door neighbor, you could set a clock by the summer storms, "Clouds rolled in around 1:00 p.m. It rained from 2:00 to 3:00 and then the skies cleared." I trusted her memory. But with climate change, there is no clock. It can rain any time. Or all night. Or at 2:00 p.m. Or not at all. I ran one July in the morning with the dogs on Campbell Mesa—not far from my house but foreign enough that I hadn't memorized the paths. I knew where the petroglyphs were and the little bridge that crossed the water running from the water treatment plant—the same water they used to water local golf courses and pump up to the snowbowl to freeze it into ski worthy ground.

Finding one's way in Flagstaff is generally easy because Dookʼoʼoosłíid and its neighboring peaks, Mount Elden most obviously, orient you around the city. If the mountains are over "there," then you are "here" in direct relation. But when a storm rolls in from the southwest or even sometimes the southeast, clouds block the peaks and between identical seeming ponderosas and paths crisscross every which way because, being proximate to a city, everybody walks through the forest, making more paths than are probably good for the trees.

With the first drop of rain, I realized we should get back to the car. With the first lightning strike, I thought we should hurry. I ran in the direction I thought the car lay. Then, I wasn't sure. Maybe I was running the wrong way.

Maybe I should go back. Or should I follow the path to my left. Where is the little red bridge that crossed the effluent stream? Were the petroglyphs, spiral sun etchings, ahead of me or behind?

The dogs hated the rain, but hate is no umbrella. They ran between trees, standing under the shelter of its branches. I knew enough, streetwise, to know standing by a single tree in a lightning storm is bad. Standing alone in the open is also bad. We should stand in the middle of the largest ponderosa pine forest in the continental United States and hope for the best. Which we did. I ran. I jumped over a snake lying across the path. I hadn't seen the snake before. Did this make me more lost or less? Is it bad luck to jump over a snake? Was it a rattler? They didn't used to be found at this elevation, but diamondback rattlesnakes inch higher as the climate warms just like trees in the east inch westward.

Eventually, I saw the pipes that convert methane produced by the collection of sewage into productive energy. The pipes hump up and down, as if making the gas slither like snakes, it will take the smell out and add extra combustibility to the mix. My Lycra running clothes were soaked through. The dogs' coats were just as wet. When we reached the car, I told the dogs I was sorry. They shook their heads. Would they trust me again?

A few years later, in 2023, I got lost cross-country skiing the year I predicted it would be the last big snowfall Flagstaff would ever see. I'm offering no meteorological data here. Just once again, I'm stepping out of my lane to say, the climate has changed so significantly in Flagstaff since I've lived here that this one snowstorm seemed like a goodbye letter, folded, white, and flattened. Winds came up as I cross-country skied through the forests behind my house. I went one way. Then another. Then way too far some way I didn't know. Then, the clouds opened for a minute and I could see Mount Elden. I knew to ski in that direction, since home was between it and here. Again, the dogs looked at me like I couldn't be trusted.

"What?" I asked them. "It was just an extra long walk. Through snow. You love snow."

The dogs and I ate a lot of cheese to celebrate eventually finding home.

Perhaps if I were a real forester or a person with Indigenous roots, I could have used the trees to help me get home. I imagine there are all kinds of details to note while wandering through a forest to help you get you back on track.

But again, knowledge is a kind of trust but I didn't plan on getting lost so I hadn't noted tree by slightly different tree on my way into the forest so even if I did have the skills, I wouldn't have thought to employ it. The trees can't do everything for us.

Really. The trees can't do everything for us. Climate researchers have marked a tipping point of global warming when, at a certain temperature, forests will start producing more carbon than they absorb. Plants will not photosynthesize as readily and the microbes in the soil will decay more quickly as the temperature warms. This is another one of those positive feedback loops that has nothing positive to it.

We look to trees for help. Can we convince them to pull more carbon from the atmosphere? We have just begun to understand the extent of what they do for the atmosphere—how they balance and juggle its chemical stew. Can we ask them to do more? If we want to do things as well as the forest does, we will have to look at the world differently. We will actually need to pull out our eyeballs and insert different ones—that's what they call a paradigm shift—a radical new way of seeing and framing, cataloging and philosophizing, medicating and organizing the world. For starters, we can't see a tree as a single tree. We must take in mosses on its bark, the ferns that feather the humus, the humus made from old, dead things, and the mycelium under the ground converting nutrients for the tendrils in the tree roots system. You have to look for things you don't even know are there. It's a lot to ask of humans, to do things in non-humany ways, to try to model something besides their singular selves. But again, maybe that's where the trees come in—trees teaching a lesson in how to think beyond our singular selves, to learn something about cross-species community health.

Lake Mary's western shore looked as far away from me as it looked a half an hour ago. I had not moved. I stood in the middle of the lake, paddling an inflatable board, with my fifty-pound dog, Zora, on the back, who is neither paddling nor steering. The more I paddled against the wind, the more nervous she became, walking back and forth, aft to stern, between my legs, worrying the boat. Worrying me.

It had been an unreasonably windy summer that year. Usually, in Flagstaff, the wind harasses us in April and May but usually by June, we're free to venture to outdoor events like picnics where all your paper plates stay on the blanket or to festivals when the tents resist turning into kites. But this year, all summer long, we battened down whatever hatch seemed likely to fly open. We hadn't been paddleboarding much. The weather had looked great that morning. But now it was after noon, and I was buffeted. I tried to be tolerant and open-minded, imagining the wind wasn't going out of its way to hinder my progress. But if you had seen me, standing out on a board, in the middle of a lake, with a dog walking back and forth between my legs, transferring my arms' tensile strength into the handle of the paddle, you might have thought the wind had it out for me. Or, you might have thought, "Stop standing in the middle of a lake on a paddleboard with your dog in the stream of forty-five mph winds." But short women have something to prove, at least when it comes to dogs, big wind, and paddleboards. Short women cannot see the forest for the trees. They can only see the bark of the tree. They can only see the low edge of a shoreline as it refuses to come any closer no matter how much energy they displace into the paddle.

Still, I knew how to paddle. Paddling once seemed like something I couldn't learn—something complex that required perfect timing, perfect dip, perfect push, perfect pull. When a graduate student of mine and I shared a kayak on Clear Creek Reservoir where we'd volunteered to teach high school students lessons on how to write braided essays, we made very little progress down the river. The high school students rowed so quickly away that the only thing they were going to learn from us was how academia stifled adequate rowing skills.

The next year, on a mid-semester, hooky-playing trip to Puerto Peñesca, my friend Shamah brought her paddleboard. I tried it. I fell into the Sea of Cortez every time I tried to stand up, but, on my knees, I figured out how to paddle forward. I did not look graceful and tall as Sarah did, riding the waves like a figurehead leading its boat, but I managed to make it back to shore without any help, tipping into the water only sixteen times or so. Climbing back onto a wave-bouncing board counts as a kind of success on its own.

Tall ponderosas line the length of Lake Mary, the lake upon which my paddleboard, Zora, and I floated. I measured with my thumb and forefinger to see how small the trees were. If I'm measuring the gap between what I think I can do and what I can actually do, it's as small as the space between my fingers but also as tall as the tree itself. Perspective is a gift. You would think we would use it more often to see the things we have a hard time seeing. How far away am I from the shore where my other dog, Bear, my husband, kids, and in-laws watched me? Were they worried that I seemed stuck? Could they see that no matter how much force I pushed into the oar, the board was not moving toward them? Wind had frothed the lake surface into white caps. Motorboats sped toward the dock to get out of the wind and waves. I held onto the board with my toes, Zora with her claws as the board bore the undulation. I should have knelt down on the board. I should have sat all the way down. I should have jumped off the back and kick-swam like an outboard motor, taking us to the shore.

But Erik had just paddled out with Zora on the back and returned to his parents and our kids no problem. I thought there was no reason I shouldn't have been able to do the same. I thought of his bigger shoulders. His thicker biceps. His extra foot of height. No. That wasn't it, I reasoned. The wind had come up stronger since he'd been out. It was hard but I would be fine. I just needed to put more energy into my paddling. We'll get there, I told Zora. I was willing to put the work in. Effort should be the great equalizer.

A paddleboard is efficient. It's light enough that you can row yourself up and down a peaceful lake like a gondolier, building muscle, the cool air wicking away your sweat. It's exercise without exhaustion. Your body weight plus the weight distribution and design of the board equals easy sailing. Adding a fifty-pound dog doesn't usually change that calculus—unless she senses you've been frozen in place, rowing against a wind so strong it makes her blink. As I dug deeper into the water, using every reserve I had to plow forward, a boat zoomed by, making big waves. One of them hit us harder than either of us was prepared for. I put the paddle hard down in the middle of the board, telling the water, Gandalf-like, that it shall not pass. But Zora had never seen *Fellowship of the Ring*. The wave whipped her like a dragon's tail into the abyss.

Zora flailed in the water, pawing at the board. I tried to pull her up but the board tipped furiously with all our weight on one side. I lay down on the board, grabbed her by her elbows. She looked at me with such panic: save me, her eyes pleaded. I jumped into the water, thinking maybe I could push her aboard but then neither she nor I had any leverage. Every time I touched the board, it drifted away from us. Zora tried to use me as her boat. She scratched my arms as I tried to hold her up, then I pushed her toward the board. It floated away again. Zora thrashed at the water, tiring. I could not get her up. I couldn't even keep the board near us. I pushed her one more time toward the boat. She clamored. She slipped off again. This time, she went under the water. She was going to drown in this lake. I was going to lose my dog.

I couldn't lose Zora. I couldn't let her drown. I screamed for help toward the shore where Erik sat, as small as the measuring space of index finger and thumb. On the far side of the lake, the actual trees loomed. We were closer than I'd noticed. I told Zora to swim. She started toward the board. "No. Swim toward the shore," I told her. She turned to paddle toward land. That's the nice thing about Zora. She speaks many languages, English being one of them.

I followed Zora, breast-stroking behind her paddle. Lake Mary is 2,000 feet across and though we were closer to the far side, we still had 700 or so feet to go. I could do that. When my sister Paige and I were pulled out by a riptide when we were kids, I swam with her on my back like I was a turtle and she was my shell until my dad swam out to save us. He took the role of turtle. I turned back to my kid self, trying to swim fast and hard. I followed them back, looking through the water until the ocean turned from blackness to silvery ocean floor.

But I was already exhausted from paddling, from trying to hoist Zora onto a slippery shuttle, from panic. I could not see the bottom of the lake any more than I could see the bottom of the ocean. I was so tired. What if I just stopped swimming?

But I didn't. Maybe I couldn't paddle against the wind. On the board, I'd been nothing but a short stump in the face of the wind. In the water, I couldn't get any leverage. Your force equals the work you do to move against water. This lake water supplied a constant coefficient. Thank goodness for dogs who make it to shore and turn to encourage you to pull your body toward them. She paced along the edge of the water until I made it to the sand. Then, she licked me like she hadn't seen me in a week.

When Erik realized I needed help, he jumped on the other paddle board, making it to me in five minutes or less. It seemed unfair, his speed, the way he didn't look back toward the shore he'd left with longing.

He came up, yelling. "What were you thinking? The wind is too strong. I told you that." Erik gets mad when he gets worried. I lay on the sand, thankful for the sound of his voice, for Zora's licking tongue, for solid ground.

But then Erik made the terrible observation that I'd have to get back on the paddleboard. "I can't take two boards, you, and Zora back across." I looked into the trees. Could I walk around the lake? Probably not before nightfall.

I climbed back onto the paddleboard, rowing on my knees. Erik took Zora. Halfway across the lake, I felt strong enough to stand up. The wind was still an asshole, but I'd made it one way across. I could make it back. I measured my breath and dug back into the water.

I am thinking about trust and why the climate crisis might be the particular global threat that, like an abysmal dragon, I obsess over. Climate change makes everyday weather untrustworthy. A sign at Warner's Nursery I read over and over again as I was stuck behind a tractor today said, "Winter doesn't last forever and spring never misses its turn." Although weather affects people—from floods to fires, dust bowls to famines—the premise is that the weather will turn fair again. Balanced. Even. But climate scientists warn the weather may become so unpredictable we can't rely on the promise that it will turn fair and balanced again. Weather, measured and prophesied by meteorologists, will become unpredictable. Normal ranges will widen until an iceberg could fit between them. And then the iceberg will melt and widen the ranges even further. Maybe spring won't follow winter. Or winter will never return.

In the plant world, success is often about height. The taller you are, the more you succeed. A succession forest grows by one-upping your fellow plants by growing faster and taller. But height doesn't always win. The bigger they are, the harder they fall, etc., etc. After a decimating fire, the plant cycle starts over again.[1] In the Pacific Northwest, at least before logging and fire suppression practices took hold, grasses, then shrubs, then pioneer species of Douglas fir gave way to hemlock and western red cedar. A climax forest is that prehistoric-seeming kind of forest like the one in which Hans and I pretended to hide from Sleestacks and dinosaurs and other threats from The *Land of the Lost*, one where you can imagine crawling into burls of redwood trunks to hide-out, snack on gigantic huckleberries, umbrella under mushrooms tall enough to stand under, hammock in the strong fronds of a giant fern. In California, the redwood forest is a climax forest. It's the rare combination of rain and soil, altitude and temperature that makes the redwoods grow 250 feet tall.

But height isn't everything. Success doesn't even have to come from trees. And forests aren't the only successful ecosystems. There are plants, like amaranth, that grow very tall, but not nearly as tall as a tree. These plants, some of which I grew in my yard in Portland, are a rusty maroon with large stamens, making them look a bit like Snuffleupagus from Sesame Street. The capacity of amaranth plants to sequester carbon is substantial. Amaranth, grown in particular terrain and climate, may even sequester more carbon than their ponderosa pine friends up the hill. If we're going to plant a billion, or a trillion trees, how many amaranth plants should we grow?

Think of a forest as being book smart—a literature major who has connected a thread from Hopkins's "Windhover" buckling in the air to Marianne Moore's "Jerboa" leaping its way through the Sahara to W. S. Merwin's advice that if you find you no longer believe, you should enlarge the temple.

Then think of a field of amaranth as being street smart—a plant so full of protein it sustained civilizations for millennia by adapting to different climates and by storing its extra energy in its seeds. Amaranth knows who to trust, which alleys to turn down, and where the best hideouts are. It's not a competition. Each kind of smart is a necessary adaptation.

Just as in the animal world, not all plant species are built the same. And not all plants thrive under the same conditions. Plants love water and sun but overwater a cactus and it will deliquesce from the inside. Plant shade-loving pea plants in too much sun, their leaves will crack and burn. Like animals, like microorganisms, plants adapt to different environments.

But unlike mammalian species who chemically convert oxygen to carbon dioxide in their lungs identically to each other, plant species can photosynthesize and respire differently from each other. We're familiar with the regular photosynthesis of trees, broadleaf plants, evergreens. These plants have it pretty easy. They find themselves with the right body in the right place. Like Erik, who paddles easily even against the wind, these plants absorb sunlight, using that energy to split carbon dioxide into carbon and oxygen. Most plants are so efficient they don't need to absorb all of the light spectrum—easy-have-it plants don't absorb weak, green wavelengths, which is why humans see most of these easy-loving plants as green. But natural selection sometimes gets bumped from easy to hard. Plants at the bottom of the ocean are nearly black because deep-water plants have to absorb every particle of light, including green wavelengths, they can. They don't reflect green leaves like surface plants. But the lucky green, sun-facing plants can afford to be inefficient. They don't need to use all their energy to build their cellulose structures.

Perhaps it had been naïve of me, with my lack of street smarts, to trust a babysitter or to trust the series of boyfriends that followed or the boys at college or humans in general, but is it now naïve to trust seasons? What is this snow? Just an unfaithful mistress who may not return again.

The problem with climate change is that other systems will become untrustworthy as well. Trees will exude carbon along with the oxygen. Microorganisms in soil will die, exhausting carbon. Sea ice, lost, will no longer reflect the sun's rays back into space and instead they will be absorbed into the ocean. The dark plants in the ocean might garner enough light to turn green right before our eyes.

The post-trauma therapist tells you your job is to rebuild trust. Therapists have a hard time specifying in what you should invest that trust. I think of people I know, some of whom I definitely trust, most of the time. I think of institutions like government, the academy, psychology. I trust them about half of the time. Natural forces? You can trust these most of the time: the sun does also rise. Winds come in April and May. But the snow? Maybe yes. Maybe no. The ground itself? It is trustworthy until seismic shifts make it shake.

In Inca and Aztec cultures, amaranth, not wheat, provided the primary food source. They relied on it, which is a kind of trust. More nutritious than even corn, amaranth can grow, once it germinates, in areas where rainfall is less than 200 millimeters a year. Mayan cultures dry-farmed amaranth. It formed the basis not only of a stable crop but was celebrated as a life-giving force and figured prominently in religious ceremonies.

When the Spanish began colonizing what is now called Guatemala and Mexico, they destroyed the amaranth crops, partly to make Indigenous people reliant on grain only the Spanish could provide and partly to destroy the ceremonial aspects of the grain, creating a gap which Catholic ceremonies would fill. It might be cynical to say you can trust that burning down people's livelihoods and destroying cultural artifacts might be the surest way to force people to buy your goods, plant your wheat, pray to your god but you can trust a street-smart cynic over a book-smart optimist any day. But I'm looking for a deeper trust. Neither cynical nor optimistic, neither street nor book. The kind of trust a person can have even lost in the forest or even if all the trees in the forest are gone. It's something like a combination of trust in the self and trust in the balance of the world. Perhaps a trust that you are part of the balance. Perhaps a trust that there is more than one kind of balance. What is the collective term for balance? An ecosystem.

I am looking for a different photosynthetic system. A different respiration system. A different efficiency. Or rather, what I am looking for is more than one—perhaps one where every calorie expresses oxygen instead of carbon. The trees have been doing all the hard work—the trees and plants of the Jurassic, chugging our cars, warming our houses, then cleaning up after us. The trees of the Holocene, absorbing their ancestors' gases, burned in the shafts of our engines. We've relied on trees for so long. Maybe it's time to share the burden. Our mammalian chemical exchanges could be persuaded to change—perhaps it's not the brute force of fossil fuel but the reflective power of the sun we could harness in our own cells: thoughtful photosynthesis. Algae as skin. A new story for these old bodies.

Amaranth sustained cultures across the Americas. Their seeds are full of protein, their plants can withstand drought, high elevations, and intense sunlight. To study the amaranth plant is to rethink how we understand the systems upon which we've come to rely. Yes, we might plant a billion trees. But perhaps we can plant a billion amaranth too. Perhaps we will find other plants to store more carbon than they exhaust as temperatures get higher. Perhaps we'll find some microorganisms to help soil sequester rather than release the carbon of their dead brethren. Perhaps we can trust in and bring back systems that have been eradicated by colonialism and capitalism but to do that, you have to search to hear the stories from voices that might be quieter than your loud and practiced voice.

Here's one bit of restoration that gives me some hope: Bringing seeds from their small farms in Guatemala, a group of Maya Achí women visited a woman named Beata Tsosie-Peña at her home in New Mexico. The seeds they carried had been hidden from soldiers who destroyed most of the crops in the civil war that had lasted the last fifty years, rerunning the Spanish colonizers original story, separating communities from their most basic livelihoods. As the soldiers advanced, Mayan farmers however collected handfuls of seeds, poured them into glass jars, and hid them under their floorboards.

Now that the war is over, for the moment at least, Qachuu Aloom (which means Mother Earth in the Maya Achí language), an Indigenous, women-led organization based in Rabinal, Guatemala travels across the country to share these native seeds. In California, they've given them to members of the Bishop Paiute tribe and with urban gardens in Los Angeles. In northern New Mexico, they've hosted gardening and cooking workshops in La Madera. Tsosie-Peña, together with Qachuu Aloom planted seeds in the community garden.[2]

Not only are these relationships between communities in the Southwest and Guatemalans restoring a crop that could sustain millions, especially those who live in high-desert climates, they're also repairing connections between people who had been severed by borders and settlers and soldiers intent on severing the connections between people.

This physical restitching. This seems like something one might be able to trust. As people move from place to place, not only do they bring heirloom seeds, they bring the microorganisms on the bottom of their shoes, the spores from the fruit of their mycorrhizae, water droplets in the corner of their eyes.

As they bring these seeds, they bring different ways of thinking. That trees aren't our only carbon saviors. Amaranth absorbs carbon differently than trees. The seeds themselves grew natively in the United States which promises a source of protein different from wheat. Mayans traveling from Guatemala mimic trading habits of the deep past. They restore old pathways and ignore militarized borders. This back-and-forth seed-sharing recovers old grooves and patterns in land and agriculture. Like Haraway's cat's cradle, this crisscrossing of paths and tracks refreshes the maps we think we know.[3] This string twisting requires a kind of trust. That things may fall apart but somewhere they come back together. These web-like paths across the American continents look a lot like a respiratory system—tracks of veins leading up and into lungs, hearts pulling chemicals from lungs, pressing back different chemicals into arteries. The planet's chemistry is out of balance, but stoichiometry is an art. We just need to think like plants.

I grew a little taller after the paddleboard experience. People say you shrink as you get older but it's not true. Height isn't about self-confidence or shame. Height is about how much you layer the stories and connect the dots. Height isn't just about trees—it's about the height of amaranth too. Height is a way of seeing. It's possible I am standing on reams and reams of paper, now measuring myself. I may indeed be standing on the remains of Giant Sequoias whose air I breathe. I take my measuring tape wherever I go. I eat amaranth for breakfast and I measure. I teach my students about Herbert and Hopkins, and I measure. I stand next to that apple tree that is still alive after three years and we're both getting taller. The more systems—apple, iambic, dog, paddle, seed—I have to measure, the taller I get, and I've learned to trust these myriad measuring sticks, bookish, street, shaky, chimera and chemical as they may be.

14

On the Trail

"Could you say it one more time. I know you don't quite feel comfortable with the word, but could we just try it?"

I nodded. I'm game for anything. The stakes are high as is my ability to compartmentalize my emotions. My ability to act like an actor, however, hasn't been tested. There are three cameras on me. A microphone hanging from a jib above. A reflector behind me. A make-up artist wasn't on hand and my own make artistry amounts to eyeliner applied often in a squiggly line and mascara on at least three of my eyelashes.

"I'll try it." I told Amrutha. She'd been the one to invite me to be part of this advertisement campaign. She had interviewed me for an hour before I came down from Flagstaff to Phoenix to be filmed. Amrutha warned me that the experience might be grueling. I have two teenagers, two dogs, three cats, a husband, a job as a writer, a teacher, program director, an editor, and a conference organizer. I know gruel, I thought. I was wrong.

"Are you ready?"

The gaffer counts down. Take 8.

"Repeat after me," Amrutha said.

"No one should have to give birth to their rapist's child," she said solemnly.

"No one should have to give birth to their rapist's child," I said, hoping I sounded as serious as she.

"I was raped," she said unequivocally.

"I was raped." I said with a small tremor in my voice.

"I would be forced to bear my rapist's child."

I breathe hard. "I would be forced to bear my rapist's child."

Ever since *Roe v. Wade* was overturned by the Supreme Court, I've been writing and speaking about how ruinous Dobbs is to reproductive freedom. There was a fundamental shift in how I perceived myself. I no longer felt that my body was my own. I saw myself as if from above and thought I looked smaller. I said "fuck them" to the court, out loud, but my voice sounded softer than I remember it sounding. I looked at my arms. How much weight could they even lift now?

I have never felt I was as powerful as a man. When I speak, I usually start strong but sometimes end up off topic or rambling. I can carry seventy pounds of groceries or of children but I'm shitty at digging holes to plant apple trees. I give up halfway down and hope that the tree's roots figure out how to attach themselves to soil—hang on like a sticky octopus, I tell the roots. They don't listen. I write and write novels and poems and essays and sometimes they get published but not often in the most visible places. I believe that words can lead to change, but I'm not sure my words ever do.

But about the molestation and the abortion, after Dobbs came down, whatever shame I'd felt fell away. No longer was I going to call what the babysitter did "sexual interference." No longer was I going to hedge or whisper when I said the word "abortion." I understood in that moment what the babysitter and what the Supreme Court had done were stripes of the same cloth. My body was subject to another's desires regardless of what I wanted. I wanted to come back to my body. I wanted to feel powerful. I wanted to feel big. I wanted my hands to type words that effected change.

But, as I sat in the living room in a house in Scottsdale lent to the film crew by a woman also willing to be filmed for an Arizona Abortion Access commercial, and was being fed lines by Amrutha, I felt disembodied. I had never called what happened with the babysitter rape. I had barely come to call it "molestation."

"I know you're uncomfortable calling what happened to you 'rape.' But would you be willing to try it?"

Listen. I will try anything once. And I would have done anything to encourage people to vote yes on proposition 139 which, in Arizona, would enshrine reproductive rights into the constitution. No longer would we be whiplashed by a state supreme court revivifying a total abortion ban from the 1864 Territorial Constitution. No longer would we have to wait for our Republican legislators to be terrified to lose their seats when it became clear most Arizonans want abortion to be safe and legal so they would renounce that state supreme court ruling. We wouldn't have to depend on having a Democratic governor to insure that for at least four years, abortion rights would rule the land.

I did say the word.

Over the last two years, I've told my abortion story to anyone who would listen.

And I'm grateful for the listening. I believe in the power of storytelling. But it's made me think too about way we use our stories. It's one thing to write a story, especially for the first time. It is empowering. You get to shape your narrative. You draw the details. You choose the verbs. You take that experience back. That which was directed by your abuser's. But what does it mean when a director tells you what to say? Turning your story into fodder for political purposes does mean you have to disconnect from your story. It's no longer your story. Now it's the public's story. The campaign's story. Even when you express your experience, you are directed to express it according to the director's directions.

I was on stage in Miami an hour before the show started. I read my piece, avoiding poet-voice, coming down hard on the words shame, as Andrea, the director, instructed me.

On August 18th, 2022, two months after the Dobbs decision came down from the Supreme Court overturning *Roe v. Wade*, I published an essay for *The New York Times*. "I predict that my seventeen-year-old daughter will become a doctor," I wrote. "She knows everything about the gut biome, dopamine and herniated disks. *She does not look away at times when others might*—like when my mother unexpectedly texted me pictures of a cyst she had removed from the back of her head, sitting bloody in a specimen cup." "That's exactly what I would do," my daughter said. "*You have to show people.*"

I ended with, "A local reporter interviewed me and asked if I had a photo of myself at eleven. For the first time since I wrote the article, I broke down. It's one thing to tell the story of a girl at eleven who went through these things. But to look at her photo and see her, alone and scared and so on the verge of something life-defining. *Or worse, a month younger, having no idea what was coming, I think, what if she had been forced to continue that pregnancy?* What would the next year's photo look like? I wouldn't have been able to recognize that girl.

Now, I can look at my twelve-year-old-girl photo and know that she's been through a lot, but that with time and love and community, she could be here with you to make it clear, none of our bodies should be subject to another body's whims, or anybody's laws."

The underlined words? They are underlined because Andrea, said, "Stop. You have to emphasize '*You have to show people.*' You. Have. To. Show. People."

I tried again.

Andrea. "No. You're swallowing your lines. Say it like this: *She does not look away at times when others might.*"

I tried again.

"OK. Better. But this time really slow down when you get to shame."

Instead of trying again, I said, "OK. I'm done. I can't do this anymore."

For a minute, I meant that I couldn't do it at all. I walked backstage, stood behind the other readers. They could take their turn having their story reframed, reshot, reemphasized. I would do a good job. I read on stage all the time. I knew how to do this.

I would explain my forcefulness to my friend and director, Andrea, later. But for now, I wanted to save that forcefulness for when the audience of the Beth Am Synagogue was packed with would-be supporters. If I was going to use my story to help Florida's Amendment 4, which needed 60 percent of the electorate to vote yes get passed, I had to do what I knew I had to do. Both Amrutha and Andrea are my friends. They're also experts on how to message effectively. But somewhere between Amrutha asking me to call the babysitter a rapist and Andrea asking me to slow down on the word shame, I had become comfortable enough sharing my story that I finally felt like I was expert on it.

The best and worst part of sharing my story was how many other stories I elicited. After the reading at the synagogue, women lined up to tell me how they too had been abused. It is horrible to know how many women have stories. It is beautiful to know they're willing to share them. Stories beget stories, and, even if the content is hard stuff, two people sharing stories forge a connection, and, if they're like everything else in the natural world, those connections will multiply.

Nature is abundance. So much oxygen. So much carbon. So many trees even if those trees are planted in places they weren't natively born. It's not that there is too much carbon in the world. It's that too much of that black carbon has burned into invisible CO_2. I almost envy early-industrial London when soot covered brick. When the gypsy moth adapted its color from light gray to black to match the now charcoal colored bark of trees. At least the results of burning so much coal were evident to the eye.

There are patches of ancient forest left to absorb what carbon they can. Their life cycle moves from soil microbes, across mycelia, pushes through hyphae which feed the roots and light itself draws those nutrients up while pushing its own sustenance down. And even these second, third, growth trees—it's not bad to plant them. They do what they can with the carbon. We are acculturated to look for trees—big, strong, manly beasts that are going to save us from this stew of burned, prehistoric, once also carbon-sucking, trees.

But trees are not the only fruit. Soil microbes themselves absorb carbon dioxide. Mushrooms store it. And amaranth plants, surviving on just those two millimeters of water, even with their reddish, Snuffleupagus color can take in more CO_2 than most green plants twice as big as them. Imagine a planet covered in red, fluffy stuffed animals—their red tails wagging as if to say, "come here, you planet hottening molecule. I'll tuck you in, under my fur, and keep you safe with me." And that's just one story by one plant. There are so many carbon lovers and each has a story to tell.

It's one thing to shape your own stories. It's another to teach students to shape theirs. It is yet another to share your story with other adults who are willing to share theirs too. I taught as part of the Diné Institute a seminar about putting your body in a place. We nearly canceled because of COVID-19 but decided to move forward with distance learning, hosting seminars via Zoom. It was extra tricky to teach a seminar about putting bodies in a place through the ethereal means of video conferencing, but these teacher-fellows committed to the process even if the process had been transformed.

Perhaps it's thanks to COVID-19's challenges that we quickly delved into stories about our lives. Even if we couldn't put our bodies in place, we could communicate how our classes and our teaching were being transformed by the pandemic. We learned a new kind of responsiveness which transcended distance and geographical boundaries and made us close peers because of our shared difficulties.

This course differed from other seminars because teacher-fellows were asked to write their own stories before they incorporated what they experienced from the seminar into their curriculum. I was incredibly lucky to work with these fellows who were willing to do two projects, write an essay and develop a curriculum unit, over those next nine months even with those fundamental challenges.

One of the early conclusions of our discussions is that when teaching, the students often deliver received stories or "stock stories" as my friend and English Education prof and expert, Angie Hansen calls them because the students assume the teacher wants to hear the perceived "correct" story. So, for example, students write from a distant, third-person point of view about New Mexican history. When DeLyssa Begay, my coauthor here, taught about the Long Walk, when the Diné were removed from their homes and force-marched to Fort Redondo, the students write the story with the exact framework and language DeLyssa had used to teach them the history. DeLyssa, in taking this seminar, wanted to find ways to invite the students to change the framework, change the reception, change the dominant narrative.

The Nigerian novelist Chimamanda Ngozi Adichie, in "The Danger of a Single Story," a popular Ted Talk, narrates example after example about how one version of a story can quash others. As a child, she read books about kids with blond hair and blue eyes whose primary fruit was apples. Thus, at first, she wrote books about kids with blond hair and blue eyes who ate apples. It wasn't until she was introduced to books written by Chinua Achebe and Camara Laye that she understood how many stories existed and could exist—ones with kids who eat mangoes instead of apples. The single story is dangerous. "But to insist on the negative stories is to flatten my experience and to overlook the many other stories that formed me," Adichie says. The numbers, as absurdly abundant as they may be, each deserve their own story.

In this seminar, teacher-fellows narrated their own life experience. One teacher-fellow wrote about the healing powers of sagebrush and how the climate crisis may change access to these important plants. Another wrote about the history of the Navajo Preparatory Academy and how its boarding school past makes an impact on its present. Another student wrote about the birthing tree her mother claimed to protect her children's placentas. These essays pushed back against the dominant narrative, creating a path for their students to do the same. By focusing on putting their individual bodies in a particular place, each writer established her own idiosyncratic voice and experience. DeLyssa Begay wrote,

> Sheep manure. I wear a different pair of shoes because the smell stays on the fabric, and it does not simply fade away. The sheep corral is made of the grey and dried old boards of a felled horse stable, along with the diamond wire mesh fence from that old stable. Recycled and reused materials from a different part of the homestead. The sheep corral partly dug into a mound of a hill, so that it insulates the sheep – cooler in the summer with a covering, and warmer in the winter as it breaks the wind. Once a year, my brother takes out the posts and fence to scrape away the manure and spread it out on the side of the hill. It does not stay long as the wind and monsoon rains carry the manure towards the yellow-white sandstone canyon.

No one but DeLyssa could write that story. The fullness of her description of the fences, the fabric, the manure are so embodied, both in place and narrator. By writing her own story, she found a way to help her students write not the canned version of their history, but their individual, unique story. Telling stories elicits stories.

It wasn't until I published the abortion essay in the *Times*, that I knew how a story with a wide-audience could affect people. But what people mainly sent were words of support.

"For the last week my neighbor's secondhand *New York Times* has been spread in sections over my kitchen table while my kid and I have navigated shifting from home school to public school and getting our home ready for two brothers who will join our family in a matter of weeks. I started reading your article last Saturday. As I drink coffee late into the morning and it has been sitting with me since I got interrupted from finishing it. The strength of your truth is palpable. Your imagery makes a hot button topic real and personal. It is an article that I hope is widely read. Finishing it this afternoon as I am easing into a long weekend has given me much needed reflection time. I look forward to reading more that you have written"—Cathy

"This is brave. This is magic. You are a bad ass." Liz

"Dear Professor Walker,

I too have a 17-year-old girl, although I think she is more likely to be a human rights lawyer than a doctor.
Your op-ed in the Times today was brave, impressive, tragic, and sad. Thank you for opening up to the world, for showing the world that the right decision is often not an easy one, for sharing the grief and pain and social opprobrium that are visited on young women for the decisions they make. And thank you for giving a personal account of how the Supreme Court has violated our trust, and reversed decades of progress.
With thanks for using your voice, and using it so powerfully,

Josh"

Lawrence O'Donnell interviewed me about the article for his news program on MSNBC. He asked me,

You begin your essay in 'The Times' asking people to look at this, acknowledging that it is difficult. It is—there are graphic passages in your piece that you want people to look at and consider because you believe that this subject needs to be discussed in this kind of detail. What have you found in your own approach to talking about it is the most effective way of making people understand this?

And I answered, "I have written about what happened to me when I was a kid, obliquely, in the books I have written. I have written about it in different magazines. But it's always sort of under the cover, under the guise of something else.

And I finally realized this is the time where we need to speak up and tell our stories. I want to encourage everyone to tell their stories."

Then, more sharply, O'Donnell asked,

You are the second woman who's written an op-ed piece like this for the 'New York Times,' about having an abortion at that age. The other has joined us on this program. And I know it is a difficult subject to write about and to discuss here. And so I want to do this with the utmost respect for how difficult it is. You make the point in your piece—and this is something that I have seen, I've seen some commentary, some comment to this effect. That some abortion rights supporters worry that devoting too much energy to the stories of young children who need abortions narrows the cause. What is your reaction to that?

I shared his concern.

Right. I mean to some degree, I agree that it does narrow the cause. Again, it says that, oh, well, there are these exceptions. The fact is that, if you look at the comments on my *Times* article today, you will see so many stories of so many young people becoming impregnated at such a young age. And that inability to imagine not accessing—to be able to access abortion—I don't want to use, necessarily, this story to say that it is only for those particular cases. And as a kid, it is different, right? Obviously, I did not have control over the situation. I did not have control over even just making my choices—I could not explain why what happened to me has happened to me. I still have a hard time explaining what had happened to me. But to imagine that our lives are supposed to be purely set based on what our bodies do naturally, and what our choices are limited by what our government says, it has become very striking to me and very different world that we are living in.

And then, O'Donnell gave me one reward for telling your hard story, "Nicole Walker gets tonight's Last Word."

Although I had the last word of the night, it was more like I had the first word. People emailed me their own stories. Their daughter's stories. For some, an abortion did not equal travesty, or even narrative. They called it "procedure," like having bunions removed. A pair of ob-gyns posted actual pictures of aborted fetuses. The truth is not the bloodied fetuses of the anti-abortion poster. The truth is, the photo of eight-week fetuses looked a lot like fish food—flat, disorganized floating flecks.

That women have been led to believe that the embryos that stitch themselves into their uterus are fully-formed babies, clenching their fists against removal not only destroys some women's futures, it ensures that even if they do choose an abortion, they will spend the rest of their lives believing they killed something that resembled them. Which that fetus does look like, if you, woman, look like fish food.

I wrote in that article that the "freedom to choose" wasn't what I experienced in 1984. The argument I mean to make is that my life was not sent on an unbending trajectory. I did not become a prostitute. I did not end up in jail. I did not become addicted to white drugs. I did not kill myself. My life unfolded variously and surprisingly.

Neither I nor my life is perfect. I have been affected. When you re-build a forest, it doesn't come back like it was. Replanted trees can grow spindly or too close together. They're prone to fire. This is not yet an old growth forest I've got running around in this head of mine. I have a hard time filtering what I say, which means on a given day, several people aren't speaking to me.

Max is still mad at me because he is still short. I said to him, "My friend at work, Mark Gula, told me that he had been a shrimp throughout junior high. Now he's one of the tallest guys I know."

I reminded him that I started smoking when I was twelve. Maybe my genes meant for me to be taller. I told him that he needed to stop sneaking out at sleepovers or he'd get arrested.

"Well, you were arrested when you were a kid."

"No, I was not, Max."

"You would have been. For smoking on school property."

"Max. It was the '80s. People did not get arrested for smoking. Even on school property." I told Beya that story. She said, "Hell, we had a smoking section at Trevor Brown," her high school in Phoenix.

I asked Max, "Do you know what is worse than smoking. Climate change. Doesn't it worry you? What do your teachers teach you about it?"

"No one really cares."

"No one really cares what?"

"I mean, no one thinks we're going to live that long."

"We didn't either when we were your age. Nuclear death. AIDS death. Reagan death. But then we lived. What are you going to do if you live but everything's even more fucked up?"

He shrugged. He's twelve. What else was he going to say?

I worry about the catastrophist's way of thinking. If the planet is going to burn down, blow up, or be hit by an asteroid, then why care about the individual stories? Why do the stories that show you might care the smallest amount about how your actions or inactions might affect the future. It's lazy to be a catastrophist and yet, I feel like most of the time, I too lie down on the ground to imagine the big end. But then you get up and get to work because there is stitching to be done for the people, your community, your story, the ground itself. I knit by talking. I should try to also knit by listening.

The forests are having a hard time. So are we. It's hard to pretend everything is normal when in 2023, we had record snowfall and in 2025, we had none, when hurricane Helene destroyed towns 500 miles inland, when fires burned over 5,000 homes and businesses in Los Angeles, when the person ostensibly in charge of the country believes windmills cause cancer and kills "an unbelievable number of birds" and wants to drill for more oil. Tech bros are suing farmers in California for not giving them land. The albedo effect is dissipating like the clouds that make it. The acidification in the ocean destroys animals' abilities to create shells using calcium carbonate. People in our so-called society are left unshelled and unhoused.

Erik and I came close to that idyll ideal of living in a forest when we moved to Flagstaff. Although there is no giant blue lake, there is the small, murky

Lake Mary where we paddle board and where some of us nearly drowned. We didn't know how bad the fires were going to become. We didn't think that our homeowner's insurance would increase by $4,000 a year. We didn't know how many pine needles we'd have to rake to keep a perimeter of safety around our house. We, being from the high mountain desert of Salt Lake thought we knew dry. We did not know dry until our lungs were filled with smoke.

It was twenty-five years ago, in graduate school, that I went to my first talk about climate change. Most scientists, Dr. Chapman laid out, predicted that the southwest will become drier although some forecasts predicted a wetter future. I missed Oregon. I would have, if I could have chosen, the future with more rain. But a single person does not, it turns out, get to choose.

Every year that Erik and I have lived here, a fire has sparked closer to town. The snow falls in inches now, not feet. The monsoon storms skipped entire years. Erik and I argue about how much rain is too little rain. Too little snow. We know that at some point, this town will be too fire prone or too out of water to stay. What do you do with a story of drought? How do you build a home when the ground under you will turn from soil to sand? Perhaps it's a *Tank Girl* kind of punk rock to live in the high mountain desert but Erik and I lost our street cred as soon as we began to utter "breast pump" on a daily basis. Now the pumps we talk about are those that pump water from wells drilled deeper every year.

The models that predicted future climate scenarios based on what we know now were clear: a half a degree in Celsius predicted some ocean rise, additional forest fires, drought, flooding. As the models raised the degrees a tenth a point by tenth of point, the more exacerbated the disasters became. It's getting wetter in the Northeast, but with rain, not snow, so ticks and other pests don't die. They feast all year on the blood of moose. Some people call these exsanguinated beasts "ghost moose," for their coats turn nearly white as the insects take their toll. In the southeast, the climate oscillates between dry and hot and wet and warm. Plants grow abundantly. Then, deprived of their native humidity, become fodder for flame. Most models show the west becoming drier, although there is one climate model though that showed the southwest climate could turn wetter, becoming more like the Pacific Northwest. As air warms, it can hold more moisture. "I'll choose that one," I told my friend,

Jeff. "I miss Portland." As if climate change planned to take my poll. I've been wishing for that model to take hold ever since.

The day after Kamala lost the election, I walked into the faculty department and burst into tears. I hadn't cried in front of Erik or Zoë or Max or Beya as the three of us watched the day become darker and darker. But something about this group of people that I've known, at least some of them, for sixteen years, and know that most of them shared in the disappointment and fear of what kind of authoritarianism was coming down, made me burst into tears. I sat in the front row of the meeting watching my friend, our department chair, watch tears run down my face as she led the meeting.

Water makes its own lens. A wet pine needle—divining rod, drinking straw, kaleidoscope pulls different metaphors from it than a dry one—accusing finger, magician's wand, firestarter—does. I have held lamb's ear to my cheek and unticked kernels from wild wheat. I have picked mushrooms in deserts and rainforests—shrimpers, little brown jobbers, milk caps, amanita muscaria, chanterelles, boletes, lobsters. The forest floor bursts with babies. The mother mycorrhizae lay underground, stretching her back, and waits for the water to tickle her into birth.

Later, I sat in my office, loudly listening to *The Clash's* "Know Your Rights," hoping my students heard the music through the door and noted both the rights and the ironies. I hoped they were dumb enough, and brave enough, to actually try free speech. If we were going to be forced to live in a police state, we should at least try to write some songs and poems about it. At least we have the "art will save us" plan to work with. LA burned as the new administration planned to burn the constitution. But, as we know, a fire can't destroy everything forever. The only way to grow another forest is to spread as much mycelia onto the ash as possible. Once I was done crying, I realized I had to do something.

I emailed every woman in my contact list and asked them to join my group called Coalescing 2025 in response to Project 2025. The first meeting, we introduced ourselves and noted one action we wanted to take. The second meeting, we talked about the only way back was through art. The third meeting,

I pitched them my idea: Send a book to anyone in an information desert in order to undermine book bans, to make some noise in places where conservative operatives take over radio stations during elections to spread fear about immigration and government intrusion, where Fox News runs nonstop, like it does on military bases. In the 1920s, the Postmaster General burned newsletters advocating for unions and promoting socialism. We're going to take our post office back. We're going to send our art into the world. Some people who receive books will toss them. But some might give it to a friend. Or someone might actually crack one open. Maybe one of the hundreds we send will be read cover to cover. It's like throwing stones into sea to get the oceans to rise, but hey look. The oceans are rising. We can pretend to thank the stones.

What has been lifesaving as we watch the US Constitution be fed through the shredder by billionaires and a man who laughs while he sends aspiring Americans to maximum security prisons in other countries is the way the resistance rises up. The Coalescing 2025 group, the Flagstaff Community Coalition, Indivisible, the lawyers and independent media who push back, the people who track every assault on democracy and post on Bluesky each shine a light that you can see from the dark abyss. In this extreme time, we send morse code in these signals of light, just as trees synchronize the electrical signals they send to each other during a solar eclipse.[1]

I walk a lot. I walked in the duff of Oregon forests. I must have millions of spores stuck to my feet. I walked along the Great Salt Lake and in the field behind my house before the Mormon ward house was built. I walked across the street to the babysitter's house. I walked up the stairs to the woman's clinic. I walked to Chadbourne Lane and I walked to Stansbury Lake where I put my spore-covered feet on the board of a windsurfer and made it halfway across the lake.

I walked among the prehistoric ferns with Hans as we hid from Sleestacks and toward that first yellow undulating cap of a chanterelle with Drew. I walked with my sisters to my dad's memorial and with my mom to my grandma's funeral. I walked around my aunt's condo the week after her death wondering whether it was in poor taste to take the Hank Williams album home for Erik. The comedian Stephen Wright joked, "Anywhere is within walking distance, if you have the time." I, who have always been in such a hurry, am surprised by how much walking I do. And still have to do.

For Erik's campaign for school board, we go door to door in a neighborhood I've never seen before. Small cities, like big ones, divide and then tuck themselves into neighborhoods. These neighborhoods take on their own character. Paradise Hills is made up of one street, but that street leads to an unending number of Forest Service trails. I live in Country Club Neighborhood with an Homeowners Association that dictates what color we can paint our houses and collects dues for a lake where we are not allowed access.

So many little mushroom spores attach to my feet. Erik and I take those spores to a neighborhood we'd never visited as we knocked on doors. Shuffling our feet along the sidewalks of this part of town where people grow grass like they missed the Midwest and who latch short gates across their front yards, mycelia roll out from the bottom of my shoe, tying one front porch to another. We knock on doors to try to get people to vote, in particular for Erik, but for other candidates too. Erik goes one way, I go another. I can practically see the white of the mycorrhizal fungi sponging underneath our feet. I knock on a door and a woman, who must have been eighty-years-old, opens it and invites me in. Her little dog barks at me. Perhaps he can smell the mycorrhizae on me.

"Just ignore him. He's just trying to protect me. He's not used to strangers."

I want to say, I'm not a stranger. I live in Flagstaff. But that kind of overfamiliarity can make people not trust me. I want to be trusted.

I unreel my spiel. "I'm just here, hoping you'll vote for my husband. He's running for school board. Public schools are for everyone, and he wants to make them great for every kid."

"Can you sit for a bit? I'm just watching this football game and having my morning beer."

A morning beer. Maybe Flagstaff *is* the kind of town you should stay in forever.

I don't take her up on the beer, but I do stay while she tells me about her husband who passed away a few years before. She tells me about her kids who went to Coconino High, the same school Zoë and Max attend. She says she had lived in Flagstaff for sixty years and hasn't called anywhere home in just as long.

When I leave, she says, "Come by, any time." And I think that maybe I will, although without the auspices of canvassing for a campaign, I don't really know how to excuse a visit.

I walk to the next house, thinking of her and her morning beer and how she must know the neighbors who I would visit next. Between her house and that, I picture mycelia filaments extending between the houses. As I walk, I can feel their gossamer tendrils stretch between house and mailbox, lawn and road. I can imagine that even on this October sidewalk, mycorrhizae could stitch itself between the cracks. Under the Kentucky bluegrass that squares the houses, the mycorrhizae inch back toward the forest at the base of Mount Elden and along the canyon walls of Schulz Pass. Threads and threads extend.

I will tell this lady's story over and over because an eighty-year-old drinking a morning beer made me happy. That story stitches its way around town like the mycorrhizae. The neighbor listens and the guys at the bar listen and my students listen, and Erik and Max and Zoë listen to me tell it ten times. This story flutters, one tiny story among billions. If I had the ears of the trees, maybe I could hear them all.

I go to that field behind my house before the church existed. I go to the ground before my house was built. I go to the field before the road. I go to the cottonwoods. I go back to a community. I go to a city. I go back to a river and a river dammed and a river undammed. I go into the forest—it's not pristine, not ancient. Maybe third, even fourth growth trees planted by timber companies when they realized that the New World forests were not actually inexhaustible. I sit on the ground. There's mullein, an invasive plant, but I tug one of its soft leaves off and rub it against my cheek. It would make good toilet paper. An ant climbs the rungs of lupine's ladder. I gather a handful of dirt. What do I know about this dirt? It doesn't feel mycorrhizal. I'm not sure what kind of microorganisms this top layer of ground might be found with a microscope—it doesn't feel very alive, but I put it back down gently, just in case.

I've been looking for you, dear soils, dear microbes, amaranths, Douglas firs, fungi, western red cedars, ponderosa pines, chanterelles, cigarettes, paintings, stories of walking, baby dolls and real babies, men who were trees and men who were parts of forests. A mother of mycelia and a mother of girls. A collection of collectives. What is the collective term for snow? What is the collective term for stories? What is the collective term for microorganisms? What does it mean to start again. We are the end of progress and the beginning. What an ancient forest we are building.

Glossary

Ecological succession is the process by which the mix of species and habitat in an area changes over time. Gradually, these communities replace one another until a "climax community"—like a mature forest—is reached, or until a disturbance, like a fire, occurs. Ecological succession is a fundamental concept in ecology.

Ecology is the study of how living organisms interact with each other and their environment. It focuses on understanding the relationships between living things and their surroundings, including other organisms and the physical world. Essentially, ecology helps us understand how organisms live together and how they affect their environment.

An **ecosystem** is a community of living organisms interacting with each other and their physical environment, forming a self-sustaining system. It includes both the living (biotic) and non-living (abiotic) components of an area, and the relationships between them.

Hyphae are long, branching, filamentous structure of a fungus, oomycete, or actinobacterium. In most fungi, hyphae are the main mode of vegetative growth, and are collectively called a mycelium.

Humus is the dark, organic material that forms in soil when plant and animal matter decays. When plants drop leaves, twigs, and other material to the ground, it piles up. This material is called leaf litter. When animals die, their remains add to the litter. Over time, all this litter decomposes.

Mycelium (pl.: mycelia) is a root-like structure of a fungus consisting of a mass of branching, thread-like hyphae. Its normal form is that of branched, slender, entangled, anastomosing, hyaline threads.

Mycorrhizae are a symbiotic relationship, meaning a mutually beneficial partnership, between the roots of a plant and a fungus. The fungus helps the plant absorb more water and nutrients from the soil, while the plant provides the fungus with sugars from photosynthesis.

Notes

Chapter 1

1   Gilles Deleuze, a French philosopher, and Felix Guattari, a French psychoanalyst, propose in their book *A Thousand Plateaus* a system of describing how literature and language can work like rhizomes. In the introduction they posit a definition of rhizome that they'll use as a metaphor in the same way Haraway uses Cat's Cradle as a metaphor for thinking. As opposed to binary thinking, which is how much of Judeo-Christian thought has organized itself: occident versus orient, white versus black, body versus mind, female versus male, Democrat versus Republican, Christian versus atheist, Deleuze and Guattari suggest that "Nature doesn't work that way: in nature, roots are taproots with a more multiple, lateral, and circular system of ramification, rather than a dichotomous one." The generosity of the multiple, the lateral, the circular is that it can destabilize power structures. In binary systems of thought, it's easy to assign positive and negative traits to occident versus orient, mind versus body, or male versus female because positive and negatives themselves are binary. In college, in the single psychology course I took, I conducted an experiment that was really just a list of words that attached to gender: men were assertive, woman aggressive. Men were strong while women were bitchy. Men were funny, women ditzy. It wasn't a great experiment because it was so obvious. Binaries create hierarchies, better runs to worse. That's why women the ones who scrub floors. Deleuze and Guattari describe a possible way of seeing that topples the hierarchy model and distributes meaning on a planar field. Everything concatenates and influences. This is where we get post-structuralism in literary criticism. There is no center, no single ideology, not one over another. Instead, fragments and pieces push and move and convey against and with each other.

Chapter 2

1   "Every Rug Tells a Story," Thrumming. https://thrumming.net/every-rug-tells-a-story (accessed September 15, 2025).

Chapter 6

1 "Could spotted owls benefit from forest fires?" Penn State University. https://www.psu.edu/news/research/story/could-spotted-owls-benefit-forest-fires (accessed September 15, 2025).

Chapter 7

1 Deleuze and Guattari highlight the hierarchical systems inherent in psychoanalytic theories. "Psychoanalysis cannot change its method in this regard: it bases its own dictatorial power upon a dictatorial conception of the unconscious. Psychoanalysis's margin of maneuverability is therefore very limited. In both psychoanalysis and its object, there is always a general, always a leader (General Freud)." If all our systems of thought reinforce binary thinking, then the "healing" of a fractured mind is to set itself whole and apart—I am an individual who is fully realized. I can see myself as separate from you, capable of self-sufficiently taking care of myself. But if you take "healing" from a more rhizomatic approach, instead of reducing or interpreting the unconscious, one could, by spinning out the fractured through multiple iterations one could "produce the unconscious, and with it new statements, different desires: the rhizome is precisely this production of the unconscious."

Chapter 9

1 Deleuze and Guattari use their post-structural, philosophical language to underpin what Stevens and Weil describe. They consider rhizomatic thinking to have immanence—a thinking that spreads out and through, just like the mycorrhizal fungi that stretch their web-like mycelia through the forest floor, giving nutrients to trees, negotiating chemical dispensation with microorganisms. The meaning comes in the connections, the abundant starting up again after wiping out. The important point is that the root-tree and canal-rhizome are not two opposed models: the first operates as a transcendent model and tracing, even if it engenders its own escapes; the second operates as an immanent process that overturns the model and outlines a map, even if it constitutes its own hierarchies, even if it gives rise to a despotic channel. It is not a question of this or that place on earth, or of a given moment in history, still less of this or that category of thought. It is a question of a model that is perpetually in construction or collapsing, and of a process that is perpetually prolonging itself, breaking off and starting up again.

2 "Inscape, Instress & Distress," Commonweal. https://www.commonwealmagazine.org/inscape-instress-distress (accessed September 15, 2025).

3 Robin Wall Kimmerer, "Speaking of Nature," *Orion Magazine*, March/April 2017.

Chapter 10

1 https://japansociety.org/news/japans-forests-good-days-and-bad-rhythms-of-damage-and-recovery.

2 "Deforestation and Forest Loss," Our World in Data. https://ourworldindata.org/deforestation (accessed September 15, 2025).

3 G. Bala, K. Caldeira, M. Wickett, T. J. Phillips, D. B. Lobell, C. Delire, and A. Mirin, "Combined climate and carbon-cycle effects of large-scale deforestation," *Proc. Natl. Acad. Sci. U.S.A.* 104, no. 16 (2007): 6550–5. https://doi.org/10.1073/pnas.0608998104.

Chapter 11

1 "Small Pests, Big Problems: The Global Spread of Bark Beetles," Yale Environment 360. https://e360.yale.edu/features/small-pests-big-problems-the-global-spread-of-bark-beetles (accessed September 15, 2025).

2 "Catholic clergy in Illinois sexually abused more than 1,900 minors, state attorney general says in report," CBS News. https://www.cbsnews.com/news/illinois-catholic-clergy-sexually-abused-over-1900-minors (accessed September 15, 2025).

3 "5 Ways Climate Change Impacts Forests," NC State University. https://cnr.ncsu.edu/news/2021/08/5-ways-climate-change-impacts-forests (accessed September 15, 2025).

Chapter 12

1 A. Gessler, M. Schaub, and N. G. McDowell, "The role of nutrients in drought-induced tree mortality and recovery," *New Phytologist* 214, no. 2 (2017): 513–20. https://nph.onlinelibrary.wiley.com/doi/10.1111/nph.14340 (accessed September 15, 2025).

2 "Meet the Woman Restoring Native American Peaches to the Southwest," Atlas Obscura. https://www.atlasobscura.com/articles/navajo-peaches (accessed September 15, 2025).

3 Ibid.

Chapter 13

1. Deleuze and Guattari see the image of the tree, especially the singular, height-bound tree, as stultifying the ways we look at things. "It is odd how the tree has dominated Western reality and all of Western thought, from botany to biology and anatomy, but also gnosiology, theology, ontology, all of philosophy: the root-foundation, Grund, racine, fondement. The West has a special relation to the forest, and deforestation; the fields carved from the forest are populated with seed plants produced by cultivation based on species lineages of the arborescent type; animal raising, carried out on fallow fields, selects lineages forming an entire animal arborescence."

2. "'It could feed the world': Amaranth, a health trend 8,000 years old that survived colonization," *The Guardian*. https://www.theguardian.com/environment/2021/aug/06/ancient-grain-amaranth-food-trend-indigenous (accessed September 15, 2025).

3. Deleuze and Guattari, conductors of rhizomatic theories of communication wrote, "A rhizome may be broken, shattered at a given spot, but it will start up again on one of its old lines, or on new lines. You can never get rid of ants because they form an animal rhizome that can rebound time and again after most of it has been destroyed."

Chapter 14

1. "'A living collective': Study shows trees synchronize electrical signals during a solar eclipse," The Conversation. https://theconversation.com/a-living-collective-study-shows-trees-synchronise-electrical-signals-during-a-solar-eclipse-255499 (accessed September 15, 2025).

About the Author

Nicole Walker is the author of *Writing the Hard Stuff* (2025), *Processed Meats* (2021), *The After-Normal* (2019), and *Sustainability* (2018). Her nonfiction includes *Where the Tiny Things Are* (2017), *Egg* (2017), *Micrograms* (2016), and *Quench Your Thirst with Salt* (2013), *This Noisy Egg* (2010). She edited *Science of Story* with Sean Prentiss and with Margot Singer, *Bending Genre*. She has written for *The New York Times* and is a notable author in several Best American Essays. (I've never had an essay republished in BAE). She edits the Crux series and nonfiction at *Diagram*, teaches creative writing at Northern Arizona University and is Writer-in-Residence for the Center for Ecosystem Science and Society.